Index Map

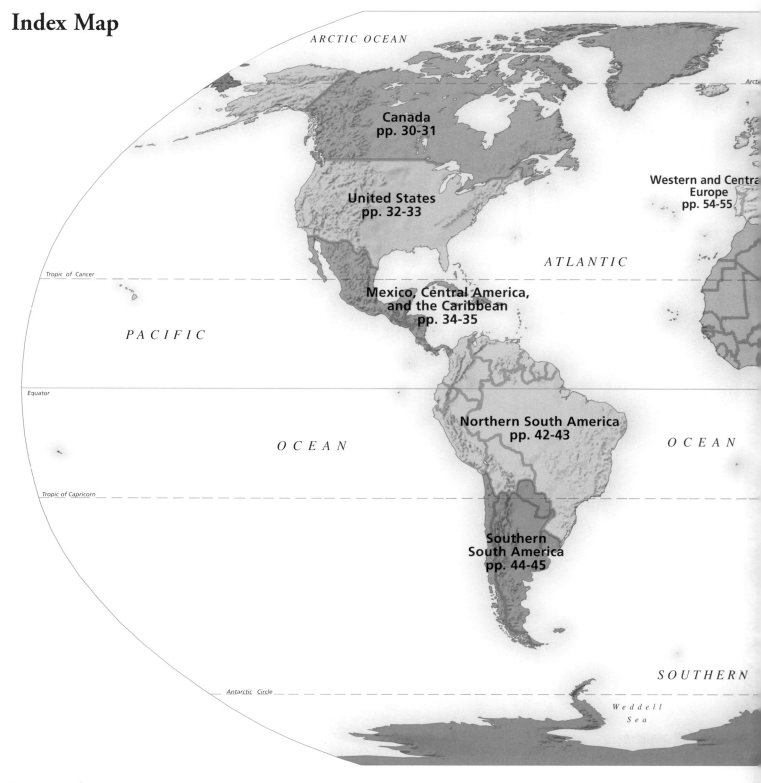

ARCTIC OCEAN

Arct

Canada
pp. 30-31

Western and Centra
Europe
pp. 54-55

United States
pp. 32-33

ATLANTIC

Tropic of Cancer

Mexico, Central America,
and the Caribbean
pp. 34-35

PACIFIC

Equator

Northern South America
pp. 42-43

OCEAN

OCEAN

Tropic of Capricorn

Southern
South America
pp. 44-45

Antarctic Circle

SOUTHERN

Weddell
Sea

Legend

Drainage Symbols

Rhine   **River**

Lake Baikal   **Fresh lake**

Salt lake

Seasonal lake

Physical Features

Features such as mountains and deserts
are indicated by certain styles of type.

△ *Mt. Kosciuszko*
7,313 Ft.   **Mountain peak/elevation**

ROCKY MOUNTAINS
Rocky Mountains   **Mountain range**

SAHARA
Sahara   **Physical region**

Cape Horn   **Cape**

KANGAROO ISLAND   **Island**

ARCTIC OCEAN

Northern Europe
pp. 52-53

Russia and Central Asia
pp. 78-79

Eastern Europe
pp. 56-57

Southeastern
Europe
pp. 58-59   Southwest Asia
pp. 76-77

East Asia
pp. 80-81

South Asia and the Middle East
pp. 84-85

Northern Africa
pp. 66-67

Southeast Asia
pp. 82-83

Southern Africa
pp. 68-69

Pacific Islands
pp. 92-93

Australia
pp. 90-91

Antarctica
pp. 94-95

PACIFIC

Tropic of Cancer

OCEAN

Equator

INDIAN

OCEAN

Tropic of Capricorn

OCEAN

Antarctic Circle

Copyright by Rand McNally & Co.
Made in U.S.A.

Boundaries

_____ International (country)

_____ State/province

_____ Tropic of Capricorn Tropics

_____ Equator

Capitals

✷ National

★ State/province

Cities

The size of the symbol and type indicates a city's relative importance.

· Nome

● Québec

● New Orleans

● NEW YORK

Editors
Anne Ford
Brett Gover
Nathalie Strassheim

Writers
Leslie Morrison
Catherine VanPatten

Photo Research
Feldman & Associates, Inc.

Cartography
Robert K. Argersinger
Gregory P. Babiak
Barbara Strassheim Benstead
Marzee Eckhoff
Robert Ferry
Susan K. Hudson
Nina Lusterman
David Simmons
Raymond Tobiaski
Thomas Vitacco

RAND M°NALLY

Children's Illustrated Atlas of the World
Copyright © 2005 by Rand McNally & Company

randmcnally.com

Published and printed in the United States of America

Library of Congress Control Number: 2005922961

For information on licensing and copyright permissions, please contact us at licensing@randmcnally.com

ISBN: 528-93458-9

10 9 8 7 6 5 4 3 2 1

Photo Credits

(l = left, c = center, r = right, t = top, b = bottom)

© Mary Altier, 72 (b l)

Animals:
© Dani/Jeske, 68 (b c)

Peter Arnold, Inc.:
© Fred Bavendam, 92 (b c); © Kevin Schafer, 46 (t); © Still Pictures/Mark Edwards, 16 (c l), 49 (t r); © Fritz Polking, 7 (t r), 68 (t l); © Bruno P. Zehnder, 90 (b r)

Black Star:
© F. Charton, 74 (b l)

© Cameramann International, Ltd., 80 (b c)

Bruce Coleman, Inc.:
© Andris Apse, 89 (c l); © Bruce Stewart, 88 (c l)

© Corbis/ *.Heaton*: 64 (b l)

Leo DeWyes, Inc.:
© DeWyes/D&J Heaton, 60 (t)

© European Space Agency, 6 (c)

FPG:
© Walter Bibikow, 31 (c r); © John Giustina, 15 (t r), 37 (b r), 81 (c r), 94-95 (b); © Mark Green, 26 (c l); © Peter Gridley, 24 (b l); © Steve Hix, 59 (b r); © G. Marche, 76 (c r); © Richard Price, 26 (c r); © Gail Shumway, 35 (b c); © Telegraph Colour Library, 70 (t), 80 (t l), 94 (t); © VCG, 15 (b r)

First Image West:
© Jim P. Garrison, 33 (b r)

© David R. Frazier Photolibrary, 49 (b l)

© Robert Fried Photography, 54 (b l)

H. Armstrong Roberts:
© B. Pogue, 56 (b l); © M. Schneider, 58 (b c); © Smith/Zefa, 88 (c r)

© Dave G. Houser, 91 (c r)

© Randall Hyman, 56 (c l)

© Jason Laure':
63 (c l); 64 (t r & b c)

Liaison International:
© Rob Johns, 27 (b l)

(c) Buddy Mays/TravelStock:
54 (t l), 88 (b), 91 (t)

© North Wind Picture Archives: 8 (Leif Ericsson, corn, iron plough), 9 (cotton gin, Abraham Lincoln, James Cook)

Odyssey Productions:
© Robert Frerck, 83 (c r)

Panoramic Images:
© China Photo Library, 70 (b); © Philip Gray, 86-87 (b); © Allen Prier, 24-25 (b); © K. Yamashita, 46 (b)

© Chip & Rosa Marie Peterson, 40 (b); 44 (c l)

© PhotoDisc, 8 (teacup), 11 (b r), 13 (b r), 33 (t r), 46 (b l), 60 (b l), 63 (b), 76 (b)

PhotoEdit:
© David Young-Wolff, 28 (b l)

Photo Researchers, Inc.:
© Tom McHugh, 89 (b l)

Photri:
77 (c l & c), 79 (cotton), 85 (Bangladesh); © Richard T. Nowitz, 74 (Muslims); © Fritz Prenzel Photo, 90 (c l)

Reuters/Archive Photos: © Yannis Behrakis, 58 (t r)

© Eugene Schultz, 69 (b c)

© The Stock Market:
41 (b r); © David Ball, 6 (b l), 55 (c r); © Peter Beck, 27 (b r); © Tom Brakefield, 79 (b r); © Tibor Bognar, 85 (b r); © Alex Cabral, 43 (b r); © Murilo Dutra, 40 (t r); © Mark Ferri, 23 (b r), 50 (b l); © H.P. Merten, 53 (t r); © James Marshall, 43 (t c); ©

M. Mastrorillo, 45 (b r); © J. Pollerross, 84 (b r); © Alan Reininger, 83 (t c); © Torleif Svensson, 83 (c), 85 (Indian man); © Ben Simmons, 49 (b r)

© Stock Montage, 10 (Atlas)

Tony Stone Images:
92 (c r), 95 (t r); © Jerry Alexander, 56 (b r); © Glen Allison, 33 (horse farm), 92 (t r); © Christopher Arnesen, 59 (t r); © Horst Baender, 31 (t r); © Alejandro Balaguer, 40 (c r); © James Balog, 28 (Inuit), 68 (b r); © David Barnes, 89 (c r); © John Beatty, 23 (t r); © Tom Bean, 34 (c l); © Oliver Benn, 28 (t r), 57 (t l); © Grilly Bernard, 66 (b l); © Randa Bishop, 39 (c r); © Gary Braasch, 14 (c l); © Ernest Braun, 21 (t r), 39 (b l); © Gary Brettnacher, 79 (b l); © Paula Bronstein, 59 (b l); © Bushnell/Soifer, 83 (t l); © Marc Chamberlain, 68 (c l); © Paul Chesley, 81 (b l), 82 (b l); © Connie Coleman, 6 (b r), 53 (b l); © Bruno De Hogues, 7 (t l), 64 (c l); © Nicholas DeVore, 53 (b c); © Florence Douyrou, 6 (b c), 50 (t l); © Wayne Eastep, 73 (t r); © Chad Ehlers, 92 (b l); © R. Elliot, 85 (t c); © Fred Felleman, 95 (b r); © Robert Frerck, 40 (t c); © Stephen Frink, 20 (b l), 89 (b r); © Louis Grandadam, 77 (b r); © Sylvain Grandadam, 7 (t r), 64 (b r), 84 (t l); © Bob Handelman, 28 (b l); © George Haling, 6 (c r), 44 (b r); © Elizabeth Harris, 6 (c l), 22 (b l), 40 (b r); © Mark Harris, 28 (playground); © Paul Harris, 7 (c r), 74 (t r); © Gary Hayes, 50 (c l); © William J. Hebert, 45 (c l); © David Hiser, 6 (c r), 33 (t l), 55 (t r); © Jeremy Horner, 9, 36 (t); © George Hunter, 83 (b r); © Warren Jacobs, 17 (t r), 63 (t r); © Jacques Jangoux, 43 (t l & t r); © Gavriel Jecan, 58 (c l), 59 (t l); © Darrell Jones, 16 (t l); © Richard Kavlin, 33 (surfers); © Paul Kenward, 44 (t l); © Jerry Kobalenko, 78 (b r); © John Lamb, 69 (b r); © Susan Lapides, 28 (waiters); © Jane Lewis, 84 (c l); © Mark Lewis, 35 (c r); © Renee Lynn, 64 (Masai); © Yves Marcoux, 30 (t c); © Sally Mayman, 66 (b r); © Steve Outram, 51 (b r); © Bryan Parsley, 21 (b r); © Richard Pasmore, 49 (c r); © Orion Press, 81 (t r); © Colin Pryor, 36-37 (b); © Kevin Schafer, 40 (t l), 79 (railway), 95 (c l); © Herb Schmitz, 76 (c l); © Ian Shaw, 56 (t r); © Hugh Sitton, 69 (t r); © Charles Sleicher, 34 (b r); © Philip & Karen Smith; 44 (b l); © Robin Smith, 90 (b l); © Sarah Stone, 35 (t r); © James Strachan, 66 (b c), 79 (t r); © Keren Su, 72 (t r); © T. Resource, 44 (t r); © Tom Till, 6 (c l), 17 (b r), 24 (t); © Traveler's Resource, 73 (b l); © P. Tweedie, 90 (t); © Marie Ueda, 7 (kangaroo); © Larry Ulrich, 32 (b l); © Steve Vidler, 57 (t r), 63 (c r); © Rosemary Weller, 63 (t c); © Randy Wells, 35 (b r); © Art Wolfe, 19 (t r), 55 (b r), 68 (b l)

© SuperStock:
6 (Galileo), 7 (c l & fan), 8 (Christopher Columbus, Normans, Medici, Gutenberg, Arab traders, Ming mask), 9 (Model T, Galileo, Isaac Newton), 18 (b l), 19 (b r), 28 (b r), 30 (c l, b l, and b c), 38 (t r), 39 (t r), 42 (b l), 48 (c l), 52 (b r), 64 (t l and c r), 70 (c l), 74 (c l, c, and monks), 75 (c r), 80 (b r), 81 (b r), 82 (c l), 86 (t); © Avid Northcott, 43 (c r)

Vandystadt/Allsport
© Jean-Marc Loubat, 55 (b l)

Viesti:
© M. Downey, 75 (t r)

Visuals Unlimited:
© Bill Kamin, 58 (b r); © Steve McCutcheon, 9, 62 (t l)

© Randy Wells, 50 (b c)

Children's Illustrated
Atlas of the WORLD

Contents

The World

World Timeline 8-9
The Basics of Maps and Cartography 10-11
How to Use This Atlas 12-13
World Climates 14-15
World Economies 16-17
World Populations 18-19
World Physical Map 20-21
World Political Map 22-23

North America

Introduction 24-25
The Land 26-27
The People 28-29
Canada 30-31
United States 32-33
Mexico, Central America, and the Caribbean 34-35

South America

Introduction 36-37
The Land 38-39
The People 40-41
Northern South America 42-43
Southern South America 44-45

Europe

Introduction 46-47
The Land 48-49
The People 50-51
Northern Europe and Western Russia 52-53
Western and Central Europe 54-55
Eastern Europe 56-57
Southeastern Europe 58-59

Africa

Introduction 60-61
The Land 62-63
The People 64-65
Northern Africa 66-67
Southern Africa 68-69

Asia

Introduction 70-71
The Land 72-73
The People 74-75
Southwest Asia 76-77
Russia and Central Asia 78-79
East Asia 80-81
Southeast Asia 82-83
South Asia and the Middle East 84-85

Australia and Oceania

Introduction 86-87
The Land 88-89
The People 90-91
The Pacific Islands 92-93

Antarctica 94-95

Country Flag and Fact File 96-103

Glossary 104

Index 105-110

World Timeline (1000 A.D. – present)

	1000-1100	1100-1200	1200-1300	1300-1400	1400-1500	
North America	**c. 1000** Leif Ericsson and the Vikings sail to North America. **c. 1100** Anasazi begin building Mesa Verde cliff dwellings in south-western North America.	**1100-1200** Hohokam of Arizona begin to build platform temple mounds for worship.	**c. 1200** Thousands live in and around Cahokia, a city of temple mounds built by the Mississippians. **1275-1300** Severe drought in Chaco Canyon hastens collapse of Anasazi communities.	**1300s** Warrior knights help make Aztecs a powerful society in Mexico. **1325** Aztecs found city of Tenochtitlán, now Mexico City.	**1492** Christopher Columbus lands in the Caribbean, but thinks he is in the East Indies.	
South America	**c. 1000** Peruvian farmers grow potatoes and corn for food.	**1100s** Incas in Peru make sculptures of their warrior chiefs.	**c. 1250** Mayan culture becomes stronger, and a new capital city is built. **c. 1250** Chimu people along northern coast of Peru expand their empire.	**c.1300s** Inca people in Peru become skilled builders. Inca culture expands into the central Andes region.	**1400s** Inca empire covers most of the west coast of South America. **c. 1450** Incas build Machu Picchu in Peru. **1470s** Chimu culture in Northern Peru collapses.	
Europe	**c. 1050** Iron plows replace wooden plows in Europe. **1066** Norman conquest of England	**1119** First European university established in Bologna, Italy **1124-1153** David I rules Scotland. **1152-1190** Frederick I rules powerful Holy Roman Empire.	**1215** King John of England signs the Magna Carta, limiting royal power. **1233** Coal is mined in Newcastle, England, for the first time. **1298** English archers use longbows to defeat Scottish army.	**1378-1381** Workers' Revolt in Florence, Italy (1378) and Peasants' Revolt in England (1381) **1397** Members of Medici family establish themselves as bankers in Florence.	**1440s** Nicolas Cusanus claims the Earth is in constant motion and space is infinite. **c. 1450** Johannes Gutenberg invents the printing press.	
Africa	**1000s** Bantu-speaking people hunt and farm in Africa. **1000s** West African kingdoms flourish with gold trade in Africa.	**c. 1100** Empire of Ghana begins to decline. **c. 1100** Arab traders settle in Africa along Indian Ocean coast. **1173** Muslim warrior Saladin declares himself sultan of Egypt.	**1200s** The town of Great Zimbabwe is built by the Shona people in southern Africa. **c. 1235** The Mali empire in West Africa becomes more powerful.	**1348** The Black Plague devastates Egyptian population. **c. 1350** Great Zimbabwe in southern Africa flourishes in gold trade. **1380** Kongo kingdom begins in the Congo River region of Zaire.	**c. 1420** Portuguese sailors explore west coast of Africa. **1468** Sanghai Empire dominates central Sudan in Africa.	
Asia	**c. 1000** Indian mathematician Sridhara recognizes the importance of zero. **c. 1000** Chinese begin to use gunpowder for warfare. **1041** Chinese printer Pi Sheng invents moveable type.	**c. 1100** Chinese explain the causes of solar and lunar eclipses. **1100s** Sultan of Baghdad becomes probably the first to use pigeons for mail system. **1191** Tea arrives in Japan from China.	**1206** Genghis Khan unites the Mongols. **1232** Chinese build first rockets, which resemble fireworks. **1259-1260** Important astronomical observatories are built in Maragha, Iran, and Beijing, China.	**c. 1300** Ottoman dynasty begins in Turkey. **1368** Ming dynasty begins in China. **c. 1390** Ottoman Turks conquer Asia Minor.	**1419-1450** Korea prospers under King Sejong. **1448-1488** Thailand expands under King Trailok. **c. 1498** Portuguese sailor Vasco de Gama reaches India.	
Australia and Oceania	**c. 1000** Maoris settle in present-day New Zealand, where they hunt and gather their food.	**1100s** Polynesians establish settlements on the island of Pitcairn.	**c. 1200** On Tonga, Tui Tonga monarchy builds coral platform for worship.	**1350** Maoris prosper on New Zealand's North Island.	**c. 1400** Tonga people build a ceremonial center at Mu'a in the South Pacific.	

1500-1600	1600-1700	1700-1800	1800-1900	1900-
1500s Europeans explore North America and claim land for their countries. **1519-1521** Hernando Cortés of Spain conquers the Aztecs. **1534** French explorer Jacques Cartier travels to Canada. **1540s** Spanish come to California.	**1607** English establish first permanent colony in North America at Jamestown, Virginia. **1608** Québec is founded by French settlers. **1619** First African slaves brought to North America. **1625** Dutch found New Amsterdam (later called New York).	**1775** American Revolution begins. **1776** Declaration of Independence is approved. **1792** New York Stock Exchange is organized. **1793** Eli Whitney invents cotton gin. **1796** Edward Jenner develops smallpox vaccine.	**1804** Lewis and Clark begin exploring route to Pacific Ocean. **1861-1865** U.S. Civil War **1863** Lincoln issues the Emancipation Proclamation. **1876** Alexander Graham Bell invents the telephone.	**1908** Ford Motor Company produces first Model T automobile. **1960s** Martin Luther King, Jr. leads civil rights protests in U.S. **1969** Moon landing **1990** Launch of Hubble Space Telescope **2001** Terrorist attack on World Trade Center
1533 Francisco Pizarro of Spain conquers the Inca empire in South America.	**1608** Jesuits establish state of Paraguay. **1654** Portuguese drive Dutch from Brazil.	**1726** Spanish found city of Montevideo in Uruguay. **1727** Coffee is first planted in Brazil. **1742** Native Americans of Peru rebel against Spaniards. **1763** Rio de Janeiro becomes Brazil's capital.	**1810** Simón Bolívar emerges to lead Latin American revolutions. **1825** Bolívar founds state of Bolivia. **1828** Uruguay becomes independent. **1879-1884** Chile, Peru, Bolivia at war **1891** Civil war in Chile	**1955** Military officials seize power from Argentinian president Peron. **1982** Falklands war between Argentina and Britain **2003** South American glaciers discovered to be melting at rapid speed.
1506-1507 First maps of the New World are printed in Europe. **1519** Ferdinand Magellan sets sail from Spain to circumnavigate the globe. **1514-1565** Explorers introduce pineapples, coffee, chocolate, sweet potatoes, corn, and tobacco to Europe.	**1608** Galileo makes astronomical observations using newly invented telescope. **1628** William Harvey describes the circulation of blood in the body. **1687** Isaac Newton describes the fundamental laws of motion.	**1715** Daniel Fahrenheit develops first mercury thermometer. **1742** Anders Celsius creates thermometer marking 0° as freezing and 100° as boiling. **1789** French Revolution begins.	**1804** Napoleon becomes emperor of the French. **1859** Charles Darwin publishes book about the evolution of species. **1884** Greenwich, England established as the zero meridian for time zones. **1896** Italian Marconi invents wireless telegraph.	**1914-1918** World War I **1917** Bolshevik Revolution in Russia **1939-1945** World War II **1957** Russians launch Sputnik space satellite. **1991** Soviet Union dissolves. **2002** Euro introduced as currency.
1530s Slave trade begins, organized by the Portuguese. **1562** African slaves are sent to the Americas as the English slave trade begins.	**c. 1650** Ethiopia expels Portuguese missionaries and diplomats. **1652** Dutch establish Cape Town in South Africa. **1680s** Asante kingdom rises in West Africa. **1686** Louis XIV of France annexes Madagascar.	**c. 1710** The 300-year-old African kingdom of Kongo collapses after Portuguese invasion. **1724-1734** African leaders stop slave trade in West Africa. **1740s** Slave trade resumes. **1755** Sailors bring first outbreak of smallpox to Cape Town.	**1822** Liberia is founded as home for freed U.S. slaves. **1830** French invade Algeria. **1873-1874** Asante and British at war **1879** Zulu and British at war **1880s** Nearly all of Africa is colonized by European countries.	**1931** Railway from Angola to Mozambique completed. **1980** Zimbabwe is the last African country to gain independence from colonial rule. **1990** Nelson Mandela is elected president of South Africa. **2005** Fossils of walking ancestor of humans found.
1520-1566 Ottoman Empire at its peak **1526** Mongols invade India, establishing Mogul Empire. **1533** Ivan the Terrible rules as the first tsar of Russia.	**1630s** Japan expels most foreigners, allowing trade only with the Dutch and Chinese. **1644** Manchus invade China and establish the Quing dynasty.	**1735-1795** Chinese empire reaches its furthest extent. **1763** Britain becomes dominant power in India. **1783-1788** Japan experiences severe famine. **1784** U.S. begins trade with China.	**1804** Russia attempts but fails to establish trade with Japan. **1854** U.S. opens Japan to trade. **1857** Native soldiers in India rebel against English rulers. **1872** First Japanese railway opens.	**1900** Boxer Rebellion in China **1949** Mao Zedong establishes communist government in China. **1965-1973** Vietnam War **1979** Islamic Revolution in Iran **2004** Massive tsunami strikes Southeast Asia.
1526 Portuguese land on Papua New Guinea. **1550s** Maoris in New Zealand build fortified enclosures.	**1600s** Dutch sailors discover the north and west coasts of Australia by accident. **1642-1644** Abel Tasman explores Tasmania and New Zealand.	**1768-1771** British Captain James Cook's first voyage to the Pacific **1788** British begin to settle Australia with prisoners, creating a penal colony.	**1801-1803** Matthew Flinders circumnavigates and names Australia. **1851** Gold found in southeastern Australia.	**1901** British colonies become states and form the Commonwealth of Australia. **1933** Australia takes control of a large part of Antarctica. **1985** New Zealand bans nuclear vessels from its ports. **2000** Sydney, Australia hosts the Olympics.

The Basics of Maps and Cartography

What is a Map?

A map is a picture — or representation — of a place. Most maps are drawn to show places from above. When you think of maps, you might picture a folded road map or a wall map that hangs in the classroom. But there are many different kinds of maps. Satellite images, or pictures of Earth taken from space, are maps. Floor plans of houses are maps too, because they show where each room is. In fact, you probably keep a lot of maps in your head. These mental maps help you remember how to get to school or your friend's house without needing to ask directions every time.

History of Mapmaking

Thousands of years ago, ancient people developed the first maps as they explored new places and settled new lands. The Chinese, the Arabs, and the Indians were among the first people to experiment with mapmaking. They created maps by drawing on animal skins and rocks and by carving on stones and in wood. In Babylon, an ancient Middle Eastern civilization, people carved maps into stone tablets. Ancient Egyptians drew maps on papyrus (a plant made into paper) and carved them into temple walls. Several thousand years ago, Europeans drew maps on paper, using the maps to help find their way across oceans to new lands and then to guide them home safely.

Ancient Greeks made and used globes, which are three-dimensional models of Earth. The Greeks divided the globe into segments, using lines of latitude and longitude. Later these lines were overlaid onto flat maps. Today we still use latitude and longitude to find places on globes and maps.

This satellite image of the San Francisco Bay area clearly shows the shape of the coastline.

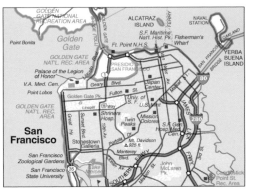

On this road map of San Francisco, you can get information on street names and points of interest.

An atlas is a book of maps. In 1570, Abraham Ortelius developed the first modern atlas, although he didn't call it by that name. Another man, Gerardus Mercator, first used the term "atlas" in 1589, when he named his collection of maps after a person from mythology named Atlas. In Greek mythology, Atlas was forced to support the world on his shoulders as punishment for warring against the gods. Although the word "atlas" is still used to mean a book of maps, atlases today may contain diagrams, tables, and text in addition to maps.

Atlas

Lines of latitude and longitude intersect on a globe to form a grid.

This map, drawn in 1587, shows what North and South America were thought to look like at the time.

People who make maps are called mapmakers or cartographers. Cartography is the art of making maps. The word comes from the Latin carta, meaning "map," and the Greek graph, meaning "write."

Major Types of Maps

Political Maps

Many of the maps you see are political maps. Political maps show how people have divided up the land on Earth. Using different colors, political maps show the borders between countries, states, provinces, and territories. The maps also show the location of cities, which are represented by different sizes of type to indicate populations, roads, parks, and other features.

Physical Maps

Physical maps use different colors to show the elevation, or height, of land and the depth of water on the surface of the earth. Physical maps help readers see mountains, valleys, oceans, lakes, and rivers. Each physical map has its own legend, which explains which colors represent various elevations of land and depths of water.

Thematic Maps

Thematic maps use different colors to give information about specific themes or topics, such as populations, climates, languages spoken, or economies in different parts of the world. You can use thematic maps to compare and contrast information on one map or between several maps. Like physical maps, each thematic map has its own legend.

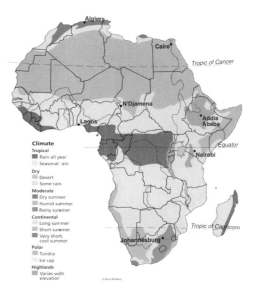

Locator Maps

Locator maps are small, simple maps that show what continent, region, or state is featured on a more detailed map. Locators point out where the maps are in relation to a larger area.

Maps Today

During the past 50 years, mapping around the world has become very precise. Sophisticated computers use information taken from satellite images — photos of Earth taken from space — and other sources to produce highly accurate maps used by people in business, government, and education. Students use maps to learn about foreign countries. Business people use maps to decide where to sell new products. And governmental agencies, like local fire and police departments, use maps to pinpoint houses and their residents who may need assistance.

Maps are available in a variety of places and formats. In addition to reading paper maps, you can use maps on your computer with special mapping software or on the Internet.

How to Use This Atlas

An atlas is a book of maps. So to use an atlas, you need to understand a few things about reading maps. The sections below explain how to use the maps in this atlas and how to use other parts of the book.

Finding Places

Finding places in an atlas is an adventure — a journey that takes you across rivers, over mountains, and into new countries. To find places in Rand McNally's *Children's Illustrated Atlas of the World*, use the following tools:

Index Map

At the very front of the book is an index map. The index map shows each of the seven continents in a different color, and it lists the pages where you'll find the maps for each continent.

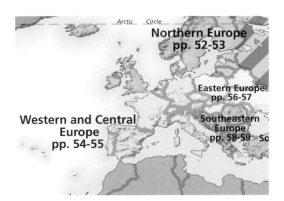

Index

At the very back of the book is the index — a list of the many places (such as cities, towns, and countries) and features (such as mountains and rivers) shown on the maps. The index tells you the page where you'll find each place or feature, and it also includes a letter-and-number code that tells you exactly where to look on the map to find the place or feature.

Place	Map Ref.	Page No.
Paraná, S.A.	D-5	45
	D-5	54
Paris, France	I-3	45
Patagonia, region, Argentina	I-8	32
Pecos, river, U.S.	I-8	32
Pennsylvania, state, U.S.	F-13	32
Pensacola, Florida, U.S.	I-11	32
Perm', Russia	E-6	78
Persian Gulf, Asia	D-6	84
Perth, Australia	G-5	90
Peru, country, South America	G-6	42
Peshawar, Pakistan	C-10	84
Philadelphia, Pennsylvania, U.S.	F-13	32
	C-6	92
		82

Map Grids

To help you locate places and features, each map includes a map grid along its four sides. Along the left side are letters, and along the top side are numbers. The letter-and-number codes in the index correspond to the letters and numbers along the sides of the maps.

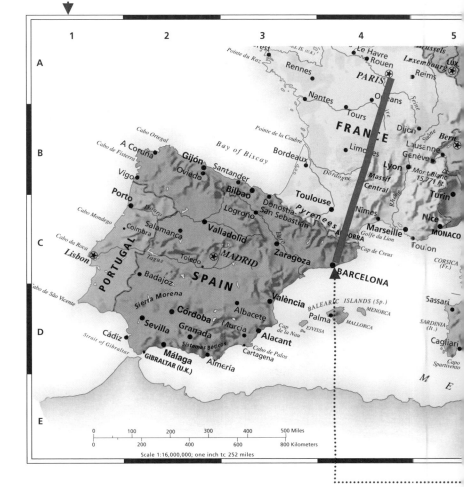

Latitude/Longitude

The imaginary lines that run vertically from the top of the earth to the bottom are called lines of longitude. These lines, which meet at the top of the earth and at the bottom, are also called meridians. The imaginary lines that run horizontally around the globe are called lines of latitude. These lines, which are parallel to one another and therefore never meet, are also known as parallels. The equator, which runs around the very middle of the earth, is the best known line of latitude.

These imaginary lines of longitude and latitude cross and form grids, which help you find places on a map or globe. In this atlas, the equator, the Tropic of Cancer, and the Tropic of Capricorn — all lines of latitude — are shown.

Knowing Direction

Each of the maps in this atlas includes something called a compass rose — a circle with arrows and the letters N, S, E, and W. These letters represent the four main points of a compass: North, South, East, and West. (On some old maps, the compass roses are beautifully illustrated and include so many direction points that they actually look like flowering roses!)

This is an example of an ornate compass rose.

Using the Legend

Maps contain all sorts of information. The legend, sometimes called the "map key," explains the symbols that appear on the maps. Symbols are icons that represent something else. For example, a black star in a circle is the symbol for a capital city. So in France, you'll find a ✷ next to Paris, the capital city. Other symbols on the maps represent rivers, lakes, mountain peaks, and borders between countries.

The main legend in this atlas is located below the index map in the very front of the book. The physical maps and thematic maps in the rest of the book all have legends next to them.

River   Fresh Lake   Salt Lake   Seasonal Lake

Understanding Terms

This atlas includes a glossary on page 104. In the glossary you will find explanations of many geographic terms used in the atlas.

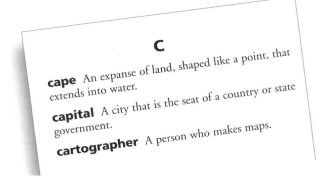

C

cape An expanse of land, shaped like a point, that extends into water.

capital A city that is the seat of a country or state government.

cartographer A person who makes maps.

Measuring Distance

Next to every map is a scale bar that shows how the size of the map relates to the real world. The scale bar also allows you to measure the distance between places. For example, let's say that one inch on a map scale represents about 250 miles in the real world, and that, using a ruler, you measured 2 inches between the cities of Paris, France, and Barcelona, Spain. Since one inch equals about 250 miles, then 2 inches must equal about 500 miles. This means that the distance between Paris and Barcelona in the real world is approximately 500 miles. Instead of using a ruler to measure distances, you can mark points along the edge of a piece of paper and then use the scale bar to measure the distance between the points.

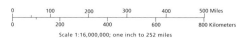

| 0 | 100 | 200 | 300 | 400 | 500 Miles |
| 0 | 200 | 400 | 600 | 800 Kilometers |

Scale 1:16,000,000; one inch to 252 miles

Learning about Countries

If you want to learn some basic facts about any country, or to see what its flag looks like, turn to the Country Flag and Fact File that begins on page 96. This section shows each country's flag and lists its size, population, and capital city.

Togo
Area: 21,925 sq mi (56,785 sq km)
Population: 5,495,000
Capital: Lomé

World Climates

This map shows the climate zones of the world. The word "climate" describes the weather conditions that occur in an area over a long period of time — not weeks and months, but years. The legend to the right of the map shows the specific climates that you can find on the map.

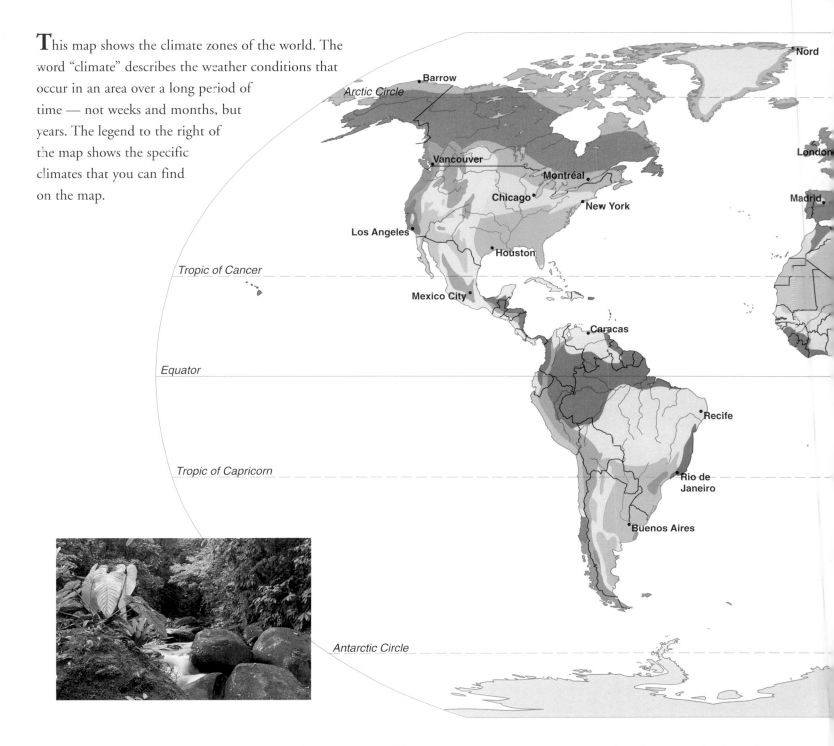

Climates are created by temperature and precipitation (such as rain and snow), and climates around the world vary for different reasons. In general, Earth's climates grow hotter as you approach the equator, and become colder as you move north or south from the equator. This is because the Sun's rays hit Earth most directly and most often in the tropics — the area between the Tropic of Cancer and the Tropic of

Capricorn. Also, climates tend to be cooler in areas with high elevations because the thinner air high up holds less heat. Finally, areas that lie along the coast of an ocean or sea often have climates much milder than that of inland areas, thanks to ocean breezes and currents.

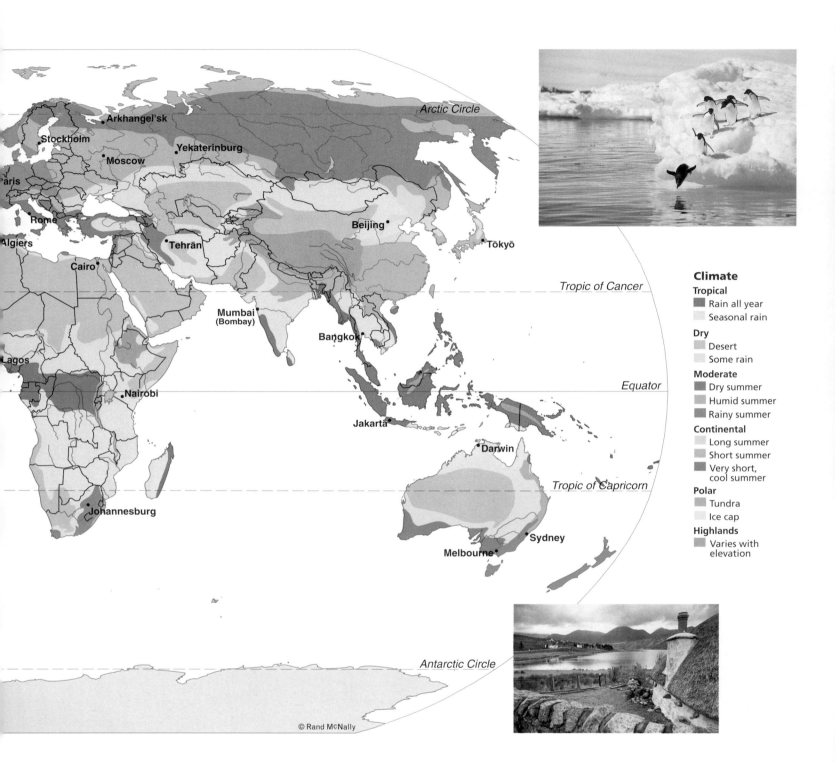

Arctic Circle

Arkhangel'sk
Stockholm
Moscow
Yekaterinburg
aris
Rome
Algiers
Beijing
Tōkyō
Cairo
Tehrān
Tropic of Cancer
Mumbai
(Bombay)
Bangkok
Lagos
Equator
Nairobi
Jakarta
Darwin
Johannesburg
Tropic of Capricorn
Sydney
Melbourne

Antarctic Circle

© Rand McNally

Climate

Tropical
- Rain all year
- Seasonal rain

Dry
- Desert
- Some rain

Moderate
- Dry summer
- Humid summer
- Rainy summer

Continental
- Long summer
- Short summer
- Very short, cool summer

Polar
- Tundra
- Ice cap

Highlands
- Varies with elevation

Precipitation is the other factor that determines climate. Usually, areas of heaviest precipitation are found along the equator, where warm tropical air holds the greatest amount of water vapor. The reddish colors on the map show areas that experience tropical climates: the great rain forests of northern South America, central Africa, and Indonesia.

The terrain, or physical features, of an area also affects precipitation. When the terrain blocks the flow of breezes, it can dramatically alter the pattern of rainfall. Tall mountain ranges force moist air currents to rise above them, and when the air descends on the other side of the mountain, it releases moisture in the form of heavy rains. This "rainshadow effect" — where one side of a mountain range receives abundant rainfall

and the other is desert — can be observed in the northwestern United States and in Chile west and east of the Andes.

The climate we live in directly affects our lifestyles. The type of clothing we wear, the foods we eat, the way we travel, and the home we inhabit — all are dictated by climate.

World Economies

This map identifies economic activity around the world. The colors of the different areas on the map indicate how most of the people in a particular area make their living.

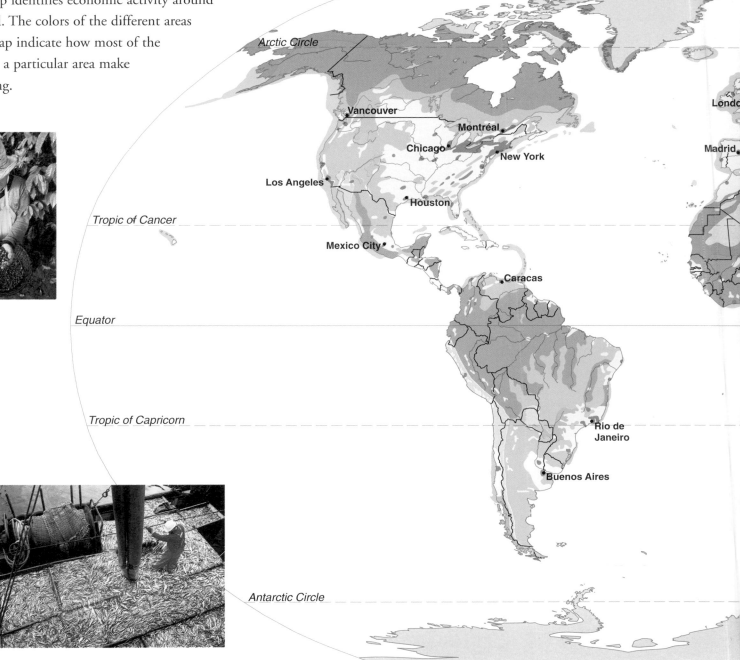

The physical characteristics of the land, such as fertile valleys and oil-rich plains, determine how people are able to use it and make livings. Compare this map to the world physical map on pages 20-21. In general, areas where farming takes place (shown in yellow on this world economies map) contain some of Earth's most fertile soils. Food harvested from the wide plains and river valleys of Europe, southeastern Asia, and central North America feeds much of the world's population. In some countries, such as India and China, agriculture is the major way to earn a living. In Brazil and the countries of eastern Europe, however, a much smaller part of the work force raises crops. This fraction is even smaller in Canada, the United States, and western Europe.

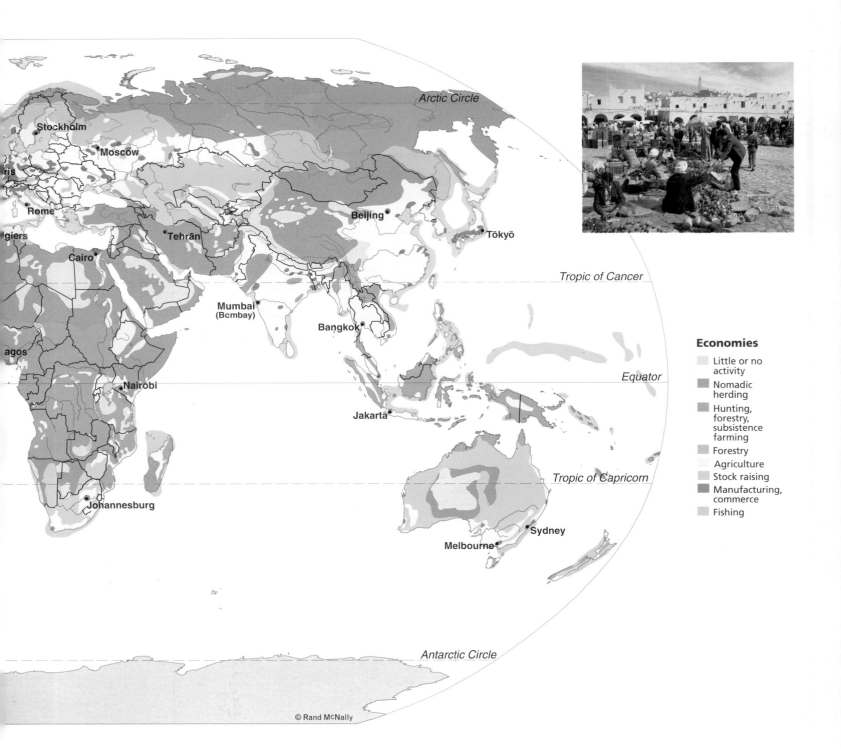

Economies

- Little or no activity
- Nomadic herding
- Hunting, forestry, subsistence farming
- Forestry
- Agriculture
- Stock raising
- Manufacturing, commerce
- Fishing

© Rand McNally

Very few regions of the world are used for manufacturing and trade. These areas are sometimes called "developed." In the United States, for instance, developed areas grew near transportation routes and land that contained natural resources such as minerals. Major manufacturing centers such as Chicago and Montréal line the shores of the Great Lakes and the St. Lawrence Seaway, an important transportation route that provides access to the Atlantic Ocean. Likewise, Germany's Ruhr Valley has long provided mineral resources, and the country's position in the center of Europe has helped it grow into a major industrial force.

In general, countries that are more economically developed have a greater range of industries than less developed countries. This is because people are able to specialize in the work that they do best, and use the money that they earn to pay for other goods and services that they need.

World Population

This map shows where people live in the world. The legend to the right of the map explains what the different colors mean in terms of population density. Population density is a measure of the number of people living in each square mile (2.59 square kilometers) of land.

Population densities vary for many reasons, including climate and terrain. For example, the continent of Antarctica — Earth's coldest region — is uninhabited, meaning that no one lives there permanently. Its harsh climate makes living there nearly impossible.

Lands with favorable climates and terrains tend to be densely populated, especially if they are good for farming. The presence of the Nile River explains the ribbon of dense population that runs through the desert lands of Sudan and Egypt in northern Africa: People live and farm close to its fertile banks. In the vast rain forests of South America, people settle along the Amazon River.

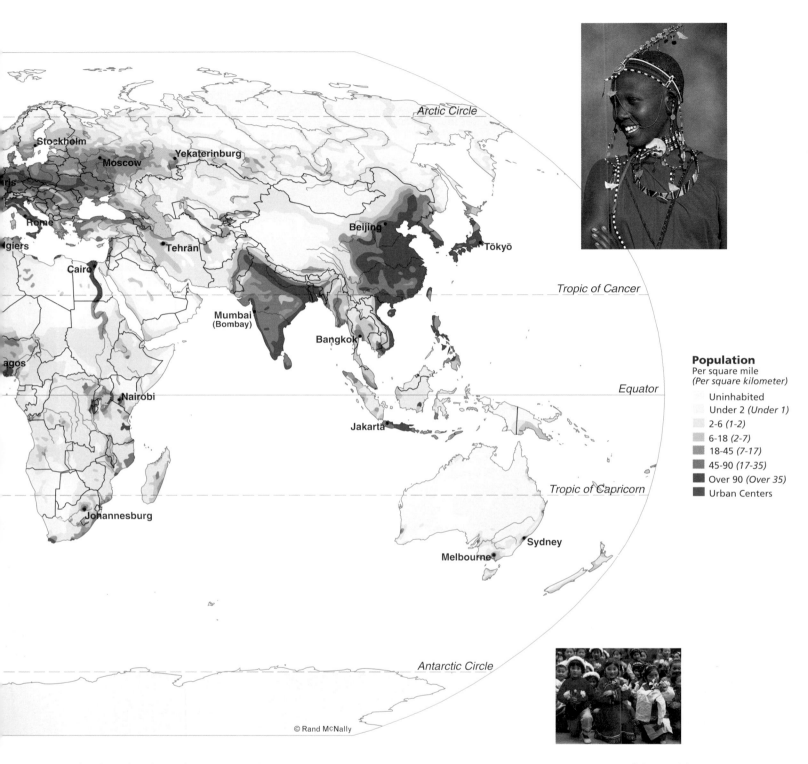

Population
Per square mile
(Per square kilometer)

- Uninhabited
- Under 2 *(Under 1)*
- 2-6 *(1-2)*
- 6-18 *(2-7)*
- 18-45 *(7-17)*
- 45-90 *(17-35)*
- Over 90 *(Over 35)*
- Urban Centers

© Rand McNally

Look for the red and purple regions — they represent the world's most densely populated areas. The huge populations of India and China are settled in Asia's rich farmlands. For the most part, most of these people still live away from cities in country, or rural, areas.

In Europe and the United States, by contrast, the most populous areas are cities, or urban areas, which grew up near farmland, resources, and trade routes, especially waterways. In the United States, people are concentrated along the Atlantic and Pacific Oceans, the shores of the Great Lakes, and the banks of the Mississippi River. Cities contain the majority of the population of Australia, Argentina, Canada, France, Japan, and the United States.

Japan is one of the world's most densely populated countries. Slightly smaller than the state of California, it holds more than 127 million people.

World Physical

This map shows the physical features found on the surface of the earth. The colors and shading on the map indicate the kind of terrain found in that area of the world. The legend to the right of the map explains what the colors mean.

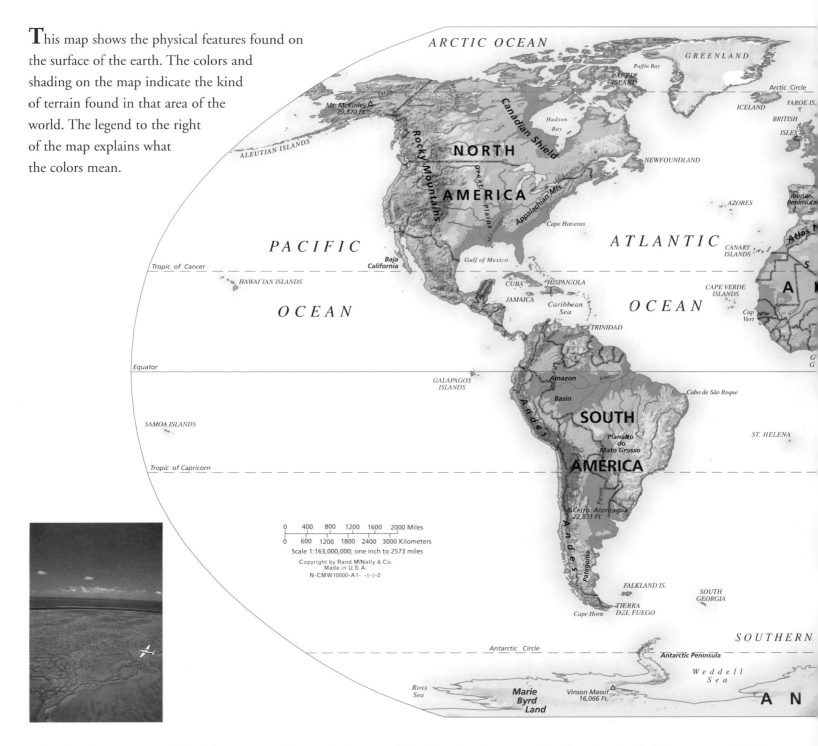

ARCTIC OCEAN

GREENLAND

Baffin Bay

BAFFIN ISLAND

Arctic Circle

ICELAND

FAROE IS.

BRITISH ISLES

Mt. McKinley 20,320 Ft.

Yukon

Mackenzie

Canadian Shield

Hudson Bay

NEWFOUNDLAND

ALEUTIAN ISLANDS

Rocky Mountains

NORTH AMERICA

Great Plains

St. Lawrence

Appalachian Mts.

Cape Hatteras

AZORES

Iberian Peninsula

Atlas M

PACIFIC

Colorado

Mississippi

Baja California

Gulf of Mexico

ATLANTIC

CANARY ISLANDS

A

S

Tropic of Cancer

HAWAI'IAN ISLANDS

CUBA

HISPANIOLA

JAMAICA

Caribbean Sea

OCEAN

CAPE VERDE ISLANDS

Cap Vert

Niger

A

OCEAN

TRINIDAD

Orinoco

G G

Equator

GALAPAGOS ISLANDS

Amazon

Amazon

Cabo de São Roque

SAMOA ISLANDS

Basin

Andes

SOUTH

Planalto do Mato Grosso

ST. HELENA

Tropic of Capricorn

AMERICA

Paraná

Cerro Aconcagua 22,831 Ft.

0   400   800   1200   1600   2000 Miles
0   600 1200 1800 2400 3000 Kilometers
Scale 1:163,000,000; one inch to 2573 miles
Copyright by Rand McNally & Co.
Made in U.S.A.
N-CMW10000-A1- -1-2-2

Andes

Patagonia

FALKLAND IS.

SOUTH GEORGIA

Cape Horn

TIERRA DEL FUEGO

SOUTHERN

Antarctic Circle

Antarctic Peninsula

Weddell Sea

Ross Sea

Marie Byrd Land

Vinson Massif 16,066 Ft.

AN

More than three-quarters of Earth is covered by water, including five oceans and many smaller seas, all made up of salt water. Fresh water — water without salt — is most often found in smaller inland lakes and rivers, such as the Great Lakes in North America.

The remaining part of Earth's surface is made up of landmasses with mountains, deserts, rivers, lakes, and plateaus. The floors of oceans and seas also have mountains and valleys, but you can't see them because they're underwater. This map shows the names and different categories of Earth's physical features.

Earth's surface is called the crust, a wrinkled layer of solid rock that is constantly changing. The crust is cracked into a dozen separate fragments called tectonic plates, which float on a sea of dense, semi-liquid rock far below the surface. Columns of this molten rock slowly rise and fall, nudging the bases of the crustal plates that float on Earth's surface. As the plates try to move, they push into neighboring plates.

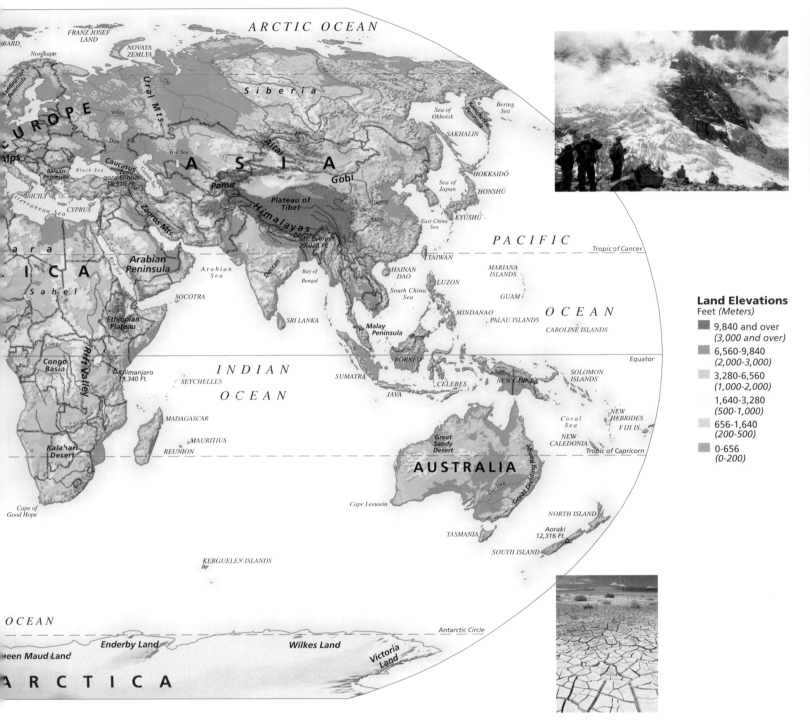

Land Elevations
Feet (Meters)

- 9,840 and over (3,000 and over)
- 6,560-9,840 (2,000-3,000)
- 3,280-6,560 (1,000-2,000)
- 1,640-3,280 (500-1,000)
- 656-1,640 (200-500)
- 0-656 (0-200)

Over millions of years, the pushing, grinding, and colliding of tectonic plates has crumpled, folded, and lifted rock, slowly building up the world's great mountain ranges. For instance, the Appalachian Mountains in eastern North America resulted from a collision between North America and Africa some 320 million years ago. Likewise, the Himalayas —

the highest mountains in the world — were forced upward when India rammed into Asia. On this map, you can see where Earth's mountains have formed.

The map also shows the world's desert regions. Deserts are dry lands with low rainfall and sparse plant and animal life. Not all deserts are hot, sandy, and sunny. They can also be cold, rocky, or ice-covered.

World Political

This map shows the countries of the world. Unlike the colors on the other maps in this section, the colors on this map do not tell you anything about a particular country. They are there to make it easier to see each country separately on the map. This type of map is called a political map because it shows the world's divisions by country.

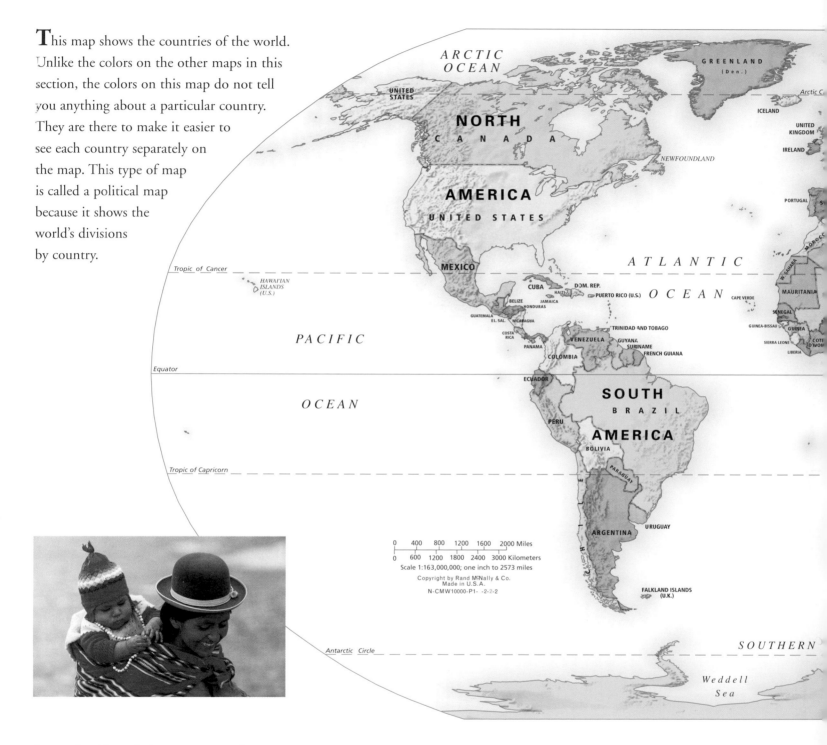

International boundaries are represented on this map by a dashed black line. These lines divide the world into separate countries. Sometimes country borders follow natural features such as rivers or mountain ranges. For example, the crooked northwestern border of China runs along a river. In many places, though, people decide where boundaries should fall — as with the straight portion of the boundary between Canada and the United States.

Although most political boundaries are well established, changes still occur. In 1990, for instance, East and West Germany reunited, and Germany became a single country. In 1991 the Soviet Union dissolved, and its 15 republics became independent countries.

Some countries, like Russia and Canada, are large and take up a lot of space on any world political map. Other countries — like Vatican City in Rome, Italy — are so tiny that they aren't usually shown on a world political map unless the map scale is very large.

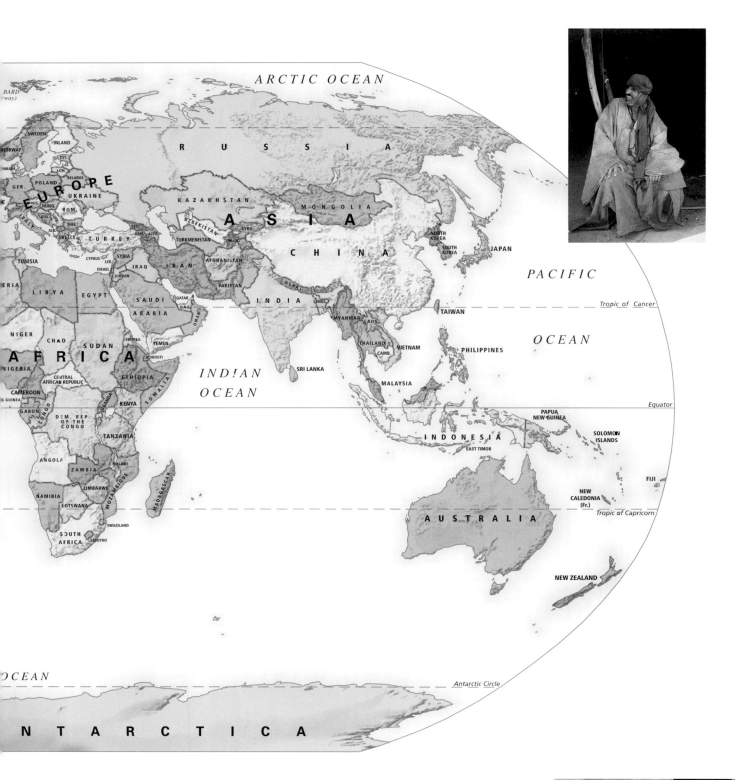

ARCTIC OCEAN

SWEDEN FINLAND
NORWAY
EST.
LAT.
LITH.
BELARUS
DENMARK
POLAND
UKRAINE
GER.
AUS.
HUNG.
ROM.
BOS.
ITALY
ALB.
BUL.
GREECE
TURKEY
GEO.
ARM. AZER.
CYPRUS
LEB.
SYRIA
ISRAEL
JORDAN
IRAQ
TUNISIA
LIBYA
EGYPT
SAUDI
ARABIA
QATAR
U.A.E.
OMAN

EUROPE

RUSSIA

KAZAKHSTAN
UZBEKISTAN
KYRG.
TURKMENISTAN
TAJIK.
IRAN
AFGHANISTAN
PAKISTAN

MONGOLIA

ASIA

CHINA

NORTH
KOREA
SOUTH
KOREA
JAPAN

PACIFIC

NEPAL
INDIA
BNGL.

TAIWAN

Tropic of Cancer

OCEAN

MYANMAR
LAOS

NIGER
CHAD
SUDAN
ERITREA
YEMEN
DJIBOUTI

AFRICA

NIGERIA
CENTRAL
AFRICAN REPUBLIC
ETHIOPIA
CAMEROON
EQ. GUINEA
GABON
CONGO
DEM. REP.
OF THE
CONGO
UGANDA
KENYA
SOMALIA
TANZANIA
ANGOLA
ZAMBIA
MALAWI
NAMIBIA
ZIMBABWE
BOTSWANA
MOZAMBIQUE
MADAGASCAR
SOUTH
AFRICA
SWAZILAND
LESOTHO

THAILAND
CAMB.
VIETNAM

SRI LANKA

MALAYSIA

PHILIPPINES

INDIAN
OCEAN

INDONESIA

EAST TIMOR

PAPUA
NEW GUINEA

SOLOMON
ISLANDS

Equator

FIJI

NEW
CALEDONIA
(Fr.)

AUSTRALIA

Tropic of Capricorn

NEW ZEALAND

OCEAN

Antarctic Circle

ANTARCTICA

BARD
(Norway)

When people study the world, they often group countries by land areas called continents. The seven continents are the great divisions of Earth's land. Nearly all of them are landmasses almost completely surrounded by water.

This atlas divides the world into the seven continents: North America, South America, Europe, Africa, Asia, Australia (including the South Pacific area of Oceania), and Antarctica.

NORTH AMERICA

North America stretches from Greenland in the Arctic Ocean to Panama on the Caribbean Sea. The far northern areas of the world's third-largest continent are permanently covered with ice and snow. Flat, fertile plains spread across the center. In the west rise the rugged chains of mountains that include the towering Rocky Mountains and Coast Ranges, and in the east are the ancient, rolling Appalachian Mountains. Deserts dominate the southwest, and tropical rain forests flourish near the equator.

North America is a continent of spectacular scenery, varied landscapes, and vast resources. It includes the Canadian Shield, where Earth's oldest rock lies; the glacier-gouged Great Lakes; the breathtaking Grand Canyon; the endless expanses of Mexico's white-sand beaches, and the lush volcanic islands of the Caribbean.

New York (above) is the largest city in the United States; El Castillo (left) at Chichen Itza, Mexico, represents ancient Mayan architecture; the lofty Alaska Range (below) soars above clouds in Denali National Park.

ARCTIC OCEAN

Bering Sea

Brooks Range

Anchorage

Alaska Range

Mt. McKinley 20,320

Alaska Peninsula

ALEUTIAN ISLANDS

U.S.

Gulf of Alaska

Mt. Logan 19,551 Ft.

QUEEN CHARLOTTE ISLANDS

VANCOUVER ISLAND

Vancouver

Cape Blanco

Cape Mendocino

PACIFIC OCEAN

Coast Ranges

Cascade Range

Sierra Nevada

Great Basin

Columbia

Snake

Great Salt Lake

LOS ANGELES

Mt. Whitney 14,494 Ft.

Colorado Plateau

UNITED STATES

Denver

Colorado

Arkansas

Red

Rio Grande

Bala California

Punta Eugenia

Gulf of California

Sierra Madre Occidental

Tropic of Cancer

Cabo San Lucas

ISLAS REVILLAGIGEDO

MEXICO

MEXICO CITY

Pico de Orizaba 18,406 Ft.

Sierra Madre Oriental

Bahía de Campeche

Yucatan Peninsula

BELIZE

GUATEMALA

Gulf of Honduras

HONDURAS

EL SALVADOR

NICARAGUA

Lago de Nicaragua

COSTA RICA

PANAMA

Istmo de Panamá

Golfo de Panamá

Beaufort Sea

Point Hope

Point Barrow

Cape Bathurst

BANKS ISLAND

Mackenzie

Great Bear Lake

Great Slave Lake

Whitehorse

Yukon

Kuskokwim

Peace

Lake Athabasca

Edmonton

Saskatchewan

Lake Winnipeg

C A N A D A

Nelson

Churchill

Albany

Great Plains

Missouri

Mississippi

CHICAGO

Lake Superior

Great Lakes

Lake Michigan

Lake Huron

MONTREAL

Ottawa

St. Lawrence

L. Ontario

Niagara Falls

Lake Erie

Ohio

Ozark Plateau

Coastal Plain

HOUSTON

GULF OF MEXICO

Cape Sable

Havana

Canal de Yucatán

CUBA

JAMAICA

CARIBBEAN SEA

QUEEN ELIZABETH ISLANDS

VICTORIA ISLAND

DEVON ISLAND

ELLESMERE ISLAND

Baffin Bay

Cape Adair

BAFFIN ISLAND

Foxe Basin

Cape Mercy

Hudson Bay

Péninsule d'Ungava

James Bay

Smallwood Resevoir

Gulf of St. Lawrence

Canadian Shield

G r e a t P l a i n s

Cape Sable

NEWFOUNDLAND

Appalachian Mts.

Cape Cod

NEW YORK

Washington

Cape Hatteras

ATLANTIC OCEAN

Cape Canaveral

Miami

BAHAMAS

Tropic of Cancer

WEST INDIES

GREATER ANTILLES

HAITI

DOMINICAN REPUBLIC

PUERTO RICO (U.S.)

LESSER ANTILLES

TRINIDAD AND TOBAGO

Kap Morris Jesup

GREENLAND (Denmark)

Arctic Circle

Kap Brewster

Kap Mosting

Ice Cap

Kap Farvel

Arctic Circle

Arctic Circle

Land Elevation
Feet (Meters)

- 9,840 and over (3,000 and over)
- 6,560 - 9,840 (2,000 - 3,000)
- 3,280 - 6,560 (1,000 - 2,000)
- 1,640 - 3,280 (500 - 1,000)
- 656 - 1,640 (200 - 500)
- 0 - 656 feet (0 - 200)

0   200   400   600 Miles
0   200   400   600   800   1000 Kilometers

Scale 1:45,000,000; one inch to 710 miles

Copyright by Rand McNally & Co.
Made in U.S.A.

N-CMW20000-A1- -1-1-1

N
W   E
S

North America Facts

Area: 9,500,000 square miles (24,700,000 square kilometers)

Highest Mountain: Mount McKinley, Alaska, United States, 20,320 feet (6,194 meters)

Lowest Point: Death Valley, California, United States, -282 feet (-86 meters)

Longest River: Mississippi-Missouri, central United States, 3,710 miles (5,971 kilometers)

Largest Lake: Lake Superior, Canada-United States 31,700 square miles (82,100 square kilometers)

Largest Desert: Chihuahuan Desert, Mexico-United States, 124,000 square miles (321,000 square kilometers)

Largest Island: Greenland, 836,331 square miles (2,156,086 square kilometers)—*world's largest island*

THE LAND

North America is a land of abundance. The continent has plentiful minerals, mighty rivers that provide hydroelectric power, and rich farmland that yields fruits, vegetables, and grain. The United States is the economic powerhouse of the continent, while Canada's economy is diversified with mining, agriculture, and tourism. Mexico's oil fields are one of that country's most important resources. The countries of Central America export a variety of tropical produce to lands farther north.

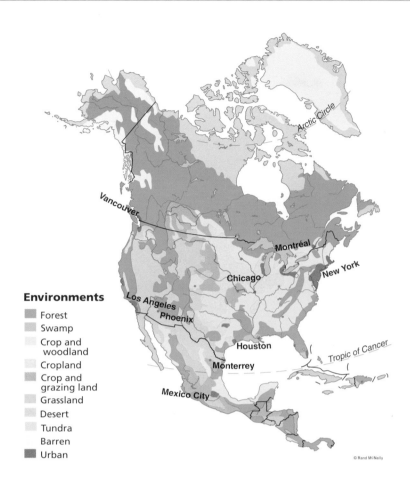

Environments

■	Forest
■	Swamp
■	Crop and woodland
■	Cropland
■	Crop and grazing land
■	Grassland
■	Desert
■	Tundra
■	Barren
■	Urban

© Rand McNally

Steel production in the United States and Canada is one of North America's best-known industries.

Industry

Industry provides a huge portion of the wealth in North America. Most industrial regions developed around port cities, where it was easy to receive raw materials and to ship out finished products. Mexico's role in manufacturing is growing as companies from the United States relocate their factories there. Canada and the United States, however, are still the leading industrial countries in North America.

Farming

North America produces more of the world's food than any other continent. In the temperate region that extends from southern Canada to northern Mexico, major crops include corn, wheat, and soybeans. Tropical and subtropical regions export bananas, cocoa, coffee, oranges, and other produce.

Environments

Forests, North America's dominant environment, cover one-third of the continent. Much of the land in the continent's midsection, especially the plains that lie between the Rocky Mountains and the Appalachian Mountains, is devoted to farming and livestock. Parched, barren deserts stretch across large parts of the southwestern United States and northwestern Mexico. Tundra spreads across most of Alaska and northern Canada. A thick sheet of ice covers nearly the entire island of Greenland. In contrast, the islands of the Caribbean support lush vegetation and dense tropical forests.

The midwestern United States is one of the world's largest producers of corn.

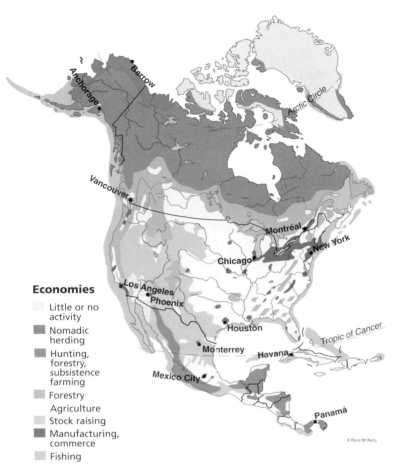

Economies

Little or no activity

Nomadic herding

Hunting, forestry, subsistence farming

Forestry

Agriculture

Stock raising

Manufacturing, commerce

Fishing

© Rand McNally

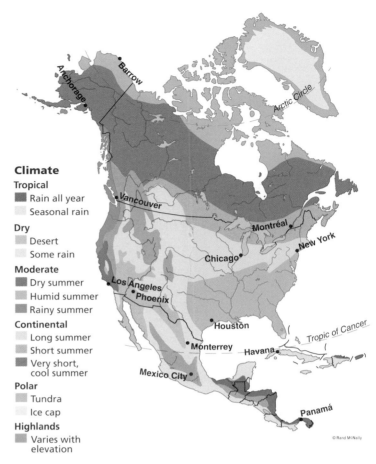

Climate

Tropical
Rain all year

Seasonal rain

Dry
Desert

Some rain

Moderate
Dry summer

Humid summer

Rainy summer

Continental
Long summer

Short summer

Very short, cool summer

Polar
Tundra

Ice cap

Highlands
Varies with elevation

© Rand McNally

Economies

North America's abundant resources provide both the continent and the world with food, raw materials such as wood and mineral ores, and manufactured goods.

Mining and Mineral Resources

Much of the world's copper, lead, iron ore, and zinc are mined in North America. Coal, oil, and natural gas are plentiful, providing fuel for the factories of Canada, the United States, and Mexico.

Coal miners wear headlamps and protective gear when they work underground.

Climate

Almost every type of climate is found in North America, from the frozen tundra in the far north to the tropical areas in the south. Much of the continent, however, enjoys a temperate climate that is just right for growing crops and raising cattle.

A logger loads cut timber onto a truck for transport.

Forestry

Canada is one of the world's major exporters of wood and wood products. Forestry also plays a major role in the economies of the Pacific Northwest, the Gulf Coast, and the southern Atlantic coastal regions of the United States.

THE PEOPLE

North America is a land settled by immigrants. Even the earliest North American Indians migrated from Asia across a land bridge that once linked the two continents. Today, much of the population is descended from Europeans. African Americans, many of whose ancestors were brought to North America as slaves from the sixteenth to the nineteenth centuries, are also an important part of North America's ethnic mix. North Americans speak Spanish and English primarily; French is spoken in the Canadian province of Québec. Many other native languages are also spoken throughout the continent. The United States has the largest population of any country in North America, and Mexico City is the continent's most populous city.

Three cowboys in Mexico City prepare to ride in a rodeo.

Children laugh on a playground in Cuba.

Montréal, Canada, has a distinctly French character.

The Inuit people of Alaska and northern Canada build igloos with blocks of ice or compacted snow.

Los Angeles, California, reflects a "melting pot" of nationalities and cultures.

Three children row on a pond in New York's Central Park.

A costumed crowd gathers for a carnival on Antigua, an island in the Lesser Antilles.

North America Facts

Population: 505,780,000

Population Density:
53 people per square mile
(20 per square kilometer)

Most Populous Country:
United States,
291,680,000 people

Largest City:
Mexico City, Mexico,
19,000,000 people
(metropolitan area)

Scale 1:45,000,000; one inch to 710 miles
Copyright by Rand McNally & Co.
Made in U.S.A.
N-CMW20000-P1- -1-1-1

Ottawa has been Canada's capital since 1857.

CANADA

Canada is the largest country in North America. A large portion of its land lies in the harsh regions of the far north, making this one of the most sparsely populated countries in the world. Most of Canada's people live in cities and towns near the country's border with the United States. In 1999, a new territory called Nunavut, which means "Our Land," was carved out of the eastern and northern portions of the Northwest Territories; it joined 10 provinces and two other territories. Most of the citizens of Nunavut are Inuit, the native people of northern Canada.

Totem poles are an integral part of the culture of western Canada's native people.

On Prince Edward Island, a lighthouse stands at Shipwreck Point.

Polar bears roam the frozen wilderness of northern Canada.

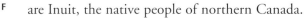

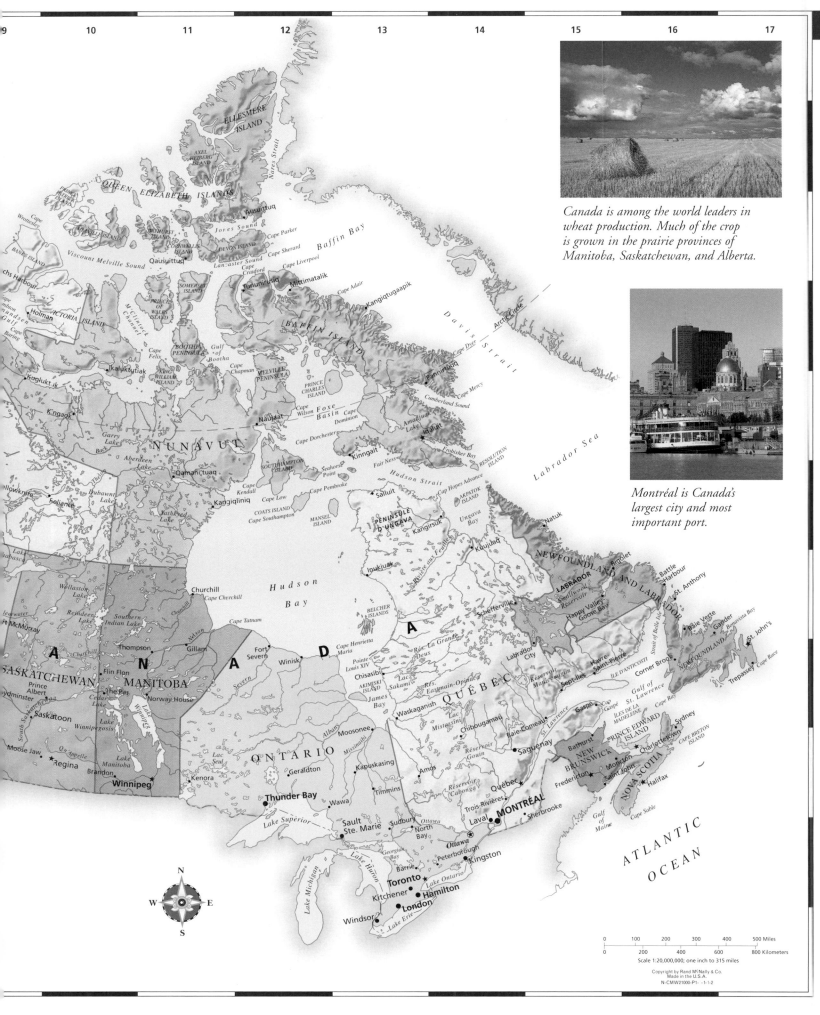

9   10   11   12   13   14   15   16   17

Canada is among the world leaders in wheat production. Much of the crop is grown in the prairie provinces of Manitoba, Saskatchewan, and Alberta.

Montréal is Canada's largest city and most important port.

ELLESMERE ISLAND

AXEL HEIBERG ISLAND

QUEEN ELIZABETH ISLANDS

PRINCE PATRICK ISLAND

MELVILLE ISLAND

BANKS ISLAND

Viscount Melville Sound

BATHURST ISLAND

CORNWALLIS ISLAND

DEVON ISLAND

Jones Sound

Ausuittuq

Nares Strait

Cape Parker

Cape Sherard

Lancaster Sound

Cape Crauford

Cape Liverpool

Baffin Bay

Cape Adair

Kangiqtugaapik

Davis Strait

Arctic Circle

Qausuittuq

SOMERSET ISLAND

PRINCE OF WALES ISLAND

M'Clintock Channel

BOOTHIA PENINSULA

Gulf of Boothia

Tununirusiq

Mittimatalik

BAFFIN ISLAND

Cape Dyer

Labrador Sea

chs Harbour

Cape Wrottesley

PRINCE ALBERT

Holman

Amundsen Gulf

VICTORIA ISLAND

Cape Baring

Cape Felix

Cape Chapman

MELVILLE PENINSULA

Pannirtuuq

Cape Mercy

Iqaluktuuttiaq

KING WILLIAM ISLAND

PRINCE CHARLES ISLAND

Cumberland Sound

Kugluktuk

Naujaat

Cape Wilson

Foxe Basin

Cape Dominion

Amadjuak Lake

Kinngait

Iqaluit

Frobisher Bay

K'ngaok

Garry Lake

Back

Aberdeen Lake

NUNAVUT

SOUTHAMPTON ISLAND

Seahorse Point

Fair Ness

Hudson Strait

RESOLUTION ISLAND

llowknife

Thelon

Dubawnt Lake

Qamani'tuaq

Cape Kendall

Cape Low

Cape Dorchester

Cape Pembroke

Salluit

Cap Hopes Advance

AKPATOK ISLAND

Reliance

Yathked Lake

Kangiqliniq

COATS ISLAND

Cape Southampton

MANSEL ISLAND

PENINSULE D'UNGAVA

Kangirsuk

Ungava Bay

Natuk

ellowknife

NEWFOUNDLAND AND LABRADOR

Rigolet

Inukjuak

Rivière aux Feuilles

Kuujjuaq

Battle Harbour

LABRADOR

St. Anthony

Wollaston Lake

Churchill

Cape Churchill

Hudson Bay

Smallwood Reservoir

Happy Valley-Goose Bay

Baie Verte

Gander

Botavista Bay

St. John's

learwater

Reindeer Lake

Southern Indian Lake

Cape Tatnam

Schefferville

NEWFOUNDLAND

Corner Brook

Cape Race

t McMurray

Churchill

Thompson

Gillam

Fort Severn

BELCHER ISLANDS

Labrador City

Strait of Belle Isle

Trepassey

A

N

A

D

A

Cape Henrietta Maria

Rés. La Grande Deux

ÎLE D'ANTICOSTI

SASKATCHEWAN

Flin Flon

MANITOBA

Winisk

Pointe Louis XIV

Rés. Eastmain-Opinaca

Réservoir Manicouagan

Sept-Îles

Prince Albert

Cedar Lake

The Pas

Nelson

Severn

Chisasibi

AKIMISKI ISLAND

Lac Sakami

QUÉBEC

Havre Saint-Pierre

Gulf of St. Lawrence

Sydney

ydminster

Saskatoon

Lake Winnipegosis

Norway House

James Bay

Waskaganish

Lac Mistassini

Baie-Comeau

St. Lawrence

Gaspé

ÎLES DE LA MADELEINE

CAPE BRETON ISLAND

South Sask.

Moose Jaw

Qu'Appelle

Lake Manitoba

Lake Winnipeg

Moosonee

Missinaibi

Chibougamau

Saguenay

PRINCE EDWARD ISLAND

Charlottetown

Regina

Brandon

Winnipeg

Kenora

Lac Seul

ONTARIO

Geraldton

Kapuskasing

Amos

Réservoir Gouin

Baie-Comeau

Bathurst

NEW BRUNSWICK

Moncton

NOVA SCOTIA

Thunder Bay

Wawa

Timmins

Réservoir Cabonga

Québec

Trois-Rivières

Fredericton

Saint John

Halifax

Lake Superior

Sault Ste. Marie

Sudbury

North Bay

Ottawa

MONTRÉAL

Laval

Sherbrooke

Gulf of Maine

Cape Sable

Lake Michigan

Georgian Bay

Lake Huron

Barrie

Peterborough

Kingston

ATLANTIC OCEAN

N

W   E

S

Toronto

Lake Ontario

Kitchener

Hamilton

London

Windsor

Lake Erie

| 0 | 100 | 200 | 300 | 400 | 500 Miles |

| 0 | 200 | 400 | 600 | 800 Kilometers |

Scale 1:20,000,000; one inch to 315 miles

UNITED STATES

The United States occupies the central portion of the continent, but also includes Alaska, next to Canada's northwest corner, and Hawaii, a chain of islands in the middle of the Pacific Ocean. The United States is the most prosperous and populous country in North America. It also has the world's most ethnically diverse population. A large number of the country's people live in or near its many large cities. In other areas, especially the west, the population is extremely sparse. The landscape of the United States is varied and beautiful, ranging from stark deserts and rockycanyons to majestic mountains and endless plains.

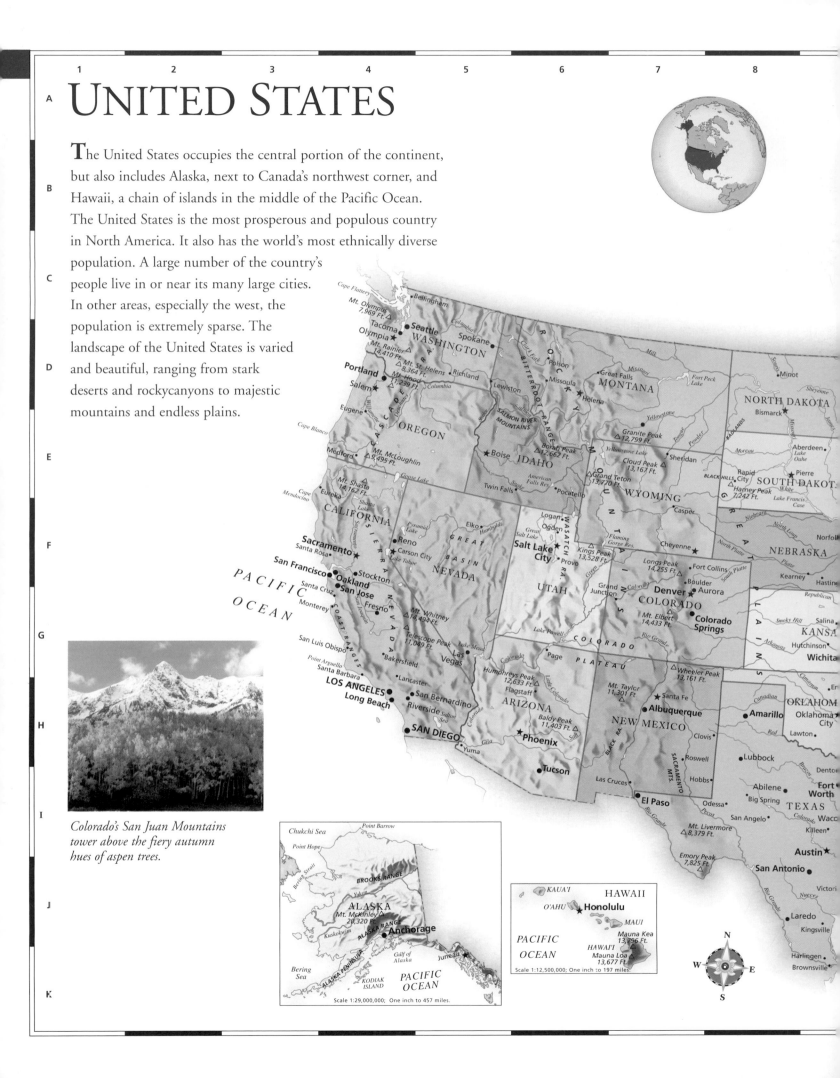

Colorado's San Juan Mountains tower above the fiery autumn hues of aspen trees.

Cape Flattery
Bellingham
Mt. Olympus 7,969 Ft.
Tacoma Seattle Spokane
Olympia WASHINGTON
Mt. Rainier 14,410 Ft.
Portland Mt. St. Helens 8,364 Ft. Richland
Mt. Hood 11,239 Ft. Lewiston
Salem Columbia
Eugene BITTERROOT RANGE
Cape Blanco OREGON SALMON RIVER MOUNTAINS
Medford Mt. McLoughlin 9,495 Ft.
Boise IDAHO Borah Peak 12,662 Ft.
Mt. Shasta 14,162 Ft. Goose Lake Twin Falls American Falls Res. Pocatello
Cape Mendocino Eureka Shasta Lake
CALIFORNIA Pyramid Lake Elko Humboldt GREAT BASIN
Sacramento Reno Carson City NEVADA
Santa Rosa Lake Tahoe
San Francisco Stockton
Oakland San Jose Fresno Mt. Whitney 14,494 Ft.
Santa Cruz San Joaquin Telescope Peak 11,049 Ft. Lake Mead
Monterey COAST RANGES Las Vegas
San Luis Obispo Bakersfield
Point Arguello Santa Barbara Lancaster
LOS ANGELES San Bernardino
Long Beach Riverside Salton Sea
SAN DIEGO Gila Yuma

Polson
Great Falls
MONTANA
Missoula
Helena
Yellowstone
Granite Peak 12,799 Ft.
Yellowstone Lake
Cloud Peak 13,167 Ft. Sheridan
Grand Teton 13,770 Ft. WYOMING
Logan Ogden Salt Lake City Provo Flaming Gorge Res. Casper
Great Salt Lake WASATCH Kings Peak 13,528 Ft.
UTAH Longs Peak 14,255 Ft. Fort Collins
Grand Junction Colorado Denver Boulder Aurora
Lake Powell Mt. Elbert 14,433 Ft. Colorado Springs
Page COLORADO PLATEAU Wheeler Peak 13,161 Ft.
Colorado Humphreys Peak 12,633 Ft. Mt. Taylor 11,301 Ft. Santa Fe
Flagstaff Albuquerque
ARIZONA Baldy Peak 11,403 Ft. NEW MEXICO
Phoenix Clovis
Salt Roswell
Tucson Las Cruces Hobbs
El Paso

Columbia Clark Fork
Milk Missouri
Fort Peck Lake
Minot
Sheyenne
NORTH DAKOTA Bismarck
BADLANDS Morean
Aberdeen Lake Oahe
SOUTH DAKOTA Pierre
BLACK HILLS Rapid City White Lake Francis Case
Harney Peak 7,242 Ft.
North Loup Niobrara Norfolk
Cheyenne North Platte NEBRASKA
Platte Kearney Hastings
GREAT Republican
Smoky Hill Salina
Rio Grande PLAINS KANSAS
Arkansas Hutchinson Wichita
Canadian Cimarron
OKLAHOMA Oklahoma City
Amarillo Lawton
Red
Lubbock Denton
Abilene Fort Worth
Big Spring TEXAS Waco Killeen
Brazos Austin
Odessa Colorado
Mt. Livermore 8,379 Ft. San Angelo
San Antonio
Pecos
Emory Peak 7,825 Ft. Victoria
Rio Grande Nueces
Laredo Kingsville
Harlingen
Brownsville

PACIFIC OCEAN

Chukchi Sea Point Barrow
Point Hope
Bering Strait Yukon BROOKS RANGE
ALASKA Mt. McKinley 20,320 Ft.
Kuskokwim ALASKA RANGE Anchorage
Bering Sea ALASKA PENINSULA Gulf of Alaska Juneau
KODIAK ISLAND PACIFIC OCEAN
Scale 1:29,000,000; One inch to 457 miles.

KAUA'I HAWAII
O'AHU Honolulu
MAUI
PACIFIC OCEAN HAWAI'I Mauna Kea 13,796 Ft.
Mauna Loa 13,677 Ft.
Scale 1:12,500,000; One inch to 197 miles.

N
W   E
S

10   11   12   13   14   15   16   17

The Navajo are one of many Native American tribes that live in the desert Southwest.

The design of many state capitol buildings imitates the dome shape of the U.S. Capitol in Washington, D.C.

Lake of the Woods

nd Forks

oorhead

Duluth

Superior

Marquette

MINNESOTA

St. Cloud

St. Paul

Wausau

Eau Claire

Green Bay

Minneapolis

Mankato

Austin

WISCONSIN

Appleton

Sheboygan

MICHIGAN

Grand Rapids

Bay City

Flint

La Crosse

Milwaukee

Madison Racine

Lansing

DETROIT

Fort Dodge

Cedar Rapids

Rockford

Ann Arbor

IOWA

Des Moines

Davenport

Moline

South Bend

Toledo

Cleveland

Des Moines

Ottumwa

CHICAGO

Gary

Fort Wayne

Akron

Canton

ncoln

Omaha

Burlington

Peoria

Kankakee

Lima

INDIANA

OHIO

Pittsburgh

St. Joseph

Quincy

ILLINOIS

Indianapolis

Dayton

Columbus

anhattan

Kansas City

Columbia

Terre Haute

Springfield

Cincinnati

eka

Jefferson City

St. Louis

Columbus

Louisville

Parkersburg

Wheeling

MISSOURI

MICHIGAN

Lake Superior

KEWEENAW PENINSULA

Whitefish Point

Mackinaw City

Lake Huron

Lake Michigan

Saginaw Bay

Lake Erie

Mt. Katahdin 5,267 Ft. △

MAINE

Bangor

Mt. Washington 6,288 Ft. △

Augusta

VERMONT

Lake Champlain

Montpelier

Lewiston

N.H.

Portland

Gulf of Maine

ADIRONDACK MTS.

Concord

NEW YORK

Rochester

Syracuse

MASS.

Boston

Cape Cod

Lake Ontario

Albany

Worcester

Providence

Niagara Falls

Buffalo

Elmira

Hartford

CONN. R.I.

NANTUCKET ISLAND

Jamestown

Scranton

PENNSYLVANIA

Paterson

NEW YORK

Youngstown

Allentown

Newark

Harrisburg

Trenton

PHILADELPHIA

Wilmington

NEW JERSEY

Baltimore

Dover

Annapolis

DELAWARE

WASHINGTON

MARYLAND

W. VA.

Charleston

VIRGINIA

Richmond

James

Chesapeake Bay

Louisville

Evansville

Frankfort

Lexington

Roanoke

Norfolk

Virginia Beach

Portsmouth

Springfield

KENTUCKY

Bowling Green

Lake Cumberland

Winston-Salem

Raleigh

Pamlico Sound

Cape Hatteras

Bartlesville

OZARK PLATEAU

Cape Girardeau

Paducah

Clarksville

Knoxville

Asheville

Mt. Mitchell 6,684 Ft. △

NORTH CAROLINA

Cape Lookout

Tulsa

Fayetteville

Jonesboro

Nashville

Cumberland

Kentucky Lake

TENNESSEE

Charlotte

Cape Fear

Muskogee

ARKANSAS

Chattanooga

Greenville

Florence

Wilmington

Cape Fear

ATLANTIC

nryetta

OUACHITA MTS.

Memphis

Huntsville

Rome

SOUTH CAROLINA

Columbia

OCEAN

oma

Little Rock

Hot Springs

Pine Bluff

Tupelo

Gadsden

Anniston

Atlanta

Charleston

rison

Paris

Texarkana

El Dorado

Greenville

Birmingham

Tuscaloosa

GEORGIA

Augusta

LLAS

MISSISSIPPI

ALABAMA

Macon

ongview

Shreveport

Meridian

Selma

Montgomery

Savannah

yan

Natchez

Jackson

Hattiesburg

Dothan

Albany

LOUISIANA

Sam Rayburn Res.

Toledo Bend Res.

Alexandria

Valdosta

Jacksonville

USTON

Beaumont

Baton Rouge

Biloxi

Mobile

Pensacola

Tallahassee

Gainesville

Daytona Beach

New Iberia

Houma

New Orleans

Panama City

Cape San Blas

Ocala

FLORIDA

Cape Canaveral

Galveston

GULF OF MEXICO

Orlando

Lakeland

Melbourne

Tampa

St. Petersburg

Fort Pierce

Sarasota

Lake Okeechobee

West Palm Beach

Fort Myers

Fort Lauderdale

Miami

Cape Sable

FLORIDA KEYS

Limestone-rich grasses in Kentucky contain a lot of calcium; horses that eat them often become strong runners.

Four surfers walk along the beach in southern California.

Prairie dogs make their homes in burrows across the central and western parts of the United States.

0   100   200   300   400 Miles
0   100   200   300   400   500   600 Kilometers

Scale 1:16,000,000; one inch to 252 miles.
Copyright by Rand McNally
Made in the U.S.A.
N-CMW24000-P1- -1-1-2

MEXICO, CENTRAL AMERICA, AND THE CARIBBEAN

A

B

N
W E
S

Tijuana
Ensenada
Mexicali
BAJA CALIFORNIA
Cerro de la Encantada △10,069 Ft.
Nogales
Agua Prieta
Ciudad Juárez
Rio Grande
SONORA
Gulf of California
ISLA CEDROS
Punta Eugenia
C
Hermosillo
CHIHUAHUA
Ciudad Acuña
Cuauhtémoc
Chihuahua
Piedras Negras
Empalme
Delicias
Nueva Rosita
Volcán Las Tres Vírgenes 6,299 Ft.
Ciudad Obregón
Hidalgo del Parral
Camargo
COAHUILA
Nuevo Laredo
D
BAJA CALIFORNIA SUR
Los Mochis
SIERRA MADRE OCCIDENTAL
Frontera
Monclova
NUEVO LEÓN
Guasave
Gómez Palacio
San Pedro de las Colonias
Reynosa
Guamúchil
Torreón Saltillo
MONTERREY
Matamoros
La Paz
DURANGO
Culiacán
Linares
Tropic of Cancer
SINALOA
Durango ZACATECAS
TAMAULIPAS
GULF OF MEXICO
Cabo San Lucas
E
Mazatlán
MEXICO
Ciudad Victoria
Matehuala
Fresnillo
SAN LUIS POTOSÍ
ISLAS MARÍAS
Zacatecas
Ciudad Mante
NAYARIT
AGUASCALIENTES
Ciudad Madero
ISLAS REVILLAGIGEDO
ISLA SAN BENEDICTO
Tepic
Aguascalientes
San Luis Potosí
Tampico
Puerto Vallarta
Tepatitlán
León
Ciudad Valles
ISLA ROCA PARTIDA
GUADALAJARA
GUANAJUATO Querétaro
Guanajuato
Tuxpan
Cabo Rojo
Mérida
F
ISLA SOCORRO
JALISCO
Irapuato
QUERÉTARO
Pachuca
Poza Rica
YUCATÁN
Cancún
Ciudad Guzmán
Uruapan
Morelia
MÉXICO
HIDALGO
Martínez de la Torre
Campeche
YUCATÁN PENINSULA
Colima
MICHOACÁN MEXICO
Toluca
TLAXCALA
Xalapa
QUINTANA ROO
COLIMA
Tecomán
Puebla
Córdoba
Veracruz
Bahía de Campeche
CAMPECHE
Chetumal
Cuernavaca
Pico de Orizaba 18,406 Ft.
Orizaba
VERACRUZ
Ciudad del Carmen
MORELOS
Tehuacán
Coatzacoalcos
TABASCO
Belize City
G
SIERRA MADRE DEL SUR
GUERRERO
PUEBLA
Minatlán
Villahermosa
Belmopan
BELIZE
Roadrunner
Chilpancingo
Oaxaca
ISLA ROAT
Acapulco
OAXACA
San Cristóbal de las Casas
Gulf of Honduras
Golfo de Tehuantepec
Juchitán
Tuxtla Gutiérrez
CHIAPAS
San Ped Sula
Volcán Tajumulco 13,845 Ft.
Venustiano Carranza
GUATEMALA
El Progr
H
Tapachula
GUATEMALA
HONDUR
Quezaltenango
Tegucig
Escuintla
Santa Ana
PACIFIC
Sonsonate
Cojutepeque
San Miguel
San Salvador
Choluteca
OCEAN
EL SALVADOR
Chinandega
León
Managu
La Nica
Cabo Sant

Mexico, settled by Spaniards, has the largest Spanish-speaking population in the world. Most Mexicans live in cities — one-fourth of them in Mexico City alone. Mexico has large oil fields and silver deposits in its arid northern and western regions, and lush rain forests in the south, near the mountainous and densely forested countries of Central America. The "Mosquito Coast," along the Caribbean shores of Honduras, Nicaragua, and Costa Rica, is a sparsely populated land of swamps and abundant wildlife. Elsewhere in Central America, agriculture, especially coffee, beans, and bananas, is an important part of the economy. To the east of Mexico and Central America in the Caribbean Sea lie hundreds of coral and volcanic islands, inhabited by a vibrant mix of Africans, Asians, and Europeans. Many Caribbean islands are still controlled by the European countries that settled them centuries ago. The islands' coral-sand beaches and turquoise waters attract many tourists and cruise ships.

A bustling outdoor market in Guadalajara, Mexico, sells fruit, clothing, and toys.

10   11   12   13   14   15   16   17

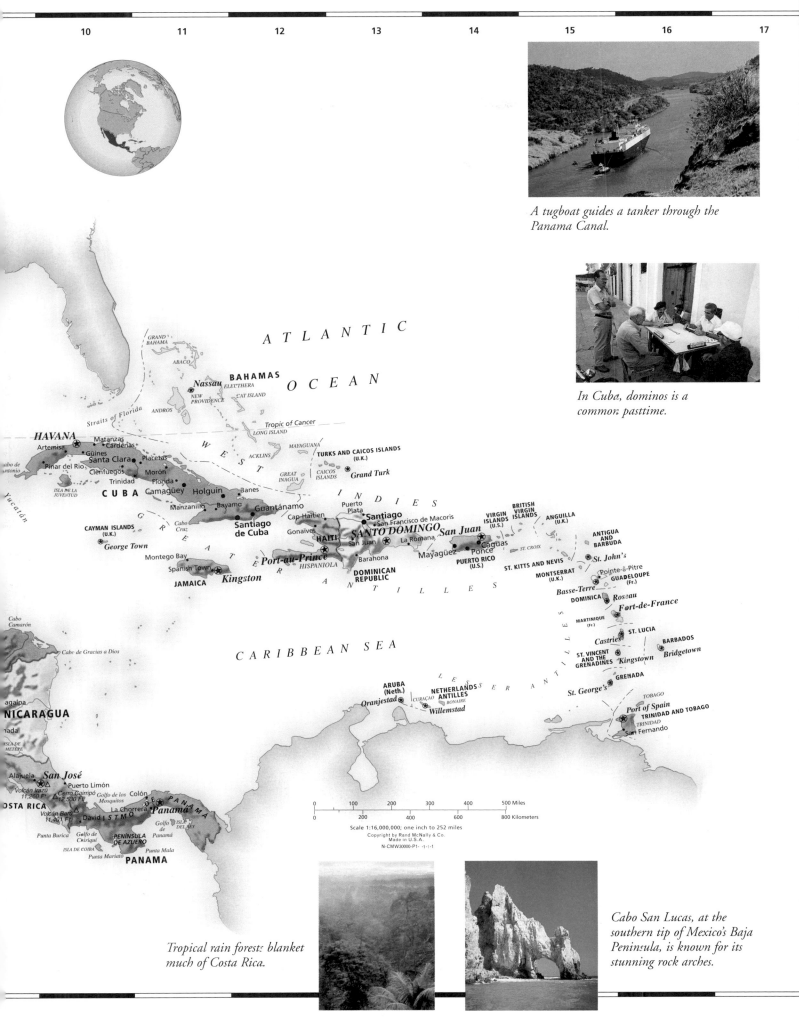

A tugboat guides a tanker through the Panama Canal.

In Cuba, dominos is a common pastime.

ATLANTIC OCEAN

GRAND BAHAMA
ABACO
BAHAMAS
Nassau
ELEUTHERA
NEW PROVIDENCE
CAT ISLAND
Straits of Florida
ANDROS
LONG ISLAND
Tropic of Cancer

HAVANA
Matanzas
Artemisa
Cárdenas
Güines
Santa Clara
Placetas
Pinar del Río
Cienfuegos
Morón
Cabo de Antonio
Trinidad
Florida
ISLA DE LA JUVENTUD
CUBA
Camagüey
Holguín
Banes
Manzanillo
Bayamo
Guantánamo
Cabo Cruz
Santiago de Cuba

ACKLINS
MAYAGUANA
GREAT INAGUA
CAICOS ISLANDS
TURKS AND CAICOS ISLANDS (U.K.)
Grand Turk

WEST INDIES

CAYMAN ISLANDS (U.K.)
George Town

Yucatán

GREATER ANTILLES

Montego Bay
Spanish Town
JAMAICA
Kingston

Cap-Haïtien
Gonaïves
HAITI
Port-au-Prince
HISPANIOLA

Puerto Plata
San Francisco de Macorís
Santiago
SANTO DOMINGO
San Juan
La Romana
Barahona
DOMINICAN REPUBLIC

VIRGIN ISLANDS (U.S.)
BRITISH VIRGIN ISLANDS
San Juan
Caguas
Mayagüez
Ponce
PUERTO RICO (U.S.)
ST. CROIX

ANGUILLA (U.K.)
ANTIGUA AND BARBUDA
St. John's
ST. KITTS AND NEVIS
MONTSERRAT (U.K.)
Pointe-à-Pitre
GUADELOUPE (Fr.)
Basse-Terre
DOMINICA
Roseau
Fort-de-France
MARTINIQUE (Fr.)
Castries
ST. LUCIA
BARBADOS
Bridgetown
ST. VINCENT AND THE GRENADINES
Kingstown
GRENADA
St. George's

LESSER ANTILLES

CARIBBEAN SEA

ARUBA (Neth.)
Oranjestad
CURAÇAO
NETHERLANDS ANTILLES
BONAIRE
Willemstad

TOBAGO
Port of Spain
TRINIDAD AND TOBAGO
TRINIDAD
San Fernando

NICARAGUA
agalpa
ada
ISLA DE OMETEPE

San José
Alajuela
Volcán Irazú 11,260 Ft.
Puerto Limón
Cerro Chirripó 12,530 Ft.
Golfo de los Mosquitos
Colón
OSTA RICA
Volcán Barú 11,401 Ft.
David
La Chorrera
ISTMO DE PANAMÁ
Panamá
Golfo de Panamá
Punta Burica
Golfo de Chiriquí
PENÍNSULA DE AZUERO
ISLA DEL REY
ISLA DE COIBA
Punta Mala
Punta Mariato
PANAMA

0 100 200 300 400 500 Miles
0 200 400 600 800 Kilometers
Scale 1:16,000,000; one inch to 252 miles
Copyright by Rand McNally & Co.
Made in U.S.A.
N-CMW30000-P1- -1-1-1

Tropical rain forest blanket much of Costa Rica.

Cabo San Lucas, at the southern tip of Mexico's Baja Peninsula, is known for its stunning rock arches.

SOUTH AMERICA

The architecture of Peru's Machu Picchu (above) reflects an advanced Inca culture; lush rain forests (below) cover Venezuela's Bolívar state; the toucan (right) lives in the rain forests of South America.

South America, a continent of geographical extremes, is known both for its tropical rain forests and for its cold, desolate Atacama Desert, the driest place on Earth. South America's northern border lies north of the equator on the Caribbean Sea. Its southernmost point at Cape Horn is only 600 miles (970 kilometers) from Antarctica. The Andes, which stretch along the entire western edge of the continent, form the longest mountain chain in the world. The highest peaks of the Andes are surpassed in height only by the Himalayas in Asia.

South America also boasts the world's largest river basin, the Amazon Basin; the world's highest waterfall, Angel Falls in Venezuela; and the world's highest lake used for transportation, Lake Titicaca on the border of Peru and Bolivia. Other principal landscape features include the broad plains of Bolivia and Paraguay's Gran Chaco and Argentina's Pampa, and the arid, rocky tablelands of Patagonia.

South America Facts

Area: 6,900,000 square miles (17,800,000 square kilometers)

Highest Mountain: Cerro Aconcagua, Argentina, 22,831 feet (6,959 meters)

Lowest Point: Laguna del Carbón, Argentina, -344 feet (-105 meters)

Longest River: Amazon, 4,000 miles (6,400 kilometers)

Largest Lake: Lago de Maracaibo, Venezuela, 5,000 square miles (13,000 square kilometers)

Largest Desert: Atacama Desert, Chile, 35,600 square miles (92,200 square kilometers)

Largest Island: Tierra del Fuego, Chile-Argentina, 18,600 square miles (48,200 square kilometers)

Highest Waterfall: Angel Falls, Venezuela, 3,212 feet (979 meters)—*world's highest waterfall*

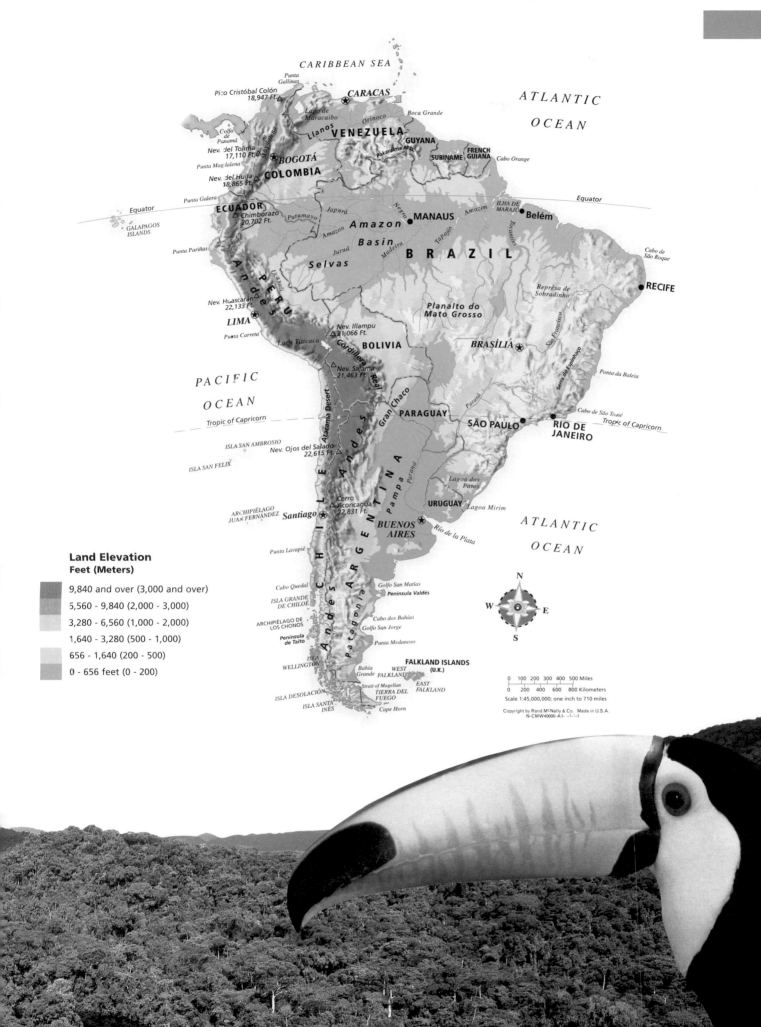

CARIBBEAN SEA

Punta Gallinas

Pico Cristóbal Colón
18,947 Ft. △

CARACAS

ATLANTIC

OCEAN

Lago de Maracaibo

Colfo de Panamá

Boca Grande

Orinoco

Llanos **VENEZUELA**

Nev. del Tolima
17,110 Ft. △

△ **BOGOTÁ**

GUYANA

COLOMBIA

Pakaraima Mts.

SURINAME **FRENCH GUIANA**

Magdalena

Cabo Orange

Punta Magdalena

Nev. del Huila
18,865 Ft. △

Equator

ECUADOR

Punta Galera

△ Chimborazo
20,702 Ft.

Japurá

Negro

MANAUS

Amazon

ILHA DE MARAJÓ

● **Belém**

Equator

GALÁPAGOS ISLANDS

Putumayo

Amazon

A m a z o n

Tapajós

B a s i n

Punta Pariñas

Amazon

Jurúa

B R A Z I L

Cabo de São Roque

Selvas

Madeira

Ucayali

P E R U

Napo

A n d e s

Nev. Huascarán
22,133 Ft. △

● **RECIFE**

Represa de Sobradinho

Planalto do Mato Grosso

LIMA ✪

Punta Carreta

Nev. Illampu
△ 21,066 Ft.

BOLIVIA

BRASÍLIA ✪

São Francisco

Lago Titicaca

Cordillera Real

PACIFIC

OCEAN

△ Nev. Sajama
21,463 Ft.

Serra do Espinhaço

Ponta da Baleia

Tropic of Capricorn

Atacama Desert

Gran Chaco

PARAGUAY

Paraná

Tropic of Capricorn

Cabo de São Tomé

ISLA SAN AMBROSIO

Nev. Ojos del Salado
22,615 Ft. △

SÃO PAULO ●

● **RIO DE JANEIRO**

ISLA SAN FELIX

Paraguay

Lagoa dos Patos

ARCHIPIÉLAGO JUAN FERNÁNDEZ

Cerro Aconcagua
△ 22,831 Ft.

A R G E N T I N A

Pampa

URUGUAY

Lagoa Mirim

ATLANTIC

Santiago ✪

C H I L E

A n d e s

BUENOS AIRES ✪

Río de la Plata

OCEAN

Punta Lavapié

Cabo Quedal

Golfo San Matías

N

ISLA GRANDE DE CHILOÉ

Península Valdés

W E

ARCHIPIÉLAGO DE LOS CHONOS

Cabo dos Bahías

Golfo San Jorge

S

Península de Taitó

Patagonia

Punta Medanoso

ISLA WELLINGTON

Bahía Grande

FALKLAND ISLANDS
(U.K.)

WEST FALKLAND

ISLA DESOLACIÓN

Strait of Magellan

TIERRA DEL FUEGO

EAST FALKLAND

ISLA SANTA INÉS

Cape Horn

Land Elevation
Feet (Meters)

- 9,840 and over (3,000 and over)
- 5,560 - 9,840 (2,000 - 3,000)
- 3,280 - 6,560 (1,000 - 2,000)
- 1,640 - 3,280 (500 - 1,000)
- 656 - 1,640 (200 - 500)
- 0 - 656 feet (0 - 200)

0 100 200 300 400 500 Miles
0 200 400 600 800 Kilometers
Scale 1:45,000,000; one inch to 710 miles

THE LAND

South America is known for its plentiful animal and plant life, most of which is found in the wilderness that covers a large part of the continent, from the jagged peaks of the Andes to the thick jungles of the Amazon Basin. Only about seven percent of the land is naturally suited for farming. South America is rich in mineral resources, but its industries are not well developed; most raw materials are exported and manufactured into products outside of the continent.

Brazil is one of the world's leading exporters of bananas.

Economies

- Little or no activity
- Nomadic herding
- Hunting, forestry, subsistence farming
- Forestry
- Agriculture
- Stock raising
- Manufacturing, commerce
- Fishing

© Rand McNally

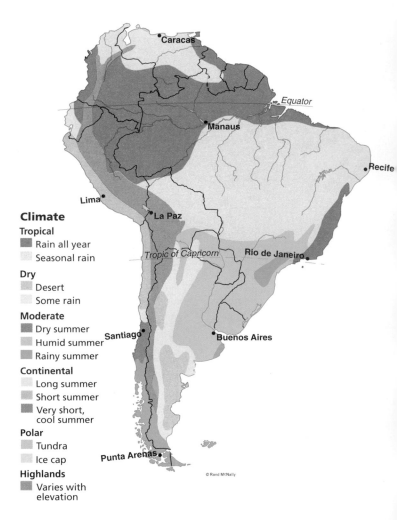

Climate

Tropical
- Rain all year
- Seasonal rain

Dry
- Desert
- Some rain

Moderate
- Dry summer
- Humid summer
- Rainy summer

Continental
- Long summer
- Short summer
- Very short, cool summer

Polar
- Tundra
- Ice cap

Highlands
- Varies with elevation

© Rand McNally

Economies

Stock raising, agriculture, and subsistence farming are important to South America's economy. Many parts of the rain forest have been burned out and cleared for farming, livestock grazing, and development. These slash-and-burn tactics have destroyed more than 200,000 square miles (518,000 square kilometers) of the Amazon rain forest in just 20 years. More than 40 square miles (103 square kilometers) vanish each day.

Climate

Tropical rain forest climates — hot and wet — and tropical savanna climates — hot with rainy and dry seasons — prevail in northern South America. Climates in the southern portion of the continent range from temperate, or moderate, to the subarctic chill of Tierra del Fuego. In parts of South America, the Andes block moist Pacific Ocean breezes from moving east, creating dry weather in the Patagonia region east of the mountains in Argentina and Chile. In other areas, the Andes rise alongside tropical regions.

Farming and Ranching

Many South Americans are involved in farming; some are subsistence farmers who grow only enough corn, beans, and potatoes to feed their families, while others work on huge commercial farms that produce crops for export. Cocoa, coffee, sugarcane, and bananas grow in abundance. Since much of the continent lies in the Southern Hemisphere — where the seasons are opposite those in the Northern Hemisphere — some countries export oranges, lemons, and grapes to the north during the northern winter. Vast cattle ranches dot the Gran Chaco of Bolivia and Paraguay, the Pampa of Argentina, and the Llanos of Venezuela and Colombia, while sheep graze the windswept landscapes of Patagonia and Tierra del Fuego.

Environments
- Forest
- Swamp
- Crop and woodland
- Cropland
- Crop and grazing land
- Grassland
- Desert
- Tundra
- Barren
- Urban

© Rand McNally

Trekkers marvel at the beauty of Peru's snow-covered Andes.

Mining and Mineral Resources

Gold and silver, which drew Europeans to South America more than 500 years ago, are now mined in much smaller quantities than they once were. More than one-quarter of Earth's copper is buried in the Andes, where Chile's Chuquicamata, the world's most expansive open-pit mine, lies over the largest known copper deposit. Iron, bauxite, manganese, zinc, lead, oil, and natural gas are among the continent's important mineral resources.

Industry

While many of South America's industries remain underdeveloped, its more industrialized countries manufacture and process food, metals, chemicals, petroleum, textiles, clothing, cars, and appliances. Brazil is by far the leading industrial and economic producer on the continent, with Argentina, Venezuela, and Chile also contributing to the industrial sector.

Hundreds of oil rigs rise from the waters of Venezuela's Lake Maracaibo.

The Itaipu Dam on the Paraña River between Brazil and Paraguay provides hydroelectric power.

Tourism

Although tourism to cities such as Rio de Janeiro, Brazil, and Caracas, Venezuela, has declined in recent years, growing interest in adventure- and nature-oriented travel is turning South America's more remote regions into prime vacation destinations. Travelers flock to study wildlife on the Galapagos Islands, experience history atop moss-covered Inca ruins high in the Andes, float down the Amazon, and trek through the starkly beautiful landscapes of Patagonia.

THE PEOPLE

Three girls in Peru wear the traditional clothing of the Quechua people.

The panpipe creates a distinctive sound in Ecuadorian music.

Rio de Janeiro celebrates Carnaval every year with lavish costumes, music, and dancing.

South America's rich heritage comes from a vibrant combination of native, European, and African peoples. From the sixteenth to the nineteenth centuries, Spain and Portugal controlled most of South America; today Spanish and Portuguese are the most widely spoken languages on the continent. Most South Americans live in crowded coastal cities — ninety percent of the population resides within 150 miles (240 kilometers) of the ocean. Native peoples, however, still dwell deep in the rain forests and the rugged high country. In the second half of the twentieth century, people from around the world emigrated to South America in search of new opportunities in trade and agriculture. Substantial Asian populations live in Brazil, Argentina, and Peru, for example. One of South America's most pressing social problems is the unequal distribution of wealth: A small percentage of rich people control most of the property, while great numbers of poor people crowd into makeshift shanty towns and squatter settlements called *favelas* that lie on the outskirts of the major cities.

Musicians serenade passers-by outside cafes and restaurants.

A Bolivian woman carries her baby on her back.

Two boys ride horses in Paraguay.

CARIBBEAN SEA

ATLANTIC

OCEAN

Punta Gallinas

Barranquilla MARACAIBO *CARACAS*

Cartagena Cúcuta Barquisimeto *Boca Grande*

Orinoco

Llanos VENEZUELA Georgetown

MEDELLÍN Bucaramanga Paramaribo

Nev. del Tolima GUYANA Cayenne

17,110 Ft. SURINAME

BOGOTÁ FRENCH

Punta Magdalena *Pakaraima Mts.* GUIANA *Cabo Cacipore*

CALI COLOMBIA Boa Vista

Nev. del Huila

18,865 Ft. Lérida *Cabo Norte*

Punta Galera *Equator* Macapá *Equator*

QUITO *Cayambe* *ILHA DE* *Baía de Marajó*

18,996 Ft. *Japurá* *Negro* *MARAJÓ*

ECUADOR *Putumayo* MANAUS *Amazon* Belém São Luis

GALÁPAGOS ISLANDS Iquitos *Tefé* Santarém *Tocantins*

(Ecuador) GUAYAQUIL *Amazon*

Punta Pariñas *Juruá* *Madeira* *Tapajós* Imperatriz Teresina *Cabo de São Roque*

Chiclayo B R A Z I L Conceição do Natal

Andes *P* Ji-Parana *Araguaia* *Represa de* *São Francisco*

Nev. Huascarán *E* *Sobradinho* RECIFE

22,133 Ft. *R* *Planalto do* Feira Aracaju

Callao *U* Cusco *Mato Grosso* de Santana

Puerto Heath SALVADOR

LIMA *Nev. Illampu* Cuiabá *BRASÍLIA* Itabuna

Punta Carreta *Lago* *21,066 Ft.*

Titicaca LA PAZ Goiânia *Serra do Espinhaço* *Ponta da Baleia*

Arequipa BOLIVIA *Represa de*

Oruro Santa Cruz Uberlândia *Três Marias*

Nev. Sajama de la Sierra

21,463 Ft. Sucre Campo BELO HORIZONTE

PACIFIC Iquique Grande *Cabo de São Tomé*

OCEAN *Gran Chaco* Londrina

Tropic of Capricorn PARAGUAY *Paraná* RIO DE JANEIRO

Antofagasta SÃO Santo André

ISLA SAN AMBROSIO *Punta Ballenita* Asunción PAULO

(Chile) *Nev. Ojos del Salado* San Miguel

22,615 Ft. de Tucumán *Paraná* Santa Florianópolis

Punta Cachos Maria

ISLA SAN FÉLIX *Lagoa dos* PORTO ALEGRE

(Chile) Goya *Patos*

A CÓRDOBA Santa Fe *Lagoa Mirim*

R *Cerro* ROSARIO URUGUAY

ARCHIPIÉLAGO G Valparaíso *Aconcagua* BUENOS MONTEVIDEO

JUAN FERNÁNDEZ E Santiago *22,831 Ft.* AIRES *Punta del Este*

(Chile) N La Plata *Río de la Plata*

Concepción T *ATLANTIC*

Punta Lavapié I *Pampa* *OCEAN*

C N Mar del Plata

Valdivia H A Bahía

I Blanca

Cabo Quedal L Neuquén

E *Golfo San Matías*

ISLA GRANDE DE CHILOÉ *Península Valdés*

ARCHIPIÉLAGO DE LOS CHONOS *Cabo dos Bahías*

Patagonia *Golfo San Jorge*

Península Comodoro Rivadavia

de Taitao *Punta Medanoso*

ISLA WELLINGTON FALKLAND ISLANDS

(U.K.)

Bahía *WEST* Stanley

Grande *FALKLAND* *EAST FALKLAND*

Strait of Magellan

Punta Arenas *TIERRA DEL*

FUEGO

ISLA SANTA INÉS *Cape Horn*

N

W E

S

0 100 200 300 400 500 Miles

0 200 400 600 800 Kilometers

Scale 1:45,000,000; one inch to 710 miles

Copyright by Rand McNally & Co. Made in U.S.A.

N-CMW40000-P1- -1-1-1

South America Facts

Population:
366,600,000

Population Density:
53 people per square mile
(21 per square kilometer)

Most Populous Country:
Brazil, 183,080,000 people

Largest City:
São Paulo, Brazil,
18,300,000 people
(metropolitan area)

A Brazilian boy holds his pet dog.

A   B   C   D   E   F   G   H   I   J   K

NORTHERN SOUTH AMERICA

Mountains and rain forests dominate the northern portion of South America. Besides the Andes, other highland areas rise in Guiana and Brazil, which lie north and south of the Amazon Basin, respectively. The tropical rain forests that fill the basins of the Amazon and Orinoco rivers provide a home for more than 1,500 species of fish, 8,000 species of insects, and 1.6 million species of plants. In the Andes, many remnants of Inca culture, including the impressive ruins at Machu Picchu, have survived for centuries.

Tapirs are strong swimmers, but they can also move quickly through their jungle habitats.

Map labels

CARIBBEAN SEA

PENÍNSULA DE LA GUAJIRA
Punta Gallinas
Punto Fijo
PENÍNSULA DE PARAGUANÁ
Santa Marta
Golfo de Venezuela
Coro
ISLA DE MARGARITA
Barranquilla
Pico Cristóbal Colón 18,947 Ft.
MARACAIBO
CARACAS
Porlamar
Carúpano
Cartagena
Valledupar
Barquisimeto
Valencia
Maracay
Barcelona
Cumaná
Sincelejo
Lago de Maracaibo
Acarigua
Calabozo
Anaco
Maturín
Monteria
Sahagún
Valera
Guanare
Valle de la Pascua
El Tigre
Tucupita
Boca Grande
Punta Marzo
Mérida
Pico Bolívar 16,427 Ft.
Barinas
San Fernando
Ciudad Bolívar
Orinoco
Cúcuta
San Cristóbal
Cerro Bolívar 2,631 Ft.
Ciudad Guayana
Barrancabermeja
Bucaramanga
VENEZUELA
Embalse de Guri
Bello
Floridablanca
LLANOS
Itagüí
Duitama
Meta
Cerro Yaví 8,009 Ft.
Angel Falls
GU
MEDELLÍN
Quibdó
La Dorada
Tomo
Puerto Ayacucho
Auyán Tepuy 9,678 Ft.
Mt. Roraima 9,432
Cabo Corrientes
Nev. del Tolima 17,110 Ft.
Vichada
LA GRAN SABANA
Manizales
Pereira
Cerro Marahuaca 8,461 Ft.
PAKARAIMA MTS.
Punta Magdalena
Armenia
BOGOTÁ
Orinoco
ISLA DE MALPELO (Colombia)
Ibagué
Villavicencio
Guaviare
Buenaventura
CALI
Palmira
COLOMBIA
Boa Vista
Nev. del Huila 18,865 Ft.
Neiva
SIERRA PARIMA
Tumaco
Popayán
Inírida
Cabo Manglares
Pasto
Florencia
SIERRA DE CURUPIRA
Esmeraldas
Florencia
Vaupés
Punta Galera
Ipiales
Pico da Neblina 9,888 Ft.
Equator
Ibarra
Apaporis
Negro
GALAPAGOS ISLANDS (Ecuador)
Cabo Pasado
QUITO
Cayambe 18,996 Ft.
Lérida
Represa Balbina
Manta
Portoviejo
Ambato
Caquetá
Cabo San Lorenzo
Chimborazo 20,702 Ft.
Putumayo
Japurá
Jipijapa
ECUADOR
Napo
AMAZON
MANAUS
PACIFIC
Punta Santa Elena
GUAYAQUIL
Milagro
Amazon
Manacapuru
Golfo de Guayaquil
Cuenca
ISLA PUNA
Machala
Tigre
Iquitos
Leticia
BASIN
Teté
Içá
OCEAN
Tumbes
Loja
Marañón
Ucayali
Teté
Talara
Sullana
Jutaí
Paraú
Punta Parinas
Piura
Juruá
SELVAS
Tapauá
Chiclayo
Cajamarca
Huallaga
Cruzeiro do Sul
Purus
Humaitá
Trujillo
Pucallpa
Madeira
Porto Velho
Chimbote
Nev. Huascarán 22,133 Ft.
Huánuco
Rio Branco
Ariquemes
Ji-Parana
Huaraz
Nevado Yerupaja 21,765 Ft.
Cerro de Pasco
Acre
Orthon
Madeira
Machado
Huacho
Tarma
PERU
Rio de las Piedras
Punta Lachay
Callao
Vitarte
Huancayo
CORDILLERA ORIENTAL
Madre de Dios
LIMA
Ayacucho
Urubamba
Puerto Maldonado
Beni
Mamoré
San Miguel
SIERRA D
Chincha Alta
Cusco
Pisco
CORDILLERA REAL
Trinidad
Punta Carreta
Ica
CORDILLERA DE HUANZO
Lago Titicaca
BOLIVIA
Nazca
Nevado Coropuna 20,686 Ft.
Puno
Nev. Illampu 21,066 Ft.
Santa Cruz de la Sierra
Punta Parada
CORDILLERA OCCIDENTAL
Volcán Misti 19,101 Ft.
Nev. Illimani 20,741 Ft.
Cochabamba
Montero
Arequipa
LA PAZ
Volcán Tutupaca 19,898 Ft.
ALTIPLANO
Oruro
Tacna
Nev. Sajama 21,463 Ft.
Lago Poopó
Sucre
ANDES
Potosí
N
W   E
S
Pilcomayo
Tropic of Capricorn
Tarija

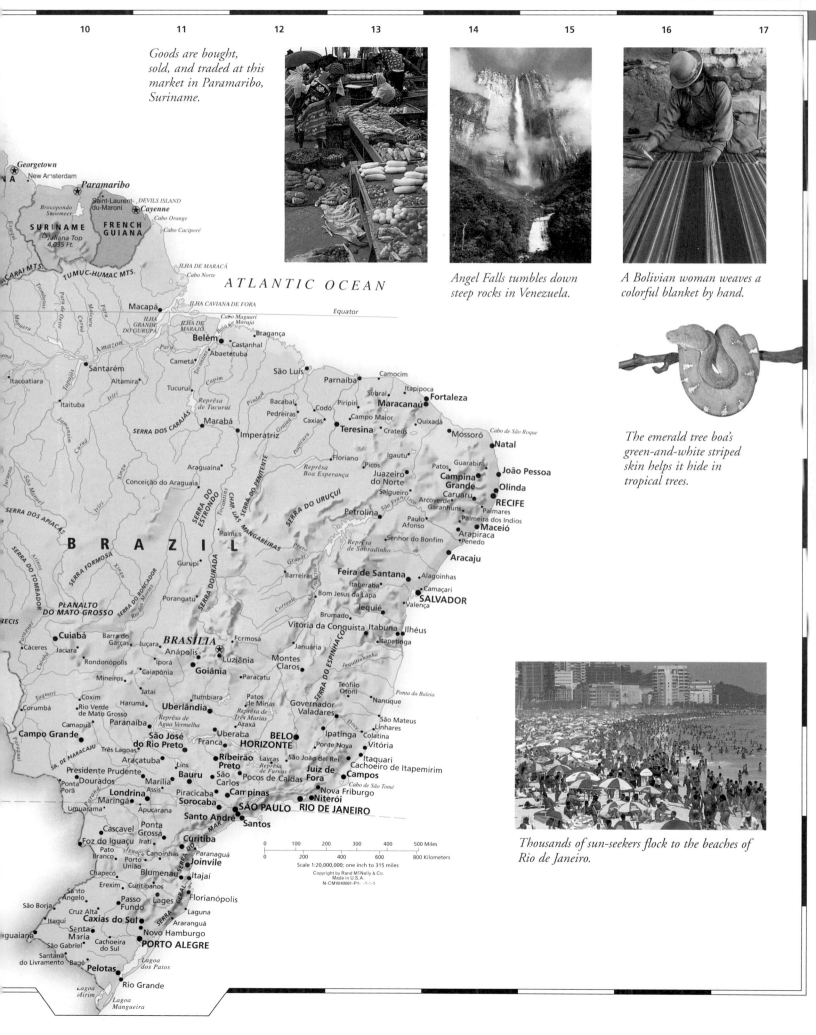

Goods are bought, sold, and traded at this market in Paramaribo, Suriname.

Angel Falls tumbles down steep rocks in Venezuela.

A Bolivian woman weaves a colorful blanket by hand.

The emerald tree boa's green-and-white striped skin helps it hide in tropical trees.

Thousands of sun-seekers flock to the beaches of Rio de Janeiro.

SOUTHERN SOUTH AMERICA

Southern South America is shaped like a long cone. The Andes span the western side of this region, separating Chile from Argentina. The landscape includes the Atacama Desert to the west of the Andes, grasslands and dry tablelands to the east, and glaciers and fjords at the southernmost tip of the continent. Spanish is the main language here, but a few native groups continue to speak their own languages.

Grapes are grown in Chile and Argentina for food and for making wine.

Los Cuernos, a series of sculpted peaks, is one of the most spectacular sights in the southern Andes.

Asunción, Paraguay's capital city, retains its Spanish colonial character.

Tango, the music and dance of Argentina, began in the slums of Buenos Aires.

Gauchos, or cowboys, have lived on the Pampa plains of Argentina for 300 years. They work on ranches and ride Criollos, a breed of wild horse.

A B C D E F G H I J K

1 2 3 4 5 6 7

PARAGUAY

CHACO BOREAL

Puerto Bahía Negra

Pedro Juan Caballero

Concepción

Montelindo

Itaipú Reservoir

Iquique

CORDILLERA OCCIDENTAL

ATACAMA DESERT

Calama

Cerro Licancábur 19,409 Ft.

Tartagal

Tropic of Capricorn

Pilcomayo

Asunción

Fernando de la Mora

Antofagasta

CORDILLERA DOMEYKO

Volcán Llullaillaco 22,110 Ft.

San Salvador de Jujuy

Salta

Bermejo

Formosa

GRAN CHACO

Paraguay

PACIFIC OCEAN

Punta Ballenita

Cerro Galán 19,396 Ft.

San Miguel de Tucumán

Presidencia Roque Sáenz Peña

Resistencia

Corrientes

Encarnación

Posadas

Nevado Ojos del Salado 22,615 Ft.

Cerro Bonete 22,546 Ft.

Santiago del Estero

Paraná

Copiapó

Punta Cachos

San Fernando del Valle de Catamarca

Reconquista

Goya

Uruguay

Vallenar

La Rioja

ANDES

Dulce

Salado

Paraná

Artigas

COXILLA DE SANTANA

La Serena

Cerro de las Tórtolas 20,735 Ft.

Mar Chiquita

Laguna Mar Chiquita

Rafaela

Santa Fe

Concordia

Rivera

Punta Lengua de Vaca

CÓRDOBA

San Francisco

Paraná

Salto

URUGUAY

Ovalle

San Juan

Cerro Aconcagua 22,831 Ft.

Río Tercero

Villa María

San Lorenzo

Paysandú

Mercedes

Melo

Laguna Merín

Quillota

Mendoza

SAN LUIS

Río Cuarto

ROSARIO

Durazno

Treinta y Tres

Valparaíso

Santiago

San Luis

Venado Tuerto

Pergamino

Zárate

San José de Mayo

San Antonio

Mercedes

Junín

Minas

Rancagua

San Rafael

BUENOS AIRES

La Plata

Río de la Plata

MONTEVIDEO

Punta del Este

Curicó

Cerro el Nevado 12,500 Ft.

Nueve de Julio

Atuel

Talca

ARGENTINA

Azul

CHILE

Chillán

Colorado

Santa Rosa

Olavarría

Tandil

Talcahuano

Concepción

Los Ángeles

PAMPA

Salado

Tres Arroyos

Mar del Plata

Punta Lavapié

Temuco

Neuquén

Bahía Blanca

Punta Alta

Necochea

General Roca

Colorado

Bahía Blanca

Valdivia

Limay

Negro

ATLANTIC

Osorno

Viedma

Punta Rasa

OCEAN

San Carlos de Bariloche

Golfo San Matías

Cabo Quedal

Puerto Montt

Monte Tronador 11,453 Ft.

PENÍNSULA VALDÉS

ISLA GRANDE DE CHILOÉ

Chubut

Trelew

Golfo Nuevo

Golfo Corcovado

Volcán Corcovado 7,546 Ft.

Cabo dos Bahías

ISLA MAGDALENA

Lago Colhué Huapi

Golfo San Jorge

ARCHIPIÉLAGO DE LOS CHONOS

Coihaique

Lago Buenos Aires

Comodoro Rivadavia

PENÍNSULA DE TAITAO

Deseado

Cerro San Clemente 13,314 Ft.

Golfo de Penas

Punta Medanosa

ISLA CAMPANA

PATAGONIA

ANDES

Cerro Chaltel 10,958 Ft.

Monte Fitzroy

ISLA WELLINGTON

Lago Viedma

FALKLAND ISLANDS (U.K.)

ISLA MADRE DE DIOS

Santa Cruz

Lago Argentino

Bahía Grande

Mount Usborne 2,312 Ft.

ISLA DIEGO DE ALMAGRO

Río Gallegos

WEST FALKLAND

Stanley

EAST FALKLAND

Falkland Sound

Strait of Magellan

ISLA RIESCO

ISLA DESOLACIÓN

Punta Arenas

TIERRA DEL FUEGO

Estrecho de le Maire

ISLA SANTA INÉS

Ushuaia

ISLA DE LOS ESTADOS

ISLA NAVARINO

ISLA HOSTE

Cape Horn

Llamas are used for carrying goods up and down the steep slopes of the Andes.

In southern Uruguay, the town of Colonia del Sacramento borders the wide river called Río de la Plata.

| 0 | 100 | 200 | 300 | 400 | 500 Miles |
| 0 | 200 | 400 | 600 | 800 Kilometers |

Scale 1:20,000,000; one inch to 315 miles

EUROPE

Europe is the second-smallest continent, but it shares a landmass with another continent, Asia. Together, they are sometimes referred to as Eurasia.

The rounded mountains, deep fjords, and fertile plains of northern Europe were shaped by the glaciers that plowed across the region during past ice ages. Picturesque uplands and rugged mountains dominate the southern part of the continent. But the Alps in central Europe are the continent's most outstanding physical feature. These mountains began forming more than 60 million years ago when geologic forces pushed Africa northward toward Europe. The Great Northern European Plain arcs from the Pyrenees to the Urals, where Asia begins.

Switzerland's Matterhorn (above) is one of the highest peaks in the Alps; St. Basil's Cathedral (below) in Moscow, Russia, dates from the 15th century; the scenic town of Cochem lies along the Mosel River in western Germany (below right).

ATLANTIC
OCEAN

Reykjavik
Reykjanes
ICELAND
Horn
Fontur
△ Hvannadalshn kur
6,952 Ft.

FAROE ISLANDS
(Den.)

HEBRIDES
ORKNEY ISLANDS
SHETLAND ISLANDS
Moray Firth
Kinnaird Head
Grampian Mts.
UNITED
KINGDOM
N O R T H
Cheviot Hills
Firth of Forth

IRELAND
Irish Sea
Mizen Head
GREAT BRITAIN
St. George's Channel
Thames
LONDON
NETHE
LAND
Land's End
English Channel
CHANNEL IS.
Strait of Dover
BELGIU

⊛PARIS
Paris Basin
FRANCE
Loire
MONA
Cabo de Fisterra
Bay of Biscay
Dordogne
Mt. Blan
15,771 Ft.
Massif Central
Cordillera Cantábrica
Douro
P y r e n e e s
ANDORRA
Golfe du Lion
Duero
Ebro
Sistema Ibérico
PORTUGAL
Iberian Peninsula
Lisbon ⊛
Tagus
SPAIN
Cabo de São Vicente
Sierra Morena
BALEARIC ISLANDS
MENORCA
MALLORCA
Cap de la Nau
EIVISSA
Strait of Gibraltar
△ Mulhacén
11,424 Ft.
GIBRALTAR
(U.K.)

N
W E
S

NORWEGIAN
SEA

Nordkapp
Arctic Circle
Kebnekaise
6,926 Ft.

LOFOTEN

Lapland

Murmansk

Kol'skiy
poluostrov

White Sea

Ponoy

Mczen

Pechora

Scandinavian

Peninsula

NORWAY
Galdhøpiggen
8,100 Ft.

SWEDEN

FINLAND

Ural Mountains

Severnaya Dvina

Northern Uvals

Kamskoye
vdkhr.

Sogna-
orden

Umeälven

Gulf
of
Bothnia

Onega

Sukhona

Kama

Lindesnes

Dalälven

ÅLAND

Ladozhskoye
ozero

Onezhskoye
ozero

RUSSIA

Stockholm

Skagerrak

Vänern

Vättern

GOTLAND

ÖLAND

SAAREMAA

Gulf of Finland

ESTONIA

Chudskoye
ozero

Rybinskoye
vodokhranilishche

Gor'kovskoye
vodokhranilishche

MOSCOW

Oka

Kuybyshevskoye
vodokhranilishche

DENMARK

Copenhagen

Kattegat

Gulf
of
Riga

Riga

LATVIA

Valdai
Hills

BALTIC SEA

BORNHOLM
(DEN.)

LITHUANIA

RUSSIA

Central
Russian
Upland

Volga Hills

KAZAKHSTAN

EA

Elbe

Great Northern European Plain

Neman

MINSK

Volgogradskoye
vdkhr.

BERLIN

Oder

GERMANY

Rhine

POLAND

Wisła

WARSAW

BELARUS

Pripyat

Dnieper Lowland

Don

Ural

Tsimlyanskoye
vodokhranilishche

Volga

Ore Mts.

Sudetes

KIEV

Dniester

Dnieper

Donets Basin

black
Forest

Bohemian
Forest

CZECH
REPUBLIC

Carpathian Mountains

UKRAINE

Lake
Constance

Danube

SLOVAKIA

TZERLAND

LIECH.

AUSTRIA
Grossglockner
12,461 Ft.

HUNGARY

Great Hungarian
Plain

MOLDOVA

CASPIAN
SEA

ALPS

SLOVENIA

Drava

ROMANIA

Sea of Azov

Po

CROATIA

Carpaţii Meridionali

Crimean
Peninsula

gora El'brus
18,510 Ft.

Caucasus

urian
Sea

SAN
MARINO

Apennines

BOSNIA AND
HERZEGOVINA

Dinaric Alps

ADRIATIC SEA

SERBIA AND
MONTENEGRO

Balkan Peninsula

Danube

BLACK SEA

ROME

ITALY

Vesuvius
4,190 Ft.

BULGARIA

MACEDONIA

Rhodope Mts.

TURKEY

Istanbul

ALBANIA

Olympos
9,570 Ft.

Sea of
Marmara

TYRRHENIAN
SEA

Mt. Etna
10,902 Ft.

SICILY

Pindos Oros

IONIAN
SEA

AEGEAN
SEA

RÓDOS

GREECE

Athens

Capo Passero

MALTA

M E D I T E R R A N E A N   S E A

CRETE

0   100   200   300   400   500 Miles
0   200   400   600   800 Kilometers
Scale 1:16,000,000; one inch to 252 miles
Copyright by Rand McNally & Co.
Made in U.S.A.
N-CMW50000-A1- -2-2-2

Europe Facts

Area: 3,800,000 square miles (9,900,000 square kilometers)

Highest Mountain: gora El'brus, Russia, 18,510 feet (5,642 meters)

Lowest Point: Caspian Sea, Russia, -92 feet (-28 meters)

Longest River: Volga, Russia, 2,100 miles (3,400 kilometers)

Largest Lake: Caspian Sea, Europe-Asia, 144,400 square miles (374,000 square kilometers)

Largest Island: Great Britain, 88,795 square miles (229,978 square kilometers)

Land Elevation: Feet (Meters)

9,840 and over
(3,000 and over)

6,560 - 9,840
(2,000 - 3,000)

3,280 - 6,560
(1,000 - 2,000)

1,640 - 3,280
(500 - 1,000)

656 - 1,640
(200 - 500)

0 - 656 feet
(0 - 200)

THE LAND

Europe has a mild climate, a wealth of natural resources, and numerous rivers that have contributed to smooth and profitable trade between countries for centuries. These factors have also made European countries some of the wealthiest in the world. Most are able to sustain mixed economies based on many types of trade and manufacture, rather than only one or two.

Soaring, jagged peaks provide a striking backdrop for hikers in the French Alps.

Economies

European countries have traded freely with each other since the 1950s, when the first common market was established. More recently, the countries of eastern Europe have also begun competing in the open marketplace. In 1999, the European Union introduced the euro, a unit of money that can be used in all member countries.

Environments

- Forest
- Swamp
- Crop and woodland
- Cropland
- Crop and grazing land
- Grassland
- Desert
- Tundra
- Barren
- Urban

Environments

Europe's environments range from frozen tundra and jagged mountains to grasslands and balmy beaches. Heavy industry and large human populations have polluted many land areas and waterways, but clean-up efforts are underway.

© Rand McNally

Economies

- Little or no activity
- Nomadic herding
- Hunting, forestry, subsistence farming
- Forestry
- Agriculture
- Stock raising
- Manufacturing, commerce
- Fishing

© Rand McNally

Climate

Tropical
- Rain all year
- Seasonal rain

Dry
- Desert
- Some rain

Moderate
- Dry summer
- Humid summer
- Rainy summer

Continental
- Long summer
- Short summer
- Very short, cool summer

Polar
- Tundra
- Ice cap

Highlands
- Varies with elevation

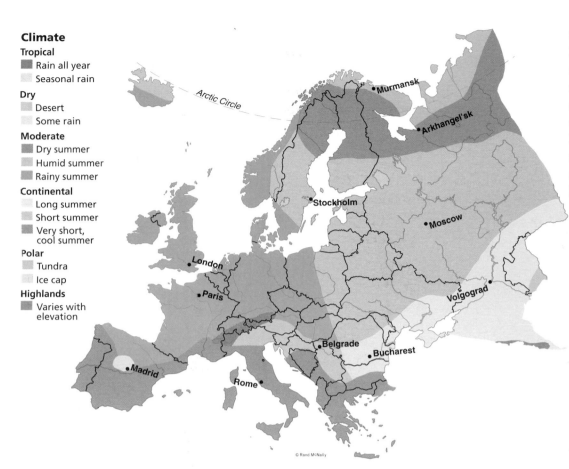

Arctic Circle

Murmansk
Arkhangel'sk
Stockholm
Moscow
London
Paris
Volgograd
Belgrade
Bucharest
Madrid
Rome

© Rand McNally

Climate

In western Europe, warm ocean air creates a climate far milder than that of northern lands elsewhere in the world. The currents don't affect eastern Europe, which experiences very cold winters. The Mediterranean climate of southern Europe has mild, wet winters and hot, dry summers.

In Denmark, a worker unloads a catch of sand eels from the North Sea.

Mining and Manufacturing

Europe's abundance of mineral resources, especially its coal, iron, and nickel reserves, fueled the Industrial Revolution of the 18th and 19th centuries and continues to supply the continent's industries today.

Germany is well known for manufacturing automobiles with state-of-the-art equipment.

Fishing and Farming

Western Europe's deeply etched coastline has long encouraged a healthy fishing industry. The European Plain supports some of the world's most fruitful farmland, while the climates and soils in Portugal, France, and Italy are perfect for growing grapes for fine wine.

Tourism

Thanks to their rich histories, pleasant climates, and stunning scenery, European countries are very popular tourist destinations. Today many countries derive most of their income from tourist spending.

Tourists and natives enjoy the atmosphere of an outdoor cafe in Paris.

Forestry

Europe used to be covered with trees, but over the centuries many forests have been cleared for farms, cities, and manufacturing plants. There are still vast forests in Norway, Sweden, and Finland, which have large paper and wood-products industries.

Harvested timber is transported on inland waterways to mills, where it is processed.

THE PEOPLE

Although farming is an important part of Europe's economy, most Europeans live and work in cities. Europe may be a small continent, but its more than 40 countries feature a tremendous diversity of cultures. Differences in language, customs, food, clothing, and religion give each European country a distinct identity. In places such as Italy and Spain, regions within the same country have very different cultures.

Bullfighter in Spain

For much of its history, Europe has been a hotbed of wars and border disputes. Two world wars wracked the continent in the first half of the 20th century and left it divided into two major parts: the western capitalist countries and the eastern Communist countries, which were loosely controlled by the Soviet Union. After the 1991 breakup of the Soviet Union, countries in eastern Europe began to reunite with their politically and economically stable neighbors in the West, a process that has spawned more wars and social and ethnic unrest in many places.

Hungarian dancers celebrate Constitution Day in Budapest.

Guards at the Tower of London are known as Beefeaters.

Meals in Italy's restaurants are often served outdoors.

Europe Facts

Population:
729,330,000

Population Density:
192 people per square mile
(74 per square kilometer)

Most Populous Country:
Russia, 144,310,000 people

Largest City:
Moscow, Russia, 10,700,000
people (metropolitan area)

Scale 1:16,000,000: one inch to 252 miles

6   7   8   9   10   11   12   13

N
W   E
S

Nordkapp

BARENTS
SEA

Murmansk

Kol'skiy
poluostrov
Pomoy

VESTERALEN

LOFOTEN

Torne älv

Kebnekaise
6,926 Ft.

Pechora

Arkhangel'sk
White Sea

Severodvinsk

Mezen

Ukhta

R   U   S   S   I   A

Ural Mountains

Trondheim

Oulu

FINLAND

Severnaya Dvina

Onega

Sukhona

Syktyvkar

Kamskoye vdkhr.

NORWAY

Galdhøpiggen
9,100 Ft.

SWEDEN

Vaasa

Petrozavodsk

Onezhskoye ozero

Kotlas

Vologda

Kirov

Glazov

PERM'

Jotunheimen

Oslo

Gävle

Tampere

Ladozhskoye ozero

Cherepovets

Rybinskoye vdkhr.

Kostroma

Votkinsk

Izhevsk

Naberezhnyye Chelny

Zlatoust

Stockholm

Daläven

Turku

Helsinki

Espoo

Gulf of Finland

ST. PETERSBURG

Rybinsk
Yaroslavl'

Ivanovo

Dzerzhinsk

NIZHNIY
NOVGOROD

Cheboksary

KAZAN'

Kuybyshevskoye vdkhr.

Dimitrovgrad

Sterlitamak

UFA

Norrköping

Uppsala

Tallinn

ESTONIA

Novgorod

Chudskoye ozero

Tartu

Pskov

Tver'

MOSCOW

Vladimir

Noginsk

Arzamas

Ul'yanovsk

Oka

Tol'yatti

SAMARA

Orenburg

Linköping

Göteborg

Vänern

Vättern

GOTLAND

Rīga

LATVIA

Velikiye Luki

Serpukhov

Kolomna

Ryazan'

Saransk

Kama

DENMARK

Copenhagen

Ålborg

Kattegat

Malmö

ÖLAND

Liepāja

Daugavpils

Smolensk

Serpukhov

Novomoskovsk

Kaluga

Tula

Tambov

Lipetsk

Saratov

Engel's

Volgogradskoye vdkhr.

Balakovo

Ural'sk

Ural

BORNHOLM (Den.)

Klaipėda

LITHUANIA

Kaunas

Vitsyebsk

Mahilyow

Bryansk

Orel

Kursk

Voronezh

Khopër

Don

Kamyshin

KAZAKHSTAN

Bremer-
haven

Kiel

Rostock

Gdańsk

RUSSIA

Kaliningrad

Vilnius

MINSK

Homyel'

Belgorod

Volzhskiy

VOLGOGRAD

Atyrau

HAMBURG

Bremen

BERLIN

Szczecin

Toruń

Wisła

Białystok

Hrodna

Baranavichy

BELARUS

Chernihiv

Sumy

Tsimlyanskoye vdkhr.

Astrakhan'

Hannover

Poznań

POLAND

Neman

Brest

Pripyat

Mazyr

KIEV

KHARKIV

Poltava

Luhans'k

Novocherkassk

ROSTOV-NA-DONU

Elista

CASPIAN
SEA

GERMANY

Essen

Magdeburg

Leipzig

Oder

Elbe

Wrocław

Łódź

WARSAW

Lublin

Pinsk

Rivne

Zhytomyr

Kirovohrad

DNIPROPETROVS'K

Horlivka

Makiïvka

DONETS'K

Taganrog

Berdians'k

Frankfurt

Dresden

Katowice

L'viv

Vinnytsia

UKRAINE

Kryvyi Rih

Zaporizhzhia

Mariupol'

Stavropol'

gora El'brus
18,510 Ft.

Mainz

Plzeň

PRAGUE

Ostrava

Kraków

Dniester

Ivano-Frankivs'k

Chernivtsi

MOLDOVA

Mykolaïv

Dnieper

Melitopol'

Krasnodar

Nevinnomyssk

Pyatigorsk

Nal'chik

Groznyy

Makhachkala

Nürnberg

Stuttgart

CZECH REPUBLIC

SLOVAKIA

Košice

Miskolc

Iaşi

Chişinău

Kherson

ODESA

Sea of Azov

Kerch

Maykop

Vladikavkaz

strasbourg

Lake Constance

VIENNA

Bratislava

Győr

BUDAPEST

Debrecen

Cluj-
Napoca

Simferopol'

Sevastopol'

Crimean Peninsula

Novorossiysk

C   a   u   c   a   s   u   s

Zürich

MUNICH

Innsbruck

AUSTRIA

Grossglockner
12,461 Ft.

Graz

HUNGARY

Szeged

ROMANIA

Carpaţii Meridionali

Mys Tarkhankut

SWITZERLAND

ALPS

MILAN

Ljubljana

SLOVENIA

Zagreb

Drava

Timişoara

BELGRADE

Ploieşti

Carpaţii Meridionali

BUCHAREST

Constanţa

BLACK SEA

Genoa

Bologna

Po

Venice

CROATIA

BOSNIA AND
HERZEGOVINA

SERBIA
AND
MONTENEGRO

Niš

Craiova

Danube

Ruse

La Spezia

Livorno

Corse

Florence

Ancona

Split

Sarajevo

Peć

SOFIA

BULGARIA

Varna

ITALY

Apennines

ADRIATIC SEA

ALBANIA

MACEDONIA

Plovdiv

Rhodope Mts.

TURKEY

VATICAN CITY

ROME

SAN
MARINO

Skopje

ISTANBUL

Vesuvius
4,190 Ft.

Bari

Tiranë

Thessaloníki

Sea of Marmara

A Greek fisherman mends a handmade net.

NAPLES

Taranto

Capo Coraino

Capo Palinuro

Lecce

Olympos
9,570 Ft.

Pindus Óros

AEGEAN SEA

TYRRHENIAN SEA

Cosenza

Capo Colonna

GREECE

Palermo

Messina

Mt. Etna
10,902 Ft.

Catania

Catanzaro

IONIAN SEA

Pátra

Athens

SICILY

I. DI PANTELLERIA (It.)

Capo Passero

Valletta

MALTA

MEDITERRANEAN SEA

RÓDOS

Irákleio

CRETE

NORTHERN EUROPE

Northern Europe is a land of surprising contrasts. North of the Arctic Circle, in parts of Scandinavia — Sweden, Norway, and Finland — some land is permanently frozen, while small palm trees dot beaches on Great Britain's southwestern coast. Vast portions of Iceland lie under *Vatnajokull*, a sheet of ice larger than all of Europe's other glaciers combined, while energy from Iceland's 250 hot springs and volcanic vents powers Reykjavik, the capital city. The Scandinavian countries are among the most sparsely populated in Europe, but the United Kingdom, which includes England, Scotland, Wales, and Northern Ireland, is one of the most densely populated. To the east, on the Baltic Sea, the countries of Latvia, Lithuania, and Estonia were once part of the former Soviet Union.

ICELAND

Arctic Circle
Horn
GRÍMSEY
Breiðafjörður
Rifstangi
Fontur
SNÆFELLSNES
Akureyri
Faxaflói
Hvannadalshnúkur 6,952 Ft.
REYKJANES
REYKJAVIK
Hekla 4,892 Ft.
Djúpivogur
Stokksnes

NORWEGIAN SEA

ATLANTIC OCEAN

RONA
ROCKALL (U.K.)

FAROE ISLANDS (Den.) Tórshavn

SHETLAND ISLANDS
Lerwick

ORKNEY ISLANDS
Cape Wrath
Duncansby Head

HEBRIDES
The Minch
Inverness
Moray Firth
Kinnaird Head
Ben Nevis 4,406 Ft.
GRAMPIAN MTS.
SCOTLAND
Aberdeen
Perth
Stirling
Dundee
BRITISH ISLES
Malin Head
Firth of Forth
Bloody Foreland
Londonderry
Ballymena
Glasgow
Kilmarnock
Edinburgh
UNITED
NORTH SEA
Erris Head
Donegal Bay
Achill Head
NORTHERN IRELAND
Bangor
Ayr
Dumfries
CHEVIOT HILLS
GREAT BRITAIN
Stranraer
Belfast
ISLE OF MAN (U.K.)
Carlisle
Newcastle upon Tyne
Dundalk
Whitehaven
Sunderland
Middlesbrough
Galway
Irish Sea
Scarborough
Dublin
Bradford
York
KINGDOM
IRELAND
Liverpool
Manchester
Kingston upon Hull
Loop Head
Chester
Sheffield
Carrauntoohil 3,406 Ft.
Stoke on Trent
ENGLAND
Limerick
Derby
Nottingham
Norwich
Shrewsbury
Leicester
Great Yarmouth
Cork
Waterford
BIRMINGHAM
Coventry
Mizen Head
WALES
Hereford
Northampton
Cambridge
St. George's Channel
Milford Haven
Swansea
Newport
Oxford
Ipswich
CELTIC SEA
Cardiff
Bristol
Thames
LONDON
Hartland Point
Southampton
Reading
Dover
Exeter
Bournemouth
Brighton
Strait of Dover
St. Austell
Land's End
Plymouth
Portsmouth
ISLES OF SCILLY
Lizard Point
Start Point
English Channel
GUERNSEY (U.K.)
CHANNEL IS.
JERSEY (U.K.)
Golfe de St. Malo

NORWAY
Tromsø
VESTERÅLEN
LOFOTEN
Kebnekaise 6,926 Ft. Kiruna
Bodø
Malmberget
Steinkjer
Trondheim
Östersund
Omsköldsvik
Ålesund
Helagsfjället 5,892 Ft.
Dombås
Otta
Ljungan
Sundsval
Hudiksval
Galdhøpiggen 8,100 Ft.
NORWAY
Lillehammer
SWEDEN
Falun
Sognafjorden
Gävle
Bergen
Borlänge
Sandvik
Haugesund
Skien
Oslo
Lillestrøm
Uppsala
Drammen
Karlstad
Västerås
Örebro
Stockho
Porsgrunn
Sandefjord
Stavanger
Eskilstuna söder
Katrineholm
Nyköp
Kristiansand
Uddevalla
Motala
Norrköp
Lindesnes
Trollhättan
Skövde
Linköping
Jönköping
Väste
Göteborg
Borås
Vetlanda
Skagerrak
Grenen
Frederikshavn
Varberg
Värnamo
Oskarshamn
Ljungby
Kalmar
Kattegat
Ålborg
Halmstad
Viborg
Randers
Holstebro
Helsingborg
Karlskrona
DENMARK
Århus
Kolding
Copenhagen
Malmö
Trelleborg
BORNHOLM (Den.)
Esbjerg
SJÆLLAND
Odense
Næstved
Rønne
Kap Arkona
Nykøbing
LOLLAND
BALTI

BALTI

Under the watchful eye of a shepherd, sheep graze on the green hills of Ireland.

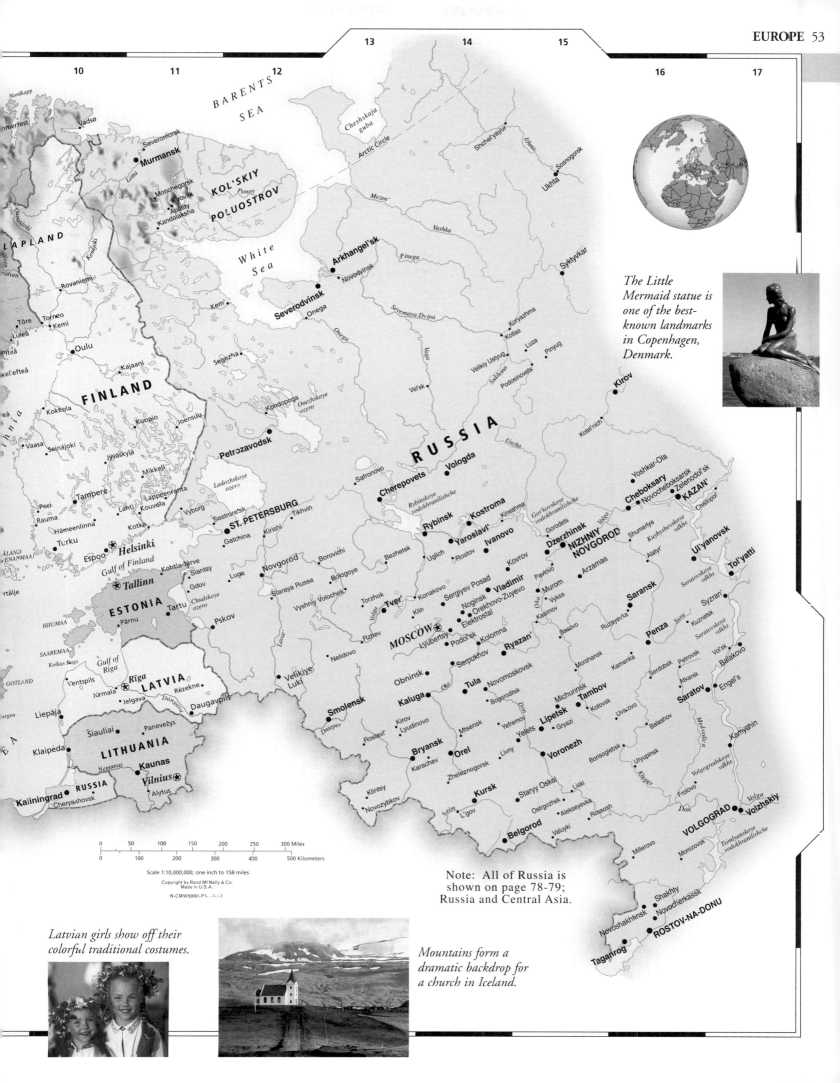

13   14   15   16   17
10   11   12

BARENTS SEA

Nordkapp
Vadsø
ammerfest
Severomorsk
Murmansk
Monchegorsk
Apatity
Kandalaksha
Kirovsk

KOL'SKIY POLUOSTROV
Ponoy

Cheshskaja guba

Arctic Circle
Shchel'yayur
Izhma
Sosnogorsk
Ukhta

White Sea

Mezen'
Vashka

Arkhangel'sk
Novodvinsk
Severodvinsk
Onega

Severnaya Dvina

Syktyvkar
Koryazhma
Kotlas
Luza
Pinyug

LAPLAND

Rovaniemi

Kem'

Oulanka

kel'efteå
Töre
Torneo
Luleå
Kemi
Oulu

Kajaani

Segezha

Kondopoga
Onezhskoye ozero
Onega

Vel'sk
Velikiy Ustyug
Sukhona
Podosinovets
Kotel'nich

Kirov

Vaasa
Seinäjoki
Kokkola
Jyväskylä
Kuopio
Joensuu

FINLAND

Petrozavodsk

Safronovo

RUSSIA
Unzha

Pori
Rauma
Tampere
Lahti
Kouvola
Lappeenranta
Mikkeli

Ladozhskoye ozero

Cherepovets
Vologda
Rybinskoye vodokhranilishche
Rybinsk
Kostroma
Kineshma
Gor'kovskoye vodokhranilishche
Gorodets
Yoshkar-Ola
Cheboksary
Novocheboksarsk
Zelenodol'sk
KAZAN'
Chistopol'

Turku
Hämeenlinna
Helsinki
Espoo
ÅLAND VENANMAA

Vyborg
Sestroretsk
ST. PETERSBURG
Gatchina
Tikhvin
Kirishi

Yaroslavl'
Ivanovo
Rostov
Kovrov
Dzerzhinsk
NIZHNIY NOVGOROD
Arzamas
Shumerlya
Alatyr'
Kuybyshevskoye vdkhr.
Ul'yanovsk
Tol'yatti

Gulf of Finland
Kohtla-Järve
Slantsy
Gdov

Novgorod
Borovichi
Bezhetsk
Uglich
Sergiyev Posad
Noginsk
Orekhovo-Zuyevo
Vladimir
Pavlovo
Murom
Vyksa
Kasimov
Sasdvo
Ruzayevka
Saransk
Penza
Syzran'
Kuznetsk
Saratovskoye vdkhr.

Tallinn
Tartu
ESTONIA
Pärnu
HIIUMAA
Chudskoye ozero

Pskov
Luga
Staraya Russa
Vyshniy Volochek
Torzhok
Tver'
Klin
Konakovo
Lyubertsy
Elektrostal
MOSCOW
Podol'sk
Kolomna
Ryazan'
Morshansk
Kamenka
Serdobsk
Petrovsk
Vol'sk
Balakovo

SAAREMAA
Kolkas Rags
Gulf of Riga

Velikiye Luki
Nelidovo
Obninsk
Serpukhov
Tula
Novomoskovsk
Bogoroditsk
Michurinsk
Uvarovo
Atkarsk
Engel's

GOTLAND

Rīga
Jūrmala
Jelgava
LATVIA
Rēzekne
Daugavpils
Daugava

Smolensk
Kaluga
Kirov
Lyudinovo
Roslavl'
Mtsensk
Yefremov
Don
Yelets
Gryazi
Lipetsk
Tambov
Kotovsk
Uryupinsk
Balashov
Borisoglebsk
Saratov
Medvedica
Khoper
Kamyshin

'entspils
Liepāja
Šiauliai
Panevėžys
Klaipėda
LITHUANIA
Kaunas
Vilnius
RUSSIA
Kaliningrad
Cheryakhovsk
Alytus

Bryansk
Karachev
Orel
Zheleznogorsk
Klintsy
Novozybkov
Kursk
L'gov
Seim
Staryy Oskol
Ostrogozhsk
Alekseyevka
Rossosh
Livny
Voronezh
Don
Millerovo
Morozovsk
Volgogradskoye vdkhr.
Frolovo

Belgorod
Valuyki

VOLGOGRAD
Volga
Volzhskiy
Tsimlyanskoye vodokhranilishche

Shakhty
Novocherkassk
Novoshakhtinsk
ROSTOV-NA-DONU
Taganrog

Dnieper

0   50   100   150   200   250   300 Miles
0   100   200   300   400   500 Kilometers

Scale 1:10,000,000; one inch to 158 miles

Copyright by Rand McNally & Co.
Made in U.S.A.

N-CMW50091-P1- -1-1-1

Note: All of Russia is shown on page 78-79; Russia and Central Asia.

The Little Mermaid statue is one of the best-known landmarks in Copenhagen, Denmark.

Latvian girls show off their colorful traditional costumes.

Mountains form a dramatic backdrop for a church in Iceland.

WESTERN AND CENTRAL EUROPE

Portuguese fisherman work on their nets before heading out to sea.

The cultures of western and central Europe are numerous and diverse, from the Islamic flavor of Spain's ancient Moorish cities to the sophisticated atmosphere of chic boutiques and sidewalk cafes in Paris, France. The region includes both the stunning beauty of the Swiss Alps and the heavy industry of Germany's Ruhr Valley. The slow, simple pace of life in a picturesque Italian hill town stands in contrast to the frenzied activity in the financial and political centers of Belgium and the Netherlands. Some of the smallest countries in the world are in this region: Andorra, San Marino, Monaco, and Vatican City, which is a tiny country entirely surrounded by the city of Rome, Italy.

Schönbrunn Palace in Vienna, Austria, was built for the Hapsburgs, a family that once ruled Austria, Germany, Spain, and other parts of Europe.

4   5   6   7   8   9   10   11

NORTH SEA

Flensburg
Kap Arkona
Kiel
Lübeck Rostock
Bremerhaven Schwerin
Groningen Oldenburg HAMBURG
NETHERLANDS Bremen Schwedt
Haarlem Hannover BERLIN
Amsterdam Braunschweig Potsdam
The Hague Osnabrück Hildesheim Magdeburg Dessau
Rotterdam Arnhem Münster Bielefeld Halle
Brugge Essen Dortmund Göttingen Cottbus
Antwerpen Wuppertal Kassel Leipzig Dresden
Gent Düsseldorf Siegen Erfurt Chemnitz
BELGIUM Maastricht Köln Zwickau ORE MTS.
Lille Brussels Liège Bonn GERMANY
Lens Namur Koblenz Frankfurt
Amiens Charleroi Wiesbaden Würzburg
LUX. Mainz BOHEMIAN FOREST
Luxembourg Trier Mannheim Nürnberg
Reims Metz Saarbrücken Heilbronn Regensburg
Châlons-sur-Marne Nancy Karlsruhe Stuttgart Danube
PARIS Strasbourg Augsburg Linz
Chartres Troyes Mulhouse Freiburg MUNICH VIENNA
Chaumont Basel Bodensee Salzburg AUSTRIA
Nevers Besançon Zürich Innsbruck Grossglockner Graz
Dijon Bern LIECHTENSTEIN 12,461 Ft. Klagenfurt
SWITZERLAND Luzern Merano Udine
Geneva Lausanne Dufourspitze Bolzano Trieste
Mt. Blanc 15,203 Ft. Trento Venice
15,771 Ft. Matterhorn Como Bergamo Verona
Grenoble 14,692 Ft. Novara MILAN Brescia

An Italian farmer inspects his grape crop.

The Colosseum in Rome was built nearly 2,000 years ago.

English Channel
Cap de la Hague Cherbourg Dieppe
Strait of Dover
Le Havre Rouen
Golfe de Caen Évreux Seine
Saint-Malo Oise
Saint-Malo Rennes Marne
Laval Le Mans Orléans
Angers Tours Vierzon
Saint-Nazaire Loire
Nantes
Poitiers
La Rochelle
FRANCE
te de la Coubre Limoges Clermont-Ferrand Villeurbanne Lyon
Périgueux MASSIF
Cap Ferret Bordeaux Aurillac Saint Étienne
Dordogne Lot CENTRAL Valence
Mont-de-Marsan Montauban Rhône
PYRENEES Montpellier Nîmes Nice MONACO
Pau Toulouse Aix-en-Provence Cannes
Donostia-San Sebastián Perpignan ANDORRA Marseille Toulon
Pamplona Golfe du Lion LIGURIAN SEA
Huesca Cap de Creus Cap Corse
Zaragoza Girona CORSICA Piombino
Sabadell (Fr.) Bastia ISOLA D'ELBA
BARCELONA Ajaccio Monte Rotondo 8,602 Ft.
Castelló de la Plana Str. of Bonifacio
ncia BALEARIC ISLANDS (Sp.) MENORCA Olbia
acant Palma MALLORCA Sassari Capo Comino
la Nau EIVISSA SARDINIA (It.)
rcia Cap de Ses Salines Punta La Marmora 6,017 Ft.
Cabo de Palos FORMENTERA Iglesias Cagliari
tagena Capo Caccia Capo Carbonara
Capo Spartivento
MEDITERRANEAN SEA

Geneva JURA Turin Piacenza Parma Ferrara
Monte Viso Genoa Bologna Po
12,602 Ft. Savona Ravenna
Golfo di La Spezia Rimini
Genova Pisa SAN MARINO
Livorno Florence Ancona
Siena A P E N N I N E S
Perugia ITALY ADRIATIC SEA
Terni Pescara
VATICAN CITY San Severo
ROME Foggia Barletta
Terracina NAPLES Bari Brindisi
Vesuvius Salerno Taranto Lecce
4,190 Ft. Golfo di Strait of Otranto
TYRRHENIAN Taranto
SEA Capo Palinuro Cosenza
Capo Vaticano Crotone
Catanzaro Capo Colonna IONIAN SEA
Messina Reggio di Calabria
Trapani Mt. Etna 10,902 Ft.
Palermo SICILY Catania
Agrigento Siracusa
Capo Passero
ISOLA DI PANTELLERIA (It.)
MALTA Valletta

During the annual Grand Prix, racecars speed through the streets of Monte Carlo in Monaco.

N
W   E
S

Ibex, a type of wild goat, graze on a hillside in Switzerland.

EASTERN EUROPE

In recent years, great changes have swept across Eastern Europe. From 1989 to 1991, the country known as the Soviet Union broke apart, and all 15 of its former republics — including Belarus, Ukraine, and Moldova — became independent countries. Then in 1993, the country called Czechoslovakia split into two separate countries: the Czech Republic and Slovakia. These newly independent republics have worked to prosper in free market trade. Industry thrives in Poland and Hungary, while other republics like Moldova and Slovakia remain largely agricultural.

Prague, in the Czech Republic, is one of Europe's loveliest and most historic cities.

The farmlands of Ukraine produce such bountiful harvests that this region is often referred to as the "Breadbasket of Europe."

Although the Carpathian Mountains skirt the borders of Poland, Slovakia, and Ukraine, most of Eastern Europe lies on the Great Northern European Plain, where there is an abundance of fertile land. The beauty and mild weather of the Crimean Peninsula, which juts into the Black Sea, makes Ukraine a popular beach destination for tourists.

Kiev, the capital of Ukraine, straddles the Dnieper River.

The Tatra Mountains are the primary range of the Carpathian Mountains.

Hungary's Magyar people have bred horses for centuries.

Poland's people have a strong national identity.

BALTIC SEA

POLAND

Gdynia
Gdańsk
Koszalin
Tczew
Elbląg
Suwałki
Szczecin
Olsztyn
Grudziądz
Bydgoszcz
Toruń
Łomża
Włocławek
Gorzów Wielkopolski
Poznań
Warta
Zielona Góra
Głogów
Kalisz
Łódź
Legnica
Piotrków Trybunalski
Radom
Liberec
Wałbrzych
Częstochowa
Wrocław
Opole
Kielce
SUDETES
Cheb
Kladno
Sümperk
Bytom
Sosnowiec
Wisła
Chełm
PRAGUE
CZECH REPUBLIC
Ostrava
Katowice
Kraków
Rzeszów
San
Plzeň
Olomouc
Bielsko-Biała
Krosno
BOHEMIAN FOREST
Písek
Brno
Žilina
CARPATHIAN MOUNTAINS
Sambir
České Budějovice
Trenčín
Prievidza
Poprad
Prešov
SLOVAKIA
Košice
Trnava
Banská Bystrica
Uzhhorod
Berehove
Bratislava
Győr
Gyöngyös
Miskolc
Nyíregyháza
Székesfehérvár
Debrecen
BUDAPEST
Kecskemét
HUNGARY
Kaposvár
Drava
Tisza
Szeged
Pécs
Danube

WARSAW
Siedlce
Lublin
Kielce

Hrodna
Lida
Białystok
Slonim
Baranavichy
Brest
Kobryn
Pinsk
Kovel'
Styr
Korosten'
Luts'k
Rivne
Dubno
L'viv
Ternopil'
Ivano-Frankivs'k
Khmel'nyts'kyi
Kamianets'-Podil's'kyi
Mohyliv-Podil's'kyi
Chernivtsi
Bălţi
MOLDOVA
Orhei
Prut
Chişinău
Tighina
Cahul
Kiliya
Dnister

Maladzyechna
MINSK
Barysaw
Orsha
Mahilyow
Krychaw
BELARUS
Slutsk
Mazyr
Chornobyl'
Nizhyn
Berdychiv
Zhytomyr
Bila Tserkva
KIEV
Uman'
Oleksandriia
Vinnytsia
Kremenchuts'ke vdskh.
Kirovohrad
Kremenchuk
Pivdennyy Buh
Kryvyi Rih
Kotovs'k
Voznesens'k
Tiraspol
ODESA
Bilhorod-Dnistrovs'kyi

Polatsk
Vitsyebsk
Dnieper
Homyel'
Hlukhiv
Chernihiv
Konotop
Sumy
Pryluky
Ckhtyrka
Lubny
Poltava
UKRAINE
KHARKIV
Kupians'k
Izium
Sieverodonets'k
Slovians'k
Kramators'k
Luhans'k
Stakhanov
Alchevs'k
Krasnyi Luch
Cherkasy
Dniprodzerzhyns'k
Horlivka
Makiïvka
DNIPROPETROVS'K
DONETS'K
Novoshakhtinsk
Zaporizhzhia
Mykolaïv
Nikopol'
Dnipro
Mariupol'
Melitopol
Berdians'k
Kherson
SEA OF AZOV
Dzhankoi
Kerch
Mys Tarkhankut
CRIMEAN PENINSULA
Ievpatoriia
Simferopol'
Sevastopol'
Yalta
Mys Sarych

BLACK SEA

0   50   100   150   200   250   300 Miles
0   100   200   300   400   500 Kilometers
Scale 1:10,000,000; one inch to 158 miles
Copyright by Rand McNally & Co.
Made in U.S.A.
N-CMW50093-P1- -1-1-1

SOUTHEASTERN EUROPE

Except for Greece, Southeastern Europe was controlled by the Soviet Union for much of the 20th century. Since the Soviet Union broke apart in 1989-1991, the countries of Southeastern Europe have embraced their newfound freedom. However, some of them have also struggled to accommodate the many ethnic and religious differences among their inhabitants. In Bosnia and Herzegovina, as well as in Serbia and Montenegro, these tensions erupted into outright war. Today the region remains unstable, despite the diplomatic efforts of the United Nations and the international community.

Albanian refugees flee the fighting in Kosovo.

This castle in the Transylvania region of northwestern Romania inspired Dracula, *the famous story about a bloodsucking count.*

Some 2,500 years ago, the city-states of ancient Greece represented one of the most highly developed and influential civilizations the world has ever known. Today Greece takes advantage of its lengthy seacoast to launch one of the world's largest merchant fleets, while its mild climate, impressive history, and lovely scenery make tourism an important part of the national economy.

The Karawanken Mountains rise behind an 11th-century castle in Slovenia.

Whitewashed homes overlook the sea on the Greek island of Santorini.

Farmhouses dot the cultivated plains
in northeast Romania.

The resort town of Kotor in Serbia and Montenegro
enjoys a peaceful setting on the Adriatic Sea.

1   2   3   4   5   6   7   8   9

A

B

C

D

Satu
Mare
Baia Mare
CARPATHIAN MTS.
Siret
Oradea
Bistriţa
Iaşi
Cluj-
Napoca
Piatra-
Neamţ
Prut
Târgu
Mureş
Bacău

E

SLOVENIA
JULIAN ALPS
Celje
Maribor
Ljubljana
Varaždin
Zagreb
Drava
CROATIA
Rijeka
Karlovac
Pula
Osijek
Sombor
Subotica
Arad
Timişoara
Sibiu
ROMANIA
Sfântu Gheorghe
Focşani
Galaţi
Bečej
Vukovar
Novi Sad
Reşiţa
Hunedoara
Braşov
Brăila
Slavonski Brod
Mureş
Bihać
Banja Luka
Tuzla
Brčko
Sava
Târgu-Jiu
Piteşti
BUCHAREST
Zadar
DINARIC ALPS
BELGRADE
Danube
Craiova
Rošiori-
de-Vede
Călăraşi
Constanţa
Šibenik
Sarajevo
Titovo Užice
Valjevo
Smederevo
SERBIA
Split
BOSNIA AND
HERZEGOVINA
Čačak
Svetozarevo
Kruševac
Ruse
Danube
Mostar
AND
Montana
Pleven
Razgrad
Dobrich

F

ADRIATIC SEA
Novi Pazar
Niš
Pirot
Türgovishte
BLACK
SEA
Nikšić
MONTENEGRO
Lovec
Veliko Tǔrnovo
Varna
Dubrovnik
Peć
Priština
Vranje
Pernik
SOFIA
BULGARIA
Stara Zagora
Bǔrgas
Podgorica
Kumanovo
Musala
9,596 Ft.
Plovdiv
Shkodër
Skopje
Štip
Blagoevgrad
Khaskovo
Kǔrdzhali
Edirne
TURKEY
Tiranë
MACEDONIA
Prilep
RHODOPE MTS.
Çorlu
İSTANBUL
Durrës
Bitola
Sérres
Xánthi
Alexandroúpoli
Sea
of
Marmara

G

ALBANIA
Berat
Kavála
IONIAN ISLANDS
PINDOS OROS
Ólympos
9,570 Ft.
Thessaloníki
Vlorë
Kozáni
Katerini
AEGEAN
Strait
of
Otranto
LÍMNOS

H

IONIAN
SEA
Kérkyra
Ioánnina
Trikala
Lárisa
Vólos
Mytilíni
SEA
GREECE
Lamia
SKÝROS
Chios
Agrínio
Chalkida
Pátra
Athens

I

PELOPONNESUS
KIKLÁDES

Scale 1:10,000,000; one inch to 158 miles
Copyright by Rand McNally & Co.
Made in U.S.A.
N-CMW56000-P1- -2-1-2

Kalamáta
Ákra
Taínaro
KÝTHIRA
Ródos
RÓDOS
KÁRPATHOS

0   50   100   150   200   250   300 Miles
0   100   200   300   400   500 Kilometers

N
W   E
S

Ákra Spánta
Chania
Irákleio
CRETE
Ákra
Líthino

J

A women crochets lace
in Bulgaria.

The ancient Greeks
built the Parthenon
high on a hill so that
they could defend it
more easily.

K

AFRICA

Africa, the world's second-largest continent, is a land of dramatic and varied terrain. Narrow plains line the coast, while wide plateaus fill much of the continent's interior. Lush tropical rain forests flank the equator near the center of the continent. Sun-scorched deserts span the north and portions of the southwest, and grasslands called savannas lie between the deserts and the rain forests.

Across this vast continent are great rivers, mountains, and valleys. It contains four major rivers, but the Nile — the longest in the world — is the most important. It flows north across more than half of the continent before emptying into the Mediterranean Sea. Africa's mountain ranges include majestic peaks such as Kilimanjaro in Tanzania. Between the mountain ranges of eastern Africa lies the Rift Valley, a long rip in the earth's surface that extends about 4,000 miles (almost 6,500 kilometers) and contains volcanoes, hot springs, and some of the world's largest and deepest lakes.

Egypt's ancient pyramids (above) have withstood the test of time; the African lion (left) is often called "King of Beasts"; Kilimanjaro (below) rises above the Amboseli Plain in Kenya.

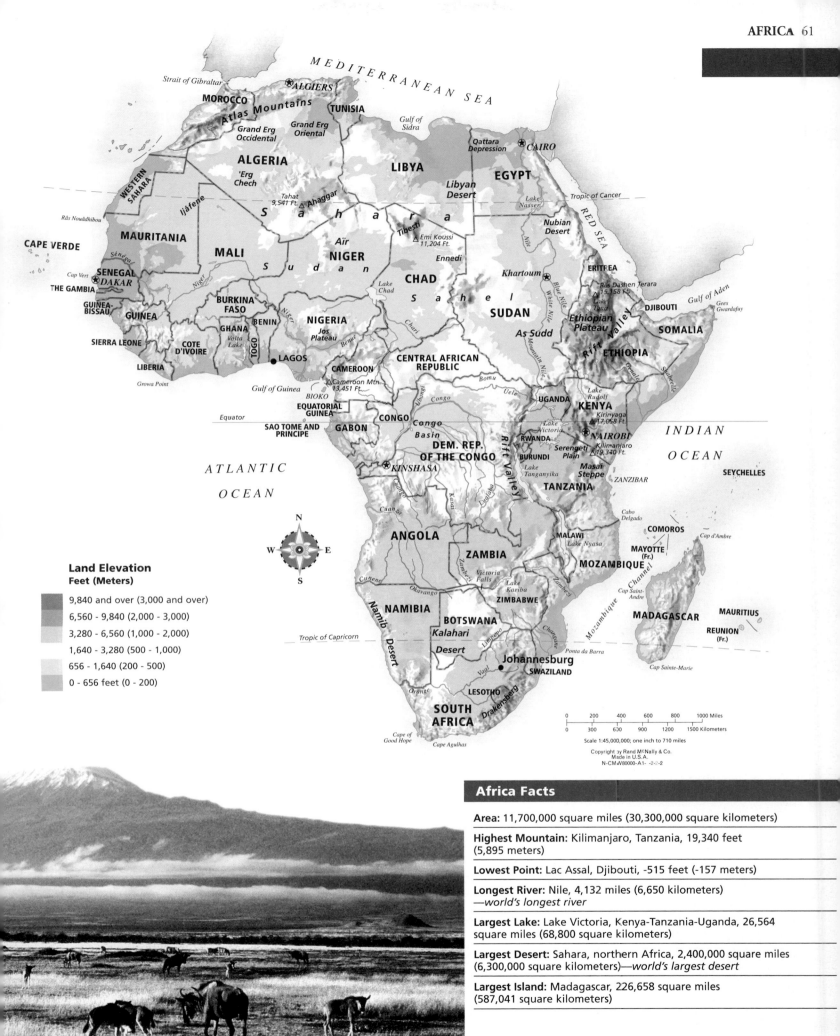

MEDITERRANEAN SEA

Strait of Gibraltar

MOROCCO
Atlas Mountains
ALGIERS
TUNISIA
Gulf of Sidra
CAIRO
Qattara Depression

Grand Erg Occidental
Grand Erg Oriental

ALGERIA
'Erg Chech
LIBYA
EGYPT
Libyan Desert

WESTERN SAHARA
Ijâfene
Tahat 9,541 Ft.
Ahaggar
Tropic of Cancer
Lake Nasser
RED SEA

Râs Nouâdhibou
S a h a r a
Nubian Desert
Nile

CAPE VERDE
MAURITANIA
Aïr
NIGER
Tibesti
Emi Koussi 11,204 Ft.
Ennedi
Khartoum
Râs Dashen Terara 15,158 Ft.
ERITREA
Gulf of Aden
Gees Gwardafuy

Senegal
MALI
S u d a n
CHAD
Lake Chad
Chari
S a h e l
SUDAN
Blue Nile
White Nile
Lake Tana
DJIBOUTI

Cap Vert
SENEGAL
DAKAR
THE GAMBIA
BURKINA FASO
Niger
NIGERIA
Jos Plateau
Benue
As Sudd
Mountain Nile
Ethiopian Plateau
SOMALIA

GUINEA-BISSAU
GUINEA
GHANA
BENIN
TOGO
Volta Lake
CENTRAL AFRICAN REPUBLIC
Bomu
Uele
Rift Valley
ETHIOPIA
Genale
Shabeelle

SIERRA LEONE
COTE D'IVOIRE
LAGOS
CAMEROON
Cameroon Mtn. 13,451 Ft.
UGANDA
Lake Rudolf
KENYA
Kirinyaga 17,058 Ft.

LIBERIA
Growa Point
Gulf of Guinea
BIOKO
EQUATORIAL GUINEA
Ubangi
Congo
Lake Victoria
NAIROBI
Kilimanjaro 19,340 Ft.
INDIAN OCEAN

Equator
SAO TOME AND PRINCIPE
GABON
CONGO
Congo Basin
DEM. REP. OF THE CONGO
Rift Valley
RWANDA
BURUNDI
Serengeti Plain
TANZANIA
Masai Steppe
ZANZIBAR
SEYCHELLES

ATLANTIC OCEAN
KINSHASA
Kwilu
Kasai
Lake Tanganyika
Lualaba
Cabo Delgado
COMOROS
Cap d'Ambre

Cuanza
ANGOLA
ZAMBIA
MALAWI
Lake Nyasa
MOZAMBIQUE
Mozambique Channel
MAYOTTE (Fr.)
Cap Saint-Andre

Cunene
Okavango
Zambezi
Victoria Falls
Lake Kariba
Zambezi
MADAGASCAR
MAURITIUS
REUNION (Fr.)

NAMIBIA
Namib Desert
BOTSWANA
Kalahari Desert
ZIMBABWE
Limpopo
Changane
Ponta da Barra
Cap Sainte-Marie

Tropic of Capricorn
Johannesburg
SWAZILAND
Vaal
Orange
LESOTHO
Drakensberg

SOUTH AFRICA
Cape of Good Hope
Cape Agulhas

Land Elevation
Feet (Meters)

- 9,840 and over (3,000 and over)
- 6,560 - 9,840 (2,000 - 3,000)
- 3,280 - 6,560 (1,000 - 2,000)
- 1,640 - 3,280 (500 - 1,000)
- 656 - 1,640 (200 - 500)
- 0 - 656 feet (0 - 200)

| 0 | 200 | 400 | 600 | 800 | 1000 Miles |
| 0 | 300 | 600 | 900 | 1200 | 1500 Kilometers |

Scale 1:45,000,000; one inch to 710 miles

Copyright by Rand McNally & Co.
Made in U.S.A.
N-CM-W80000-A1- -2-2-2

Africa Facts

Area: 11,700,000 square miles (30,300,000 square kilometers)

Highest Mountain: Kilimanjaro, Tanzania, 19,340 feet (5,895 meters)

Lowest Point: Lac Assal, Djibouti, -515 feet (-157 meters)

Longest River: Nile, 4,132 miles (6,650 kilometers) —*world's longest river*

Largest Lake: Lake Victoria, Kenya-Tanzania-Uganda, 26,564 square miles (68,800 square kilometers)

Largest Desert: Sahara, northern Africa, 2,400,000 square miles (6,300,000 square kilometers)—*world's largest desert*

Largest Island: Madagascar, 226,658 square miles (587,041 square kilometers)

THE LAND

The land in Africa offers an assortment of riches — from gold and minerals found deep within the earth to the crops that grow at its surface. Different industries dominate different parts of the continent: Economic activity depends on the quality of the land and variations in regional climate. Many African countries depend on a single industry to drive the economy, but people in other areas are looking for new ways to make the most of their natural resources.

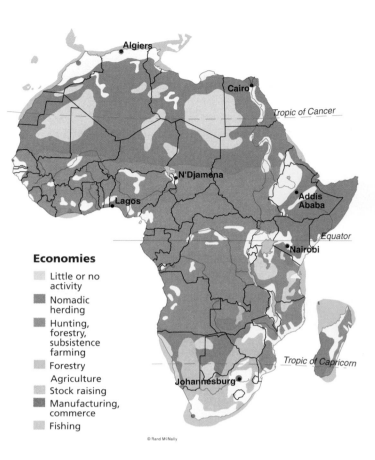

Economies

- Little or no activity
- Nomadic herding
- Hunting, forestry, subsistence farming
- Forestry
- Agriculture
- Stock raising
- Manufacturing, commerce
- Fishing

© Rand McNally

Economies

Most Africans are either farmers or herders. Many live as their ancestors did for thousands of years, continually moving across the land to follow animal herds or living in small villages to raise crops and animals.

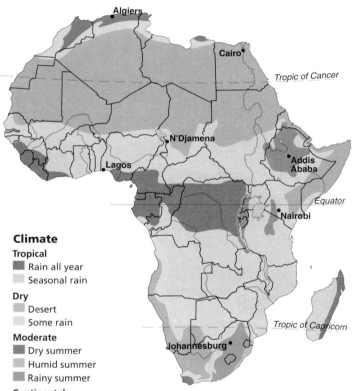

Climate

Tropical
- Rain all year
- Seasonal rain

Dry
- Desert
- Some rain

Moderate
- Dry summer
- Humid summer
- Rainy summer

Continental
- Long summer
- Short summer
- Very short, cool summer

Polar
- Tundra
- Ice cap

Highlands
- Varies with elevation

© Rand McNally

Climates

Africa is the world's hottest continent. One-third of Africa's land area is desert, but near the equator a tremendous amount of rain falls. The tropical rain forests of central Africa are hot and humid.

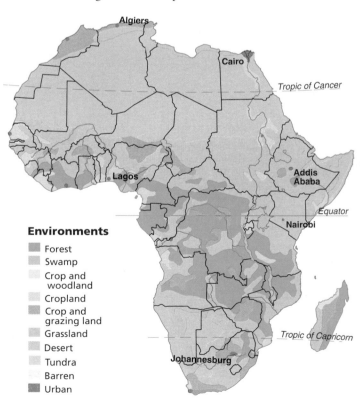

Environments

- Forest
- Swamp
- Crop and woodland
- Cropland
- Crop and grazing land
- Grassland
- Desert
- Tundra
- Barren
- Urban

© Rand McNally

Mining

Africa has some of the largest mineral reserves in the world, most of them untapped. The world's largest uranium mine is in Namibia, and copper is Zambia's major export. There are extensive oil fields in the forbidding deserts of northern Africa and large gold, platinum, and diamond mines in South Africa.

This open-air bazaar in Algeria is a thriving marketplace.

World Gold Production

All others
32%

Russia
7%

Canada
8%

Australia
11%

United States
14%

South Africa
28%

World Platinum Production

All others
8%

Russia
42%

South Africa
50%

Farming

Three out of four Africans work in agriculture. There are two major types of farming in Africa. The first is subsistence farming, when people grow enough food to feed themselves and their families. The second is commercial farming, when major companies grow large quantities of crops for sale. Commercial farms throughout central and southern Africa produce crops such as coffee, bananas, tobacco, and cocoa. Some of these items are sold only in African markets. Other yields, called cash crops, are grown specifically for canning, freezing, or refining, and are sold overseas.

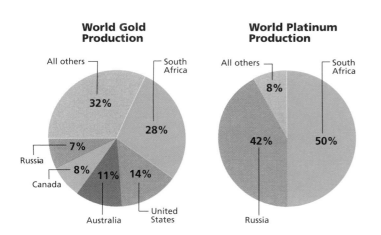

Africa possesses approximately 40 percent of the world's hydroelectric potential. Kenya's Lake Kariba Dam provides power for the surrounding region.

Johannesburg is a prosperous South African city.

Tourism

Tourism is a major industry for many African countries that are not industrialized. Every year, hundreds of thousands of people flock to the deserts of Egypt to see the colossal pyramids and the mighty Sphinx, built thousands of years ago. The wildlife preserves in Kenya and Tanzania attract thousands of people from around the world who come to see and photograph the magnificent wildlife there.

The Great Sphinx of Egypt is one of Africa's most hallowed tourist destinations.

THE PEOPLE

Africa's 50-some countries represent a complex mixture of peoples and cultures, with hundreds of ethnic groups and at least 1,000 different languages. For thousands of years, Africans organized themselves into tribal nations. From the 1600s to the 1960s, Europeans colonized most of the continent, but today the colonies are gone and nearly every country is independent. Although civil war has torn apart many of these countries, and Africa's population continues to face great challenges, the continent remains a place of opportunity due to the diversity of its cultures and resourcefulness of its people.

Schoolchildren wave the flag of South Africa on the steps of Parliament.

These Masai women from Kenya wear colorful, traditional native dress.

In Burundi, men form a ceremonial circle to play tambor drums.

A young woman walks among a herd of camels in Morocco.

Africans travel and transport goods by camel because the animals are well adapted to desert life.

A little girl stands in front of a restaurant in a small town in Namibia.

The bowl lyre is a popular musical instrument in northern Africa.

	1	2	3	4	5	6	7	8	9

MEDITERRANEAN SEA

Strait of Gibraltar
ALGIERS
Rabat
Wahran Qacentina Tunis
CASABLANCA MOROCCO TUNISIA
Marrakech Ghardaïa Tripoli Gulf of Sidra Banghāzi ALEXANDRIA
CAIRO Suez
EL Aaiún ALGERIA LIBYA EGYPT Asyūt
WESTERN SAHARA Tropic of Cancer Aswân Lake Nasser
RED SEA
MAURITANIA MALI NIGER CHAD Port Sudan
CAPE VERDE Nouakchott Timbuktu Omdurman ERITREA
Sénégal Khartoum Asmera
SENEGAL Bamako Niamey Lake Chad SUDAN Lake Tana
DAKAR BURKINA FASO N'Djamena Blue Nile DJIBOUTI Gulf of Aden
THE GAMBIA Ouagadougou Kano Djibouti
GUINEA-BISSAU GUINEA BENIN NIGERIA ADDIS ABABA SOMALIA
Conakry GHANA Abuja Benue Mountain Nile ETHIOPIA
Freetown COTE D'IVOIRE TOGO Chari Mogadishu
SIERRA LEONE Volta Lake Cotonou CENTRAL AFRICAN REPUBLIC
Monrovia Accra LAGOS CAMEROON Bangui UGANDA Lake Rudolf
LIBERIA ABIDJAN DOUALA Bomu Equator
EQUATORIAL GUINEA Yaoundé Uele Kampala KENYA
SAO TOME AND PRINCIPE Libreville CONGO Kisangani Lake Victoria NAIROBI INDIAN
GABON DEM. REP. OF THE CONGO RWANDA OCEAN
ATLANTIC Brazzaville Kigali SEYCHELLES
Congo Bujumbura BURUNDI TANZANIA Mombasa
OCEAN KINSHASA Mbuji-Mayi Lake Tanganyika Dodoma DAR ES SALAAM
Cuango Lulaba LUANDA Lubumbashi COMOROS
Cuanza MALAWI Lake Nyasa MAYOTTE (Fr.)
Lobito ANGOLA ZAMBIA Ndola Lilongwe
Huambo Lusaka Lake Kariba Harare MOZAMBIQUE ANTANANARIVO
Cunene Zambezi ZIMBABWE MADAGASCAR MAURITIUS
NAMIBIA Okavango Changane Beira REUNION (Fr.)
BOTSWANA Mozambique Channel Tropic of Capricorn
Windhoek Gaborone Limpopo Pretoria MAPUTO
Johannesburg SWAZILAND
Orange LESOTHO Durban
SOUTH AFRICA Maseru
Cape Town Port Elizabeth

N W E S

Africa Facts

Population:
866,305,000

Population Density:
74 people per square mile
(29 per square kilometer)

Most Populous Country:
Nigeria, 135,570,000 people

Largest City:
Cairo, Egypt, 11,100,000 people
(metropolitan area)

0	200	400	600	800	1000 Miles
0	300	600	900	1200	1500 Kilometers

Scale 1:45,000,000; one inch to 710 miles

Copyright by Rand McNally & Co.
Made in U.S.A.
N-CMW80000-P1- -2-2-2

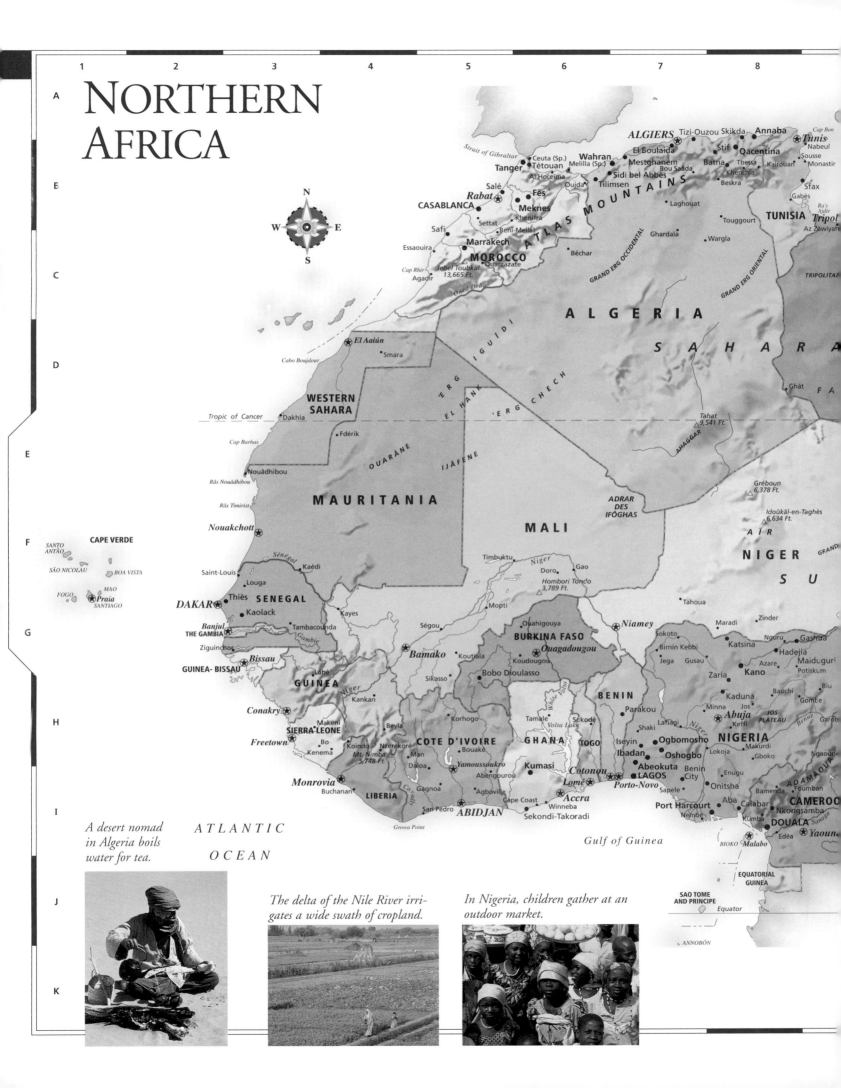

NORTHERN AFRICA

1 2 3 4 5 6 7 8

A B C D E F G H I J K

Map labels:

ALGIERS · Tizi-Ouzou · Skikda · Annaba · Cap Bon · Tunis · Nabeul · Sousse · Monastir

El Boulaida · Wahran · Mestghanem · Stif · Qacentina · Batna · Tbessa · Kairouan

Ceuta (Sp.) · Tanger · Tétouan · Melilla (Sp.) · Sidi bel Abbès · Tilimsen · Khenchla · Beskra · Sfax

Strait of Gibraltar · Al Hoceima · Oujda · Gabès · Ra's Ajdir

Salé · Rabat · Fès · ATLAS MOUNTAINS · Laghouat · Touggourt · TUNISIA · Tripol

CASABLANCA · Meknes · Khenifra · Settat · Beni-Mellal · Ghardaïa · Wargla · Az Zawiyah

Safi · Marrakech · MOROCCO · Béchar · GRAND ERG OCCIDENTAL · TRIPOLITAN

Essaouira · Ouarzazate · GRAND ERG ORIENTAL

Cap Rhir · Jebel Toubkal 13,665 Ft. · ALGERIA · SAHARA

Agadir · Oued Drâa

El Aaiún · Smara

Cabo Boujdour

WESTERN SAHARA · ERG IGUIDI · Ghāt · FA

Tropic of Cancer · Dakhla · EL HANK · ERG CHECH · Tahat 9,541 Ft. · AHAGGAR

Cap Barbas · Fdérik · OUARÄNE · IJÄFENE · Gréboun 6,378 Ft.

Rās Nouâdhibou · Nouâdhibou · ADRAR DES IFÔGHAS · Idoûkâl-en-Taghès 6,634 Ft.

Rās Timirist · MAURITANIA · MALI · AÏR · NIGER · GRAND

Nouakchott · SU

CAPE VERDE · SANTO ANTÃO · SÃO NICOLAU · BOA VISTA · MAO · FOGO · Praia · SANTIAGO

Sénégal · Kaédi · Timbuktu · Niger · Doro · Gao · NIGER

Saint-Louis · Louga · Hombori Tondo 3,789 Ft. · Tahoua · Zinder

DAKAR · Thiès · SENEGAL · Kayes · Mopti · Maradi · Nguru · Gashua

Kaolack · Ségou · Ouahigouya · Niamey · Sokoto · Katsina · Hadejia

Banjul · THE GAMBIA · Tambacounda · Gambie · BURKINA FASO · Birnin Kebbi · Kano · Maiduguri

Ziguinchor · Bamako · Koutiala · Ouagadougou · Jega · Gusau · Potiskum

GUINEA-BISSAU · Bissau · Labé · Sikasso · Koudougou · Zaria · Bauchi · Biu

GUINEA · Kankan · Bobo Dioulasso · BENIN · Kaduna · Gombe

Conakry · Niger · White Volta · Parakou · Minna · Jos · Abuja · JOS PLATEAU · Benue · Garo

SIERRA LEONE · Makeni · Beyla · Korhogo · Tamale · Volta Lake · Sekodé · Keffi · Shaki · Lafiagi · Niger

Freetown · Bo · Kenema · Koindu · Nzérékoré · Man · Bouaké · GHANA · TOGO · Iseyin · Ogbomosho · NIGERIA · Ngaoun

Mt. Nimba 5,748 Ft. · Daloa · COTE D'IVOIRE · Ibadan · Oshogbo · Lokoja · Makurdi · ADAMAOUA

Monrovia · Buchanan · Yamoussoukro · Abengourou · Kumasi · Cotonou · Abeokuta · Benin City · Enugu · Bamenda · Foumban · CAMEROO

LIBERIA · Gagnoa · Agboville · Lomé · LAGOS · Porto-Novo · Onitsha · Aba · Calabar · Nkongsamba

San-Pédro · ABIDJAN · Cape Coast · Accra · Winneba · Sapele · Port Harcourt · Kumba · DOUALA

Growa Point · Sekondi-Takoradi · Nembe · Edéa · Yaoun

ATLANTIC OCEAN · Gulf of Guinea · BIOKO · Malabo

EQUATORIAL GUINEA

SAO TOME AND PRINCIPE · Equator · ANNOBÓN

N W E S (compass)

A desert nomad in Algeria boils water for tea.

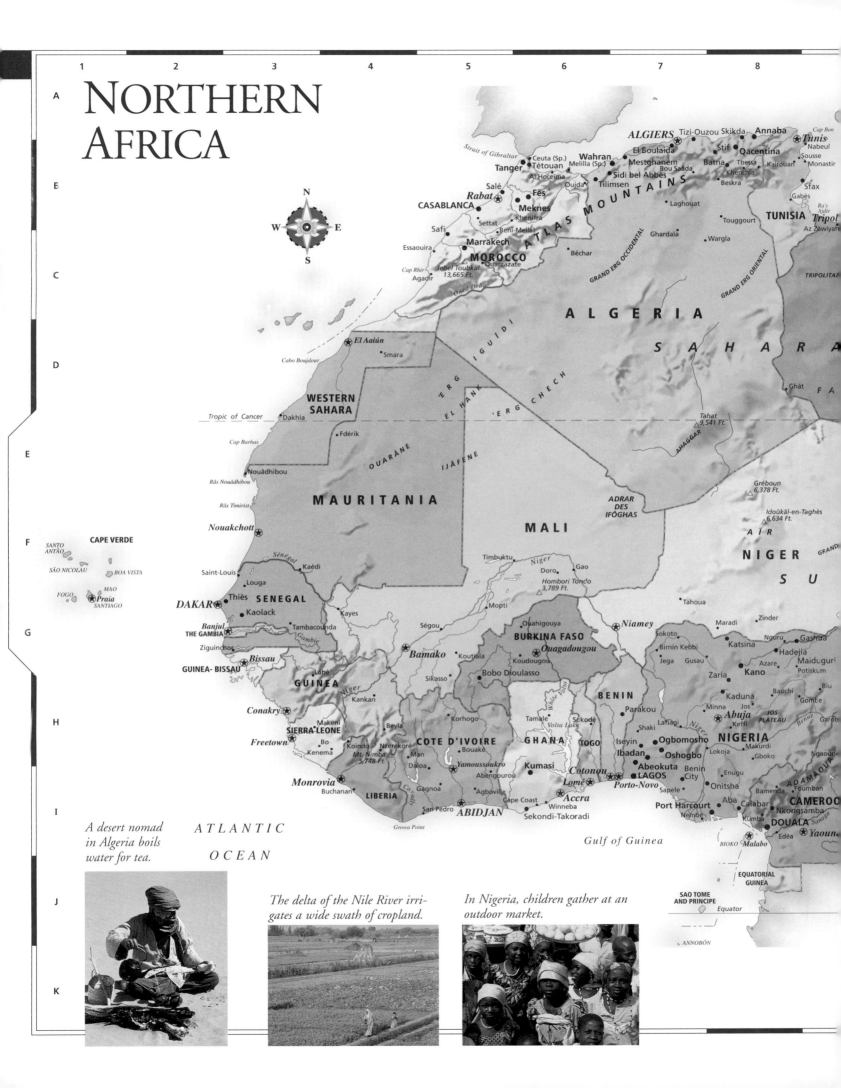

The delta of the Nile River irrigates a wide swath of cropland.

In Nigeria, children gather at an outdoor market.

10 11 12 13 14 15 16 17

Most of Northern Africa is dry, barren desert. The Sahara — the largest desert in the world — spreads across more than half of the region. Algeria and Libya are almost entirely covered by desert. Most of the people who live in this harsh environment are nomads. They travel from place to place with their herds of goats, sheep, and camels in search of water and grazing pastures. The southern Sahara gives way to the Sahel, a wide band of dry grasslands. Some crops grow there, but overfarming is causing the land to lose soil and become desert. The valleys of the Atlas Mountains offer some fertile land, but most of the richest land in Northern Africa is found to the east, in the Nile River Valley. People have farmed this fruitful land for more than 7,000 years. Farther south, the Sahel yields to the steamy tropical rain forests of central Africa. Even though the region is ripe for farming and oil reserves have been discovered in the area around the Gulf of Guinea, most of the people still struggle with poverty.

MEDITERRANEAN SEA

Misrātah
Al Baydā'
Banghāzī
Darnah
Gulf of Sidra
Tubruq
ALEXANDRIA
Port Said
Tanta
El Mansûra
CAIRO
Ismailia
Giza
Suez
El Fayoum
Maghâgha
Beni Suef
El Minya
Beni Mazâr
Mallawi
Manfalût
Asyût
Tahta
Suhag
Girga
Qena
Luxor
Isna
Nile
Kom Ombo
Aswân
Lake Nasser
Râs Banâs
Tropic of Cancer
Ra's al Ḥaḍāribah

CYRENAICA
QATTARA DEPRESSION
LIBYA
Al Jawf
WESTERN DESERT
EGYPT
ARABIAN DESERT
LIBYAN DESERT
RED SEA

NUBIAN DESERT
Port Sudan
Ra's Kasr

Bikkū Bitti 7,438 Ft.
Pic Toussidé 10,876 Ft.
TIBESTI
Emi Koussi 11,204 Ft.
ENNEDI

'Aṭbarah

CHAD
Abéché
Al Fâshir
Al Junaynah
ke Chad
SAHEL
N'Djamena
Nyala

Nile
Omdurman
Al Kharṭām Baḥrī
Khartoum
Kassala
SUDAN
Wad Madanī
Ad Duwaym
Al Qadârif
Al Ubayyid
Sannâr
An Nuhûd
White Nile
Khazzān ar Ruṣayris
Blue Nile
Malakāl

ERITREA
Akordat
Keren
Mitsiwa
Asmera
Mekele
Ras Dashen Terara 15,158 Ft.
Gonder
DENAKIL
Aseb
Lake Tana
Bahir Dar
Talo 14,478 Ft.
ETHIOPIA
Dese
DJIBOUTI
Djibouti
Gulf of Aden
Gees Gwardafuy
Debre Markos
PLATEAU
Ra's Khaanziir
Boosaaso
Berbera
ETHIOPIAN
Dire Dawa
Harer
Hargeysa

AS SUDD
Mountain Nile
Wâw
ADDIS ABABA
Debre Zeyt
Asela
Jima
RIFT VALLEY
Lake Abaya
Guge 13,780 Ft.
OGADEN
SOMALIA
Shebele
Dhuusa Mareeb

CENTRAL AFRICAN REPUBLIC
Bambari
MASSIF DES BONGO
Sarh
Kelo
Moundou
Mbomod
Bangui
Oubangui
Birao
Juba
Baïdoa
INDIAN OCEAN

Chari
Logone

Shabeelle
Mogadishu
Equator
Kismaayo
Raas Jumbo

0 100 200 300 400 500 600 Miles
0 200 400 600 800 1000 Kilometers
Scale 1:20,000,000; one inch to 315 miles

SOUTHERN AFRICA

Cheetah

Like the land to the north, Southern Africa is known for a number of outstanding natural features. In the eastern part of the region, the Rift Valley, a great gash in the earth's surface, stretches about 4,000 miles (almost 6,500 kilometers) from Ethiopia south to Zambia. Mountain ranges rise along both sides of the valley. In the surrounding savannas, or grasslands, large herds of zebras, elephants, rhinoceroses, giraffes, wildebeests, and other animals roam the land. South of the grasslands are the Kalahari and Namib Deserts. Most people in Southern Africa live in small villages, but the region also contains the major cities of Nairobi, Kenya, and Kinshasa, Democratic Republic of the Congo.

In Tanzania's Serengeti National Park, acacia trees rise up from the grasslands.

African animals come in all sizes and shapes.

Fennec Fox

Bongo

African Elephant

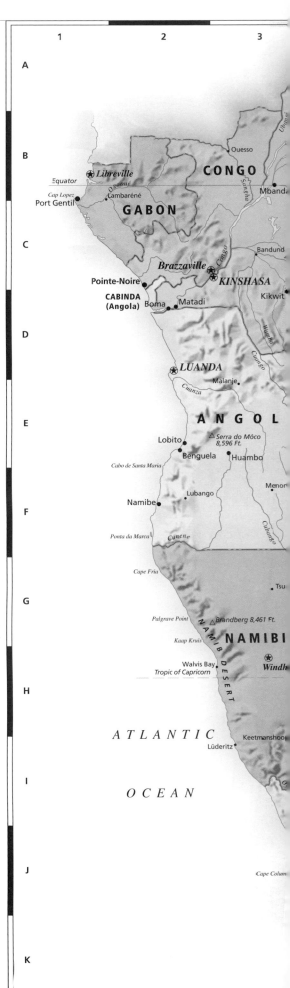

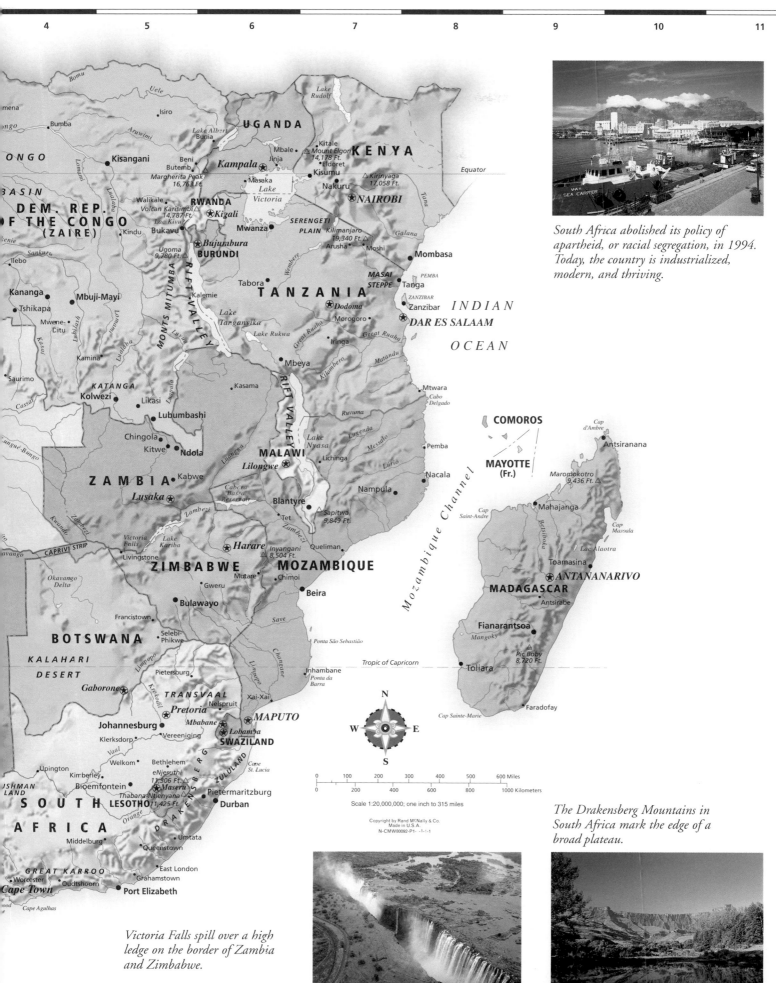

4   5   6   7   8   9   10   11

Bomu
mena
Isiro
Bumba
ongo
Aruwimi
Uele
UGANDA
Lake
Rudolf
Kisangani
Beni
Butemb
Bunia
Lake Albert
Mbale
Kitale
△ Mount Elgon
14,178 Ft.
Jinja
Eldoret
KENYA
BASIN
Margherita Peak
16,763 Ft.
Kampala
Masaka
Kisumu
Nakuru
△ Kirinyaga
17,058 Ft.
Equator
DEM. REP.
OF THE CONGO
(ZAIRE)
Walikale
Volcan Karisimbi
14,787 Ft.
RWANDA
Kigali
Lake
Victoria
NAIROBI
Lac Kivu
Kindu
Bukavu
Mwanza
SERENGETI
PLAIN
Kilimanjaro
19,340 Ft. △
Galana
Tana
Kananga
Mbuji-Mayi
Ugoma
9,780 Ft.
BURUNDI
Bujumbura
Arusha
Moshi
Mombasa
Tshikapa
Sankuru
Kalemie
Tabora
Wembere
TANZANIA
MASAI
STEPPE
Tanga
PEMBA
Mwene-
Ditu
Lake
Tanganyika
Dodoma
Zanzibar
ZANZIBAR
INDIAN
Kamina
Lake Rukwa
Morogoro
Great Ruaha
DAR ES SALAAM
Saurimo
KATANGA
Kolwezi
Kasama
Mbeya
Iringa
Great Ruaha
OCEAN
Likasi
Kilombero
Matandu
ngue-Bango
Lubumbashi
Mtwara
Cabo
Delgado
Chingola
Kitwe
Ndola
Ruvuma
MOZAMBIQUE CHANNEL
Cap
d'Ambre
ZAMBIA
Kabwe
Lake
Nyasa
Lichinga
Lugenda
Messalo
Pemba
COMOROS
Maromokotro
9,436 Ft. △
Antsiranana
MALAWI
Lilongwe
Cabora
Bassa
Reservoir
Lurio
MAYOTTE
(Fr.)
Lusaka
Blantyre
△ Sapitwä
9,849 Ft.
Nampula
Nacala
Cap
Masoala
Zambezi
Tet
Zambezi
Mahajanga
Cap
Saint-André
Lac Alaotra
Victoria
Falls
Lake
Kariba
Harare
Inyangani
8,504 Ft. △
Quelimane
Betsiboka
CAPRIVI STRIP
Livingstone
ZIMBABWE
MOZAMBIQUE
Toamasina
avango
Okavango
Delta
Gweru
Mutare
Chimoi
Beira
ANTANANARIVO
MADAGASCAR
Bulawayo
Save
Antsirabe
Francistown
Ponta São Sebastião
BOTSWANA
Selebi-
Phikwe
Changane
Fianarantsoa
Mangoky
KALAHARI
DESERT
Pietersburg
Limpopo
Inhambane
Ponta da
Barra
Tropic of Capricorn
Pic Boby
8,720 Ft. △
Gaborone
Limpopo
Xai-Xai
Toliara
TRANSVAAL
Nelspruit
N
Krokodil
Pretoria
Mbabane
MAPUTO
Cap Sainte-Marie
Faradofay
Johannesburg
Lobamba
Vereeniging
SWAZILAND
W   E
Klerksdorp
Vaal
Welkom
Cape
St. Lucia
S
Upington
Kimberley
Bethlehem
eNjesuthi
11,306 Ft.
ZULULAND
JSHMAN
LAND
Bloemfontein
Maseru
Pietermaritzburg
SOUTH
Thabana Ntlenyana
11,425 Ft.
LESOTHO
Durban
0   100   200   300   400   500   600 Miles
AFRICA
Orange
Middelburg
Umtata
0   200   400   600   800   1000 Kilometers
Scale 1:20,000,000; one inch to 315 miles
Queenstown
GREAT KARROO
East London
Worcester
Oudtshoorn
Grahamstown
Copyright by Rand McNally & Co.
Made in U.S.A.
N-CMW80092-P1- -1-1-1
Cape Town
Port Elizabeth
Cape Agulhas

ONGO
Kananga
Lomami
Lualaba
Lomela
Kasai
Cassat
Lubilash
Lulua
Luvua
MONTS MITUMBA
RIFT VALLEY
RIFT VALLEY
Luangwa
Luangwa
Lambezi
Kwando
Zambezi
Kwando
Okavango
DRAKENSBERG

South Africa abolished its policy of
apartheid, or racial segregation, in 1994.
Today, the country is industrialized,
modern, and thriving.

The Drakensberg Mountains in
South Africa mark the edge of a
broad plateau.

Victoria Falls spill over a high
ledge on the border of Zambia
and Zimbabwe.

ASIA

Asia is by far the largest and the most populous continent. It represents one-third of the world's land and holds nearly three-fifths of the world's people. Its terrain is tremendously varied but dominated by mountains, including the world's highest range, the Himalayas. Mountains, in fact, help to define the continent: The Ural Mountains separate Asia from Europe, which occupies the western part of Eurasia.

Asia is notable for its extremes. Mount Everest, on the Nepal-China border, is the world's highest mountain. The Tibetan Plateau is the world's largest and highest plateau. The shore of the salty Dead Sea, which lies between Israel and Jordan, is the lowest point on Earth. Lake Baikal in Siberia is the world's deepest lake.

India's Taj Mahal (above) was built to honor an emperor's wife; Japanese fans (left) are ornate works of art; the Great Wall of China (below) is the largest man-made structure in the world

Asia Facts

Area: 17,300,000 square miles (44,900,000 square kilometers)

Highest Mountain: Mount Everest, China-Nepal, 29,028 feet (8,848 meters) — *world's highest mountain*

Lowest Point: Dead Sea, Israel-Jordan, -1339 feet (-408 meters) — *world's lowest point*

Longest River: Yangtze, China, 3,900 miles (6,300 kilometers)

Largest Lake: Caspian Sea, Asia/Europe, 144,400 square miles (374,000 square kilometers)

Largest Desert: Gobi, China-Mongolia, 386,000 square miles (1,000,000 square kilometers)

Largest Island: New Guinea, Asia/Oceania, 309,000 square miles (800,000 square kilometers)

Land Elevation Feet (Meters)

- 9,840 and over (3,000 and over)
- 6,560 - 9,840 (2,000 - 3,000)
- 3,280 - 6,560 (1,000 - 2,000)
- 1,640 - 3,280 (500 - 1,000)
- 656 - 1,640 (200 - 500)
- 0 - 656 feet (0 - 200)

ARCTIC OCEAN

SEVERNAYA ZEMLYA

KARA SEA

LAPTEV SEA

NEW SIBERIAN ISLANDS

EAST SIBERIAN SEA

BERING SEA

pol. Yamal

poluostrov Taymyr

Noril'sk

Central Siberian Uplands

Arctic Circle

poluostrov Kamchatka

Mys Lopatka

R U S S I A

West Siberian Lowland

Ural Mountains

Verkhoyanskiy khrebet

NOVOSIBIRSK

Ob

Yenisey

Angara

S i b e r i a

Stanovoy khrebet

SEA OF OKHOTSK

SAKHALIN

KURIL ISLANDS

Irtysh

Lake Baikal

Amur

Tatar Strait

Sikhote-Alin'

Ishim

Tobol

Sayan Mts.

Selenge

Greater Khingan Range

Manchuria

HOKKAIDŌ

SEA OF JAPAN

HONSHŪ

JAPAN

TŌKYŌ

KAZAKHSTAN

Aral Sea

Ust-Urt Plateau

Kirghiz Steppe

Lake Balkhash

Syr Darya

Altai

Junggar Pendi

MONGOLIA

Gobi

NORTH KOREA

SOUTH KOREA

Korea Strait

SHIKOKU

KYŪSHŪ

YELLOW SEA

Caspian Sea

Kara Kum

TURKMENISTAN

UZBEKISTAN

KYRGYZSTAN

Amu Darya

TAJIKISTAN

Tien Shan

Pamir

Tarim Pendi

Qilian Shan

BEIJING

Mt. Fuji 12,388 Ft.

Kopet-Dag

dasht-e Kavir

AFGHANISTAN

Hindu Kush

K2 28,250 Ft.

Altun Shan

Qaidam Pendi

Kunlun Shan

C H I N A

Qin Ling

Huang

EAST CHINA SEA

SHANGHAI

PACIFIC OCEAN

Dasht-e Lut

PAKISTAN

Plateau of Tibet

H i m a l a y a s

Yangtze

Nan Ling

Wuyi Shan

Taiwan Strait

TAIWAN

Tropic of Cancer

Gulf of Oman

New Delhi

Great Indian Desert

Indus

NEPAL

Mt. Everest 29,028 Ft.

BHUTAN

Ganges

Brahmaputra

BANGLADESH

Red

Luzon Strait

LUZON

Kāthiāwār Peninsula

INDIA

Godāvari

D e c c a n

Western Ghats

Eastern Ghats

MYANMAR

LAOS

Indochina

Gulf of Tonkin

HAINAN DAO

Manila

PHILIPPINES

MUMBAI (BOMBAY)

ARABIAN SEA

Bay of Bengal

THAILAND

BANGKOK

CAMBODIA

VIETNAM

SOUTH CHINA SEA

MINDANAO

Mekong

LAKSHADWEEP

Cape Comorin

ANDAMAN ISLANDS

Andaman Sea

Gulf of Thailand

Mui Ca Mau

Sulu Sea

MALDIVES

SRI LANKA

NICOBAR ISLANDS

Malay Peninsula

Str. of Malacca

BRUNEI

Celebes Sea

MOLUCCAS

NEW GUINEA

Equator

MALAYSIA

SINGAPORE

BORNEO

CELEBES

CERAM

SUMATRA

GREATER SUNDA ISLANDS

Banda Sea

I N D I A N   O C E A N

Equator

Java Sea

INDONESIA

Jakarta

JAVA

EAST TIMOR

TIMOR

Arafura Sea

Timor Sea

0   100   300   500 Miles
0   200   400   600   800 Kilometers
Scale 1:45,000,000; one inch to 710 miles

Copyright by Rand McNally & Co.
Made in U.S.A.
N-CMW60000-A1- -2-2-2

N
W   E
S

THE LAND

Only about a fifth of the continent is suitable for agriculture, but a large portion of Asia's people make their living off the land. In Asia's three most populous countries — China, India, and Russia — two-thirds of workers are farmers. Raising livestock is also an important job, especially in the central Asian grasslands. Given Asia's size, it is not surprising that the continent holds some of the world's largest reserves of oil, natural gas, and coal.

By building terraces that capture rainfall, farmers can grow rice on even the steepest hillsides.

Environments

Asia has a wide variety of environments, including large areas of arctic and subarctic tundra, broad deserts, heavy forests, and dry grasslands.

Environments

- Forest
- Swamp
- Crop and woodland
- Cropland
- Crop and grazing land
- Grassland
- Desert
- Tundra
- Barren
- Urban

Wood products are one of Indonesia's main exports.

Mineral Resources

In addition to its huge oil and coal reserves, Asia is also rich in metals such as iron ore, tin, lead, zinc, and bauxite. The continent furnishes raw materials for its own industries with plenty left over to export to the rest of the world.

Farming

Rice is Asia's most important crop: Asia produces 90 percent of the world's supply. Rice grows both in flooded fields called paddies and on terraced hillsides. With plentiful rainfall and fertile lowlands, countries such as India, Thailand, and China are the perfect places to grow rice—in fact, some areas grow three separate rice crops each year.

Forestry

In chilly Siberia, forests cover more than one-third of the land. In southeast Asia, the exotic hardwood trees of the rain forests are used mainly for making furniture. Unfortunately, the trees are being cut down faster than they can grow back, and entire Asian forests are in danger of disappearing.

Tourism

Tourism is an important source of income for many Asian countries. The continent offers a broad range of travel destinations, including the Taj Mahal, China's Great Wall, Mount Everest and other high Himalayan peaks, the ancient temples of Myanmar, and holy sites of the Middle East.

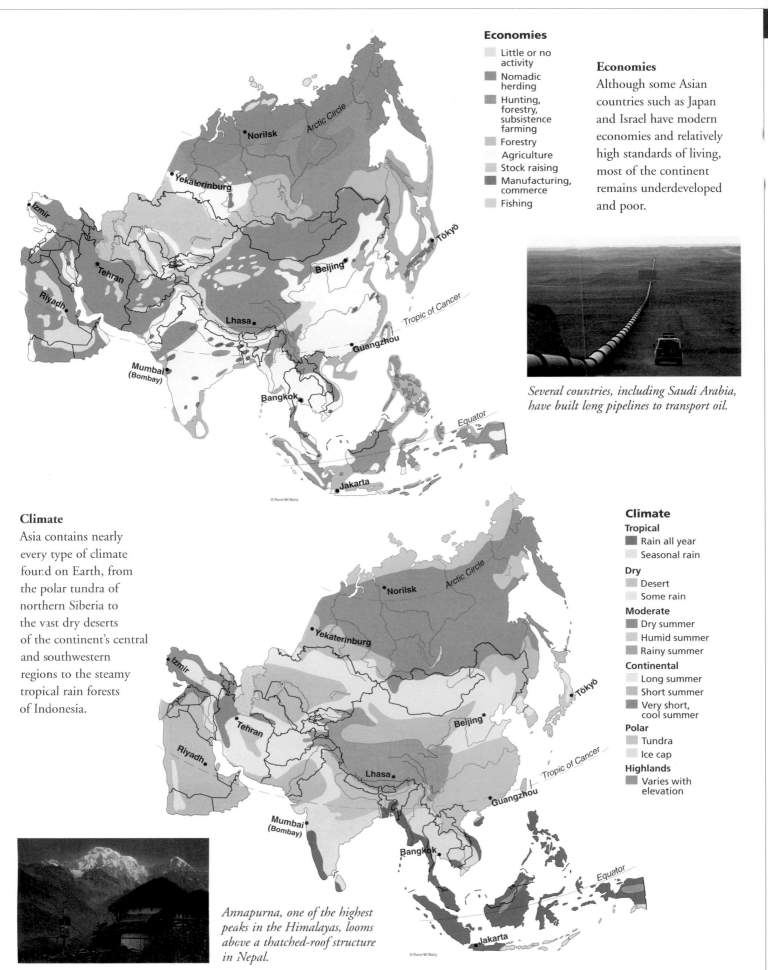

Economies

Economies

- Little or no activity
- Nomadic herding
- Hunting, forestry, subsistence farming
- Forestry
- Agriculture
- Stock raising
- Manufacturing, commerce
- Fishing

Economies

Although some Asian countries such as Japan and Israel have modern economies and relatively high standards of living, most of the continent remains underdeveloped and poor.

Several countries, including Saudi Arabia, have built long pipelines to transport oil.

Climate

Asia contains nearly every type of climate found on Earth, from the polar tundra of northern Siberia to the vast dry deserts of the continent's central and southwestern regions to the steamy tropical rain forests of Indonesia.

Climate

Tropical
- Rain all year
- Seasonal rain

Dry
- Desert
- Some rain

Moderate
- Dry summer
- Humid summer
- Rainy summer

Continental
- Long summer
- Short summer
- Very short, cool summer

Polar
- Tundra
- Ice cap

Highlands
- Varies with elevation

Annapurna, one of the highest peaks in the Himalayas, looms above a thatched-roof structure in Nepal.

© Rand McNally

THE PEOPLE

Asia is the most culturally and ethnically diverse continent, mainly because of its enormous size. Three out of every five people on Earth live in Asia. While many Asians are farmers and live in the countryside or in small villages, the continent's cities are among the world's largest and most crowded. Tokyo, Japan, is the most populous metropolitan area on Earth. China, with more than one billion people, is the world's most populous country.

Sleds drawn by reindeer help Siberians travel across the deep snow.

In India, a merchant keeps track of business transactions in a ledger.

Chinese children perform at a festival.

As part of their Islamic faith, Muslims observe the holy month of Ramadan.

Buddhist monks gather outside a temple in Bangkok, Thailand.

A young herder tends sheep and cattle in the mountains of Uzbekistan.

Asia Facts

Population: 3,839,320,000

Population Density:
222 per square mile
(86 per square kilometer)

Most Populous Country:
China, 1,298,720,000 people

Largest City:
Tokyo-Yokohama, Japan,
35,300,000 people
(metropolitan area)

4 5 6 7 8 9 10 11

ARCTIC OCEAN

SEVERNAYA
ZEMLYA

NEW SIBERIAN
ISLANDS

EAST SIBERIAN
SEA

BERING
SEA

LAPTEV
SEA

KARA SEA

Arctic Circle

• Noril'sk

Lena

Indigirka

Yana

• Magadan

poluostrov
Kamchatka

Petropavlovsk-
Kamchatskiy

SEA OF
OKHOTSK

KURIL ISLANDS

SAKHALIN

Tatar Strait

R U S S I A

• Surgut

Ob'

Yenisei

Angara

• Yakutsk

YEKATERINBURG

CHELYABINSK

Ural

• Tyumen

Ishim

OMSK

NOVOSIBIRSK

• Krasnoyarsk

Lake
Baikal

• Chita

Amur

• Khabarovsk

Astana
(Aqmola) ⊛

Qaraghandy •

• Barnaul

• Irkutsk

Selenge

QIQIHAR •

HARBIN •

Vladivostok •

SAPPORO •
HOKKAIDŌ

Aral
Sea

Irtysh

KAZAKHSTAN

• Semey

Ulan Bator ⊛

MONGOLIA

CHANGCHUN •

SHENYANG •

NORTH
KOREA
P'YONGYANG ⊛

SEA OF
JAPAN

HONSHŪ

JAPAN

TŌKYŌ

Caspian
Sea

Lake
Balkhash

Syr Darya

ALMATY •

Bishkek ⊛

ÜRÜMQI •

BEIJING ⊛ • TIANJIN

SEOUL ⊛

SOUTH
KOREA

OSAKA •

NAGOYA •

BAKU •

TASHKENT ⊛

TURKMENISTAN

UZBEKISTAN

KYRGYZSTAN

TAIYUAN •

• JINAN

YELLOW
SEA

PUSAN •

SHIKOKU

KYUSHŪ

MASHHAD •

Ashgabat ⊛

Amu Darya

TAJIKISTAN

Dushanbe ⊛

LANZHOU •

Huang

NANJING •

• SHANGHAI

EAST

Tropic of Cancer

PACIFIC OCEAN

IRAN

KABUL ⊛

AFGHANISTAN

Islāmābād ⊛

C H I N A

XI'AN •

CHENGDU •

• CHONGQING

WUHAN •

HANGZHOU •

CHINA
SEA

Fuzhou •

T'AIPEI ⊛

TAIWAN

PAKISTAN

LAHORE •

DELHI •

Lhasa •

Yangtze

KUNMING •

KAOHSIUNG •

Taiwan Strait

KARACHI •

New
Delhi ⊛

KĀNPUR •

NEPAL

Kathmāndu ⊛

Thimphu ⊛

BHUTAN

Brahmaputra

GUANGZHOU •

HONG
KONG

Luzon Strait

Gulf of Oman

Muscat ⊛

Ganges

INDIA

BANGLA-
DESH

DHAKA ⊛

Chittagong

Ha Noi ⊛

LUZON

AHMADĀBĀD •

KOLKATA
(CALCUTTA) •

MYANMAR
(BURMA)

LAOS

Gulf of
Tonkin

HAINAN DAO

MANILA ⊛

MUMBAI
(BOMBAY) •

NĀGPUR •

Godāvari

Viangchan ⊛

Da Nang •

PHILIPPINES

ARABIAN
SEA

PUNE •

HYDERĀBĀD •

YANGON ⊛

Mekong

VIETNAM

SOUTH

Cebu •

MINDANAO

THAILAND

CHINA

BANGALORE •

CHENNAI
(MADRAS) •

Bay of
Bengal

BANGKOK ⊛

CAMBODIA

SEA

Sulu Sea

Davao •

ANDAMAN
ISLANDS
(India)

Phnum
Penh ⊛

THANH PHO
HO CHI MINH

SRI LANKA

Gulf of
Thailand

MALDIVES

Colombo ⊛

Equator

Malay
Peninsula

Bandar Seri
Begawan ⊛

Celebes Sea

• Manado

NEW GUINEA

Male' ⊛

NICOBAR
ISLANDS
(India)

BRUNEI

CELEBES

CERAM

Str. of Malacca

Kuala
Lumpur ⊛

MALAYSIA

BORNEO

Banda Sea

Arafura Sea

MEDAN •

SINGAPORE ⊛

INDIAN OCEAN

Equator

SUMATRA

PALEMBANG •

Java Sea

Banjarmasin •

I N D O N E S I A

EAST TIMOR

TIMOR

Timor Sea

JAKARTA ⊛

BANDUNG •

JAVA

SURABAYA •

N
W   E
S

0   200   400   600   800   100C Miles

0   300   600   900   1200   1500 Kilometers

Scale 1:45,000,000; one inch to 710 miles

Copyright by Rand McNally & Co.
Made in U.S.A.
N-CMW60000-P1- -2-2-2

India's Ganges River is
sacred to Hindus, who
believe that bathing in its
waters will wash away
their sins.

These young people
in Turkey show off
colorful traditional
clothing.

SOUTHWEST ASIA

Southwest Asia borders Europe — in fact, a small part of Turkey actually falls within Europe. Turkey's most fertile farmlands spread along its lengthy coast, although wheat and barley grow in the dry plateau area in the center of the country. Armenia, Azerbaijan, and Georgia, which all lie in the mountainous region between the Black Sea and the Caspian Sea, possess abundant mineral wealth.

The rugged Troodos Mountains dominate the center of the island of Cyprus.

A Turkish farmer rides a donkey across a wheat field.

Sheep graze near an ancient Roman temple in western Armenia.

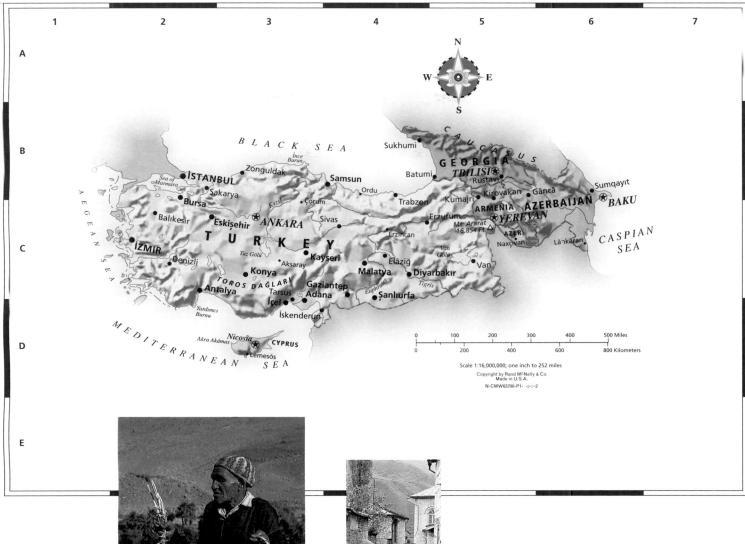

N
W   E
S

BLACK SEA

Sukhumi

CAUCASUS

GEORGIA
TBLISI ✪
Rustavi

İnce
Burun

Zonguldak

İSTANBUL

Sea of Marmara

Sakarya

Batumi

Bursa

Samsun

Ordu

Kumajri
Kirovakan
Gänca

Sumqayıt

Balıkesir

Kızıl

Çorum

Trabzon

ARMENIA

AZERBAIJAN

✪**BAKU**

Eskişehir

✪*ANKARA*

Sivas

Erzurum

Mt. Ararat
16,854 Ft. △

✪**YEREVAN**

AZER.

CASPIAN
SEA

A E G E A N   S E A

İZMİR

Denizli

T U R K E Y

Tuz Gölü

Aksaray

Erzincan

*Van
Gölü*

Naxçıvan

Länkäran

Kayseri

Elâziğ

Konya

TOROS DAĞLARI

Malatya

Diyarbakır

Van

Gaziantep

Tarsus

Euphrates

Tigris

Antalya

İçel

Adana

Şanlıurfa

*Yardımcı
Burnu*

İskenderun

M E D I T E R R A N E A N

Akra Akámas

Nicosia ✪

CYPRUS

Lemesós

S E A

0   100   200   300   400   500 Miles
0   200   400   600   800 Kilometers

Scale 1:16,000,000; one inch to 252 miles
Copyright by Rand McNally & Co.
Made in U.S.A.
N-CMW63700-P1- -2-2-2

Dates, the fruit of date palm trees, have been a staple food in Southwestern Asia for thousands of years.

Residents of a small town in Azerbaijan walk along an ancient cobblestone street.

Istanbul's magnificent Church of Hagia Sofia rises above the Bosporus Strait, which separates Asia and Europe.

RUSSIA AND CENTRAL ASIA

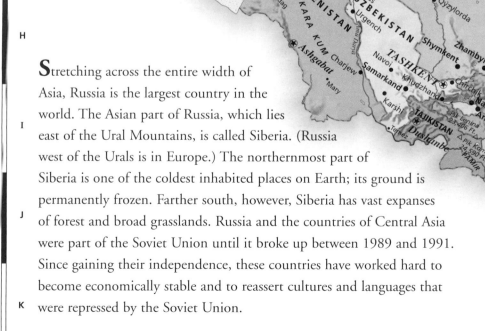

Kaliningrad

ST. PETERSBURG
Pskov
Novgorod
Velikiye Luki
MOSCOW
Smolensk
Kaluga
Bryansk
Tula
Orel
Kursk
Lipetsk
Belgorod
Voronezh
Ryazan'
Tambov
Vladimir
Ivanovo
Saransk
Penza
NIZHNIY
Cheboksary
KAZAN'
Ul'yanovsk
Tol'yatti
SAMARA
Saratov
Balakovo
Volzhskiy
VOLGOGRAD
Kamyshin
Astrakhan'
Atyrau
Aqtöbe
Orsk
Orenburg
Magnitogorsk
Sterlitamak
UFA
Miass
YEKATERINBURG
Izhevsk
PERM'
Kirov
Syktyvkar
Ukhta
Vorkuta
Salekhard
Noril'sk
Dikson

Murmansk
Severodvinsk
Arkhangel'sk
Petrozavodsk
Cherepovets
Rybinsk
Yaroslavl'
Tver'
Vologda
Kostroma

BARENTS SEA
White Sea
KARA SEA
NOVAYA ZEMLYA
ZEMLYA FRANTSA-IOS
POLUOSTROV YAMAL
WEST SIBERIAN LOWLAND
URAL MOUNTAINS
RUS

BLACK SEA
Taganrog
Krasnodar
ROSTOV-NA-DONU
Novocherkassk
Maykop
Sochi
Stavropol'
Nevinnomyssk
CAUCASUS
gora Elbrus 18,510 ft.
Vladikavkaz
Grozny
Makhachkala
Aqtaū
CASPIAN SEA
CASPIAN DEPRESSION
UST-URT PLATEAU
Turkmenbashy
Nebitdag
KARA KUM
TURKMENISTAN
Ashgabat
Mary
Charjew
Nukus
Urgench
UZBEKISTAN
Samarkand
Karshi
TASHKENT
Khudzhand
TAJIKISTAN
Dushanbe
PAMIR
Pik Kommunizma 24,590 ft.
Pik Lenina 23,406 ft.
KYRGYZSTAN
Bishkek
Andizhan
Namangan
Chirchik
Navoi
Shymkent
Zhambyl
ALMATY
Pik Pobeedy 24,406 ft.
Taldyqorghan
Lake Balkhash
Balqash
Ayaköz
KIRGHIZ STEPPE
KAZAKHSTAN
Aral Sea
Qyzylorda
Zhezqazghan
Qaraghandy
Temirtau
Astana (Aqmola)
Kökshetau
Pavlodar
Rüdnyy
Qostanay
Petropavlovsk
OMSK
NOVOSIBIRSK
Barnaul
Biysk
Rubtsovsk
Semey
Oskemen
Kuiten-Uul 14,350 ft.
ALTAI MTS.
SAYAN MTS.
Abakan
Kyzyl
Ulaastay
Novokuznetsk
Kiselevsk
Leninsk-Kuznetskiy
Prokop'yevsk
Kemerovo
Anzhero-Sudzhensk
Tomsk
Achinsk
Krasnoyarsk
Kansk
Kolpashevo
Surgut
Nizhnevartovsk
Khanty-Mansiysk
Tyumen'
Nizhniy Tagil
CHELYABINSK
Kurgan
Kamensk-Ural'skiy
Serov
Tobol'sk
Yartsevo

Volga
Don
Oral
Ishim
Irtysh
Ob'
Yenisey

Stretching across the entire width of Asia, Russia is the largest country in the world. The Asian part of Russia, which lies east of the Ural Mountains, is called Siberia. (Russia west of the Urals is in Europe.) The northernmost part of Siberia is one of the coldest inhabited places on Earth; its ground is permanently frozen. Farther south, however, Siberia has vast expanses of forest and broad grasslands. Russia and the countries of Central Asia were part of the Soviet Union until it broke up between 1989 and 1991. Since gaining their independence, these countries have worked hard to become economically stable and to reassert cultures and languages that were repressed by the Soviet Union.

Kyrgyzstan's Pamir Mountains flank a turquoise lake.

ARCTIC OCEAN

OSTROV KOMSOMOLETS
SEVERNAYA ZEMLYA
OSTROV
BOL'SHEVIK

NEW SIBERIAN ISLANDS

OSTROV NOVAYA SIBIR'
OSTROV BOL'SHOY LYAKHOVSKIY
OSTROV KOTEL'NYY

LAPTEV SEA

EAST SIBERIAN SEA

CHUKCHI SEA

Bering Strait

CHUKOTSKIY POLUOSTROV

Providenya

BERING SEA

mys Navarin

POLUOSTROV TAYMYR
GORY BYRRANGA

mys Svyatoy Nos

mys Buor-Khaya

Tiksi

Kazach'ye

Ambarchik

Arctic Circle

Omolon

Anadyr

Matochi

ANYUYSKIY KHREBET

mys Shelagskiy

gora Izvestkovaya
8,406 Ft.

Kovacha

Khatanga

Yessey

ZENTRAL

gora Kamen'
5,581 Ft.

SIBERIAN PLANDS

Zhigansk

Srednekolymsk

Kolyma

gora Pobeda
10,325 Ft.

pik Aborigen
8,484 Ft.

mys Tolstoy

OSTROV KARAGINSKIY

OSTROV KOMANDORSKIYE OSTROVA

vulkan Klyuchevskaya Sopka
15,584 Ft.

OSTROV BERINGA

OSTROV MEDNYJ

SIBERIA

Nizhnyaya Tunguska

Yakutsk

mys Shipunskiy

SREDINNYY KHREBET

Petropavlovsk-Kamchatskiy

Lena

Lensk

Aldan

Ayan

Okhotsk

Magadan

SEA OF OKHOTSK

vulkan Ichinskaya Sopka
11,880 Ft.

POLUOSTROV KAMCHATKA

mys Lopatka

OSTROV PARAMUSHIR

Ust'-Ilimsk

Angara

ALDANSKOYE NAGOR'YE

gora Inyaptuk
8,458 Ft.

STANOVOY KHREBET

Neryungri

Tynda

Nikolayevsk-na-Amure

mys Yelizavety

Okha

SAKHALIN

gora Lopatina
5,279 Ft.

OSTROV ONEKOTAN

KURIL ISLANDS

mys Terpeniya

OSTROV SIMUSHIR

OSTROV URUP

Ust'-Kut

Bratsk

Nizhneudinsk

STANOVOYE NAGOR'YE

Vitim

Svobodnyy

Komsomol'sk-na-Amure

Sovetskaya Gavan'

Tatar Strait

Yuzhno-Sakhalinsk

Korsakov

OSTROV ITURUP

Zima

Lena

Lake Baikal

Amur

Blagoveshchensk

gora Tardoki-Jani
6,814 Ft.

Khabarovsk

La Perouse Strait

OSTROV KUNASHIR

Isolye-Sibirskoye

Angarsk

Irkutsk

Ulan-Ude

Chita

Birobidzhan

SIKHOTE-ALIN

gora Munku-Sardyk
11,453 Ft.

Borzya

Selenga

Orhon

Ulan Bator

Choybalsan

Ussuriysk

Vladivostok

Nakhodka

MONGOLIA

Erdene

GOBI

0   100   200   300   400   500 Miles
0   200   400   600   800 Kilometers

Scale 1:24,000,000; one inch to 379 miles

Copyright by Rand McNally & Co.
Made in U.S.A.
N-CMW60091-P1- -2-2-2

Many people in Central Asia live in yurts—circular tents covered with animal hides.

The train station at Vladivostok, Russia, marks the eastern end of the Trans-Siberian Railroad. The route begins in Moscow and runs 5,800 miles (9,280 kilometers) through Russia.

Cotton, one of Central Asia's main cash crops, is grown on flat grasslands known as steppes.

A man in Uzbekistan engraves ornate patterns into decorative plates.

Siberian tigers can withstand the brutal cold of northern winters.

EAST ASIA

Tokyo, Japan, is the most populous city in the world.

China, the most populous country in the world and the third largest in land area, dominates East Asia. Much of western China's landscape is harsh and barren, encompassing the high, rugged Tibetan Plateau and two vast deserts, the Gobi and the Takla Makan. Most of China's people live in the eastern part of the country, where there are fertile plains, river valleys, and deltas. Japan is a mountainous island country. Although little of its land is suitable for farming, rice grows in lowland areas and on terraced hillsides. Despite having few natural resources, Japan has become one of the world's wealthiest and most highly industrialized countries.

South Korea and North Korea occupy a peninsula east of China. Once a single country, Korea was divided into North and South Korea following World War II. South Korea has most of the farmland, while North Korea is highly industrialized.

ALTAI

JUNGGAR PENDI

Yining
Manas   ÜRÜMQI
TIEN SHAN
Pik Pobedy
24,406 Ft.
Kashi   Aksu   Hami

BEI SHAN

GO

Shache

TARIM PENDI

Hotan   ALTUN SHAN   QILIAN SHAN   Yumen   Zhangye
K2   Zhangye   Wuwei
28,250 Ft.
△ Muztag   QAIDAM PENDI
Bangong Co   25,338 Ft.   Golmud   Qinghai Hu
KUNLUN SHAN   Xining
△ Leli Shan   LANZHOU
21,020 Ft.   PLATEAU   △ Yagradagzê Shan   A'NYÊMAQÊN SHAN
17,854 Ft.
Kangrinboqê Feng   OF   TIBET   BAYAN HAR SHAN
△ 22,028 Ft.   Huang   Tian
Nam Co   CHINA   Guangy
Salween
Xigazê   Lhasa   Namjagbarwa Feng   CHENGDU   Nancho
Brahmaputra   △ 25,446 Ft.   Guanxien   Suining
Mt. Everest   Gongga Shan   Zigo
△ 29,028 Ft.   24,790 Ft. △
Wutongqiao   Yibi
Xichang   Zhaotong
Anshun
KUNMING
Baoshan
Tropic of Cancer   Tonghai   Wenshan
Gejiu   Yo
Mekong

With an excellent natural harbor, Kaosiung is the fastest-growing city in Taiwan.

Kabuki theater in Japan dates from the early 1600s.

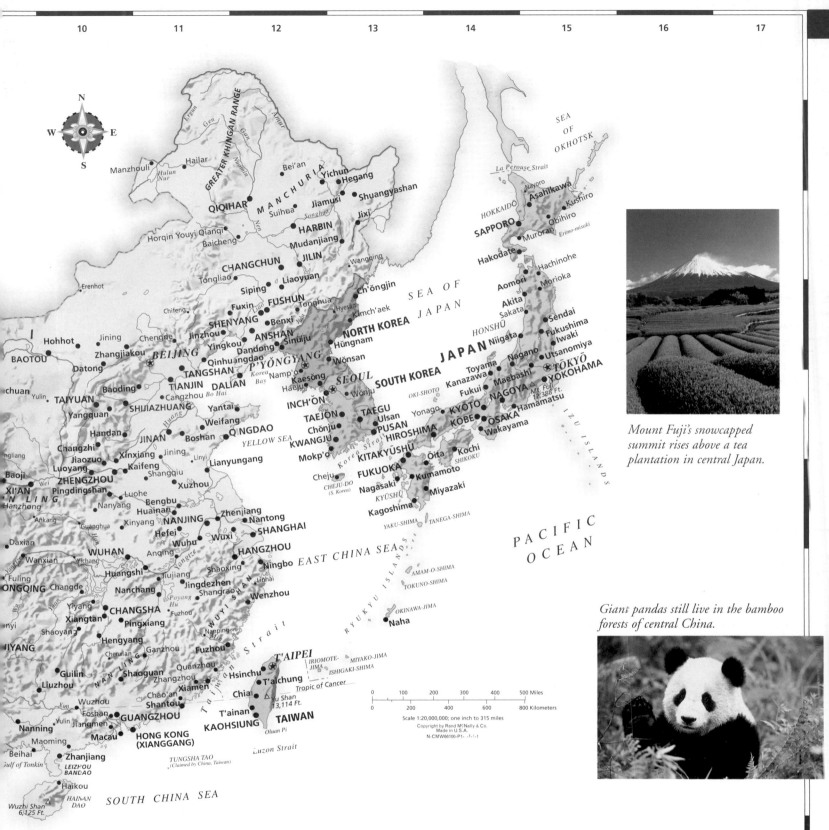

Mount Fuji's snowcapped summit rises above a tea plantation in central Japan.

Giant pandas still live in the bamboo forests of central China.

Almost all of the world's large-scale silk production takes place in Asia, where shops like this one in South Korea display hundreds of brightly colored fabric bolts.

Bicycles are a popular way to travel through the crowded streets of Chinese cities.

SOUTHEAST ASIA

Hot, humid Southeast Asia consists of an enormous peninsula — known as Indochina — and some 20,000 islands. Rice is the major crop, but other tropical crops grow here, too. Palm oil from Malaysia, rubber from Indonesia, coconuts and sugarcane from the Philippines, and hardwoods from throughout the region contribute significantly to the regional economy. Mineral resources, including oil, coal, natural gas, and tin, are also abundant. In fact, oil and natural gas reserves in Brunei have made this small country one of the world's richest. In recent years, tiny Singapore has become an important international center of business and finance.

Thailand's long coast is lined with many secluded inlets, like this one near Phuket.

Bicycles are a way for fruit vendors in Hanoi, Vietnam, to distribute their produce.

Tropic of Cancer

PATKAI RANGE
Chindwinn
Nmai
Myitkyina
Bhamo
CHIN HILLS
Monywa
Ayeyarwady
Mandalay
Maymyo
Phongsali
Phan Si Pang
10,312 Ft.
Ha Noi
Hong Gai
Pakokku
Meiktila
Hoa Binh
Hai Phong
Mt. Victoria
10,016 Ft.
Chauk
Taunggyi
Louangphrabang
Nam Dinh
Sittwe
Yenangyaung
MYANMAR
(BURMA)
Chiang Rai
Thanh Hoa
Salween
ARAKAN YOMA
Prome
Toungoo
Chiang Mai
Phou Bia
9,249 Ft.
LAOS
Gulf of Tonkin
Lampang
Viangchan
Vinh
Nong Khai
Udon Thani
Dai Inthanon
8,530 Ft.
VIETNAM
Henzada
Bago
Uttaradit
Mekong
Khon Kaen
Savannakhét
Dong Hoi
YANGON
Phitsanulok
Kalasin
Hue
Pathein
Pa Sak
THAILAND
Ubon Ratchathani
Pakxé
Da Nang
Pagoda
Point
Nakhon Sawan
Takhli
Ngoc Linh
8,524 Ft.
Quang Ngai
Mawlamyine
Nakhon Ratchasima
THIU KHAO
PHANOM DONGRAK
Kon Tum
Gulf of
Martaban
Phra Nakhon Si Ayutthaya
Play Cu
Qui Nhon
Dawei
BANGKOK
BILAUKTAUNG RANGE
Chon Buri
Bâtdâmbâng
Tuy Hoa
Andaman Sea
Rayong
Bœng Tônlé
Sab
Buon Me Thuot
Hua Hin
Chanthaburi
CAMBODIA
Kâmpóng
Cham
Da Lat
Nha Trang
Mergui
Gulf of
Thailand
Phnum Aôral
5,948 Ft.
Phnum Pénh
Bien
Hoa
Phan Thiet
Kâmpóng Saôm
My
Tho
THANH PHO HO CHI MINH
ISTHMUS
OF KRA
Long Xuyen
Rach Gia
Can Tho
Vung Tau
Soc Trang
Ca Mau
Surat Thani
Mui Ca Mau
Nakhon Si Thammarat
SPRATLY ISLA
Thung Song
Phuket
Phatthalung
Trang
Songkhla
Hat Yai
Kangar
Yala
Narathiwat
Great Channel
Alor Setar
Kota Bharu
Banda Aceh
George Town
Strait of Malacca
Kuala Terengganu
Butterworth
Gunong Tahan
7,175 Ft.
KEPULAUAN
NATUNA
BESAR
Taiping
Dungan
Gunung Abongatong
9,793 Ft.
Ipoh
MALAYSIA
Kuantan
Binjai
Binjai
MEDAN
Kuala Lumpur
KEPULAUAN
ANAMBAS
Tebingtinggi
Tanjungbalai
Pahang
Pematangsiantar
Kelang
Tanjung Datu
Seremban
PALAU SIMEULUE
Danau
Toba
Melaka
Muar
Kuching
MALAY
Sibolga
Dumai
Johor Bahru
Keluang
Gunung Niut
3,581 Ft.
Sibu
Kajang
Padangsidempuan
SINGAPORE
SINGAPORE
PALAU NIAS
Pekanbaru
Tanjungpinang
Singkawang
Kampar
Equator
Bukittinggi
Tembilahan
Pontianak
SUMATRA
Tanjung Jabung
Kapuas
Padang
PULAU BANGKA
Hari
PALAU SIBERUT
Gunung Kerinci
12,467 Ft.
Jambi
Palangka
Musi
Pangkalpinang
BELITUNG
PEGUNUNGAN BARISAN
Tanjungpandan
Tanjung
Sambar
Tanjung Puting
PALEMBANG
Lahat
Perabumulih
Tanjung Lumut
Bengkulu
Gunung Dempo
10,364 Ft.
Kotabumi
I
N
Bandar
Lampung
JAVA SE
Tanjung Cina
JAKARTA
Karawang
GREATER S
Bogor
Cirebon
Kudus
Cianjur
SEMARANG
SURABA
BANDUNG
Garut
Magelang
Purwokerto
Surakarta
Ma
JAVA
Yogyakarta

Black
Red
Red
PARACEL ISLAN
(Claimed By China: T
and Vietnam)

Chindwinn
Ayeyarwady
Salween
Mekong

INDIAN OCEAN

10   11   12   13   14   15   16   17

A family of monkeys sits in front of a temple in Myanmar.

A low sun illuminates the silhouettes of Buddhist temples in Myanmar.

N
W   E
S

Luzon Strait

BABUYAN ISLANDS

Mayraira Point
Escarpada Point

Laoag
Vigan
Ilagan
San Fernando
Baguio
LUZON
SIERRA MADRE
Dagupan
Tarlac
Cabanatuan
Angeles

MANILA ⊛ **Quezon City**
Laguna de Bay

PHILIPPINE

SEA

Lucena
Naga
Legaspi

SOUTH
CHINA SEA

MINDORO
Bohol Sea

PHILIPPINES

Libro Point

PANAY
LEYTE
Iloilo **Bacolod**
Cebu
Tacloban
SAMAR

PALAWAN
Puerto Princesa
NEGROS
Tagbilaran
Dumaguete
Sibuyan Sea
Butuan

SULU SEA

Cagayan de Oro
Pagadian
Marawi
Bislig
MINDANAO
Davao

Balabec Strait

Cotabato

Zamboanga
Koronadal
Mount Apo
9,692 Ft. Cape San Agustin

Gunong Kinabalu
13,455 Ft.
Kota Kinabalu
Sandakan
Jolo
General Santos

Tanjong Hog
Tinaca Point

PACIFIC

OCEAN

KEPULAUAN TALAUD

BRUNEI
⊛ Bandar Seri Begawan

t Pagon
070 Ft.
Tawau
PEG IRAN

Tarakan

CELEBES SEA

MOROTAI

Tanjung Kandi

Manado Gunung Klabat
6,634 Ft.

HALMAHERA

Two cattle pull a farmer through a rice paddy in Bali, Indonesia.

Elementary schoolchildren play in Zamboanga on the Philippine island of Mindanao.

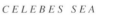

Kuala Lumpur began as a small mining settlement, but today it is the bustling capital of Malaysia.

Tanjung Mangkalihat

Bukit Malino
8,015 Ft.
Gorontalo

Equator

MULLER

Samarinda
Teluk Tomini
Tanjung Api

Molucca Sea

Tanjung Libobo
Sorong
JAZIRAH DOBERAI

BORNEO
Balikapan
Palu
Danau Poso
CELEBES

KEPULAUAN SULU
KEPULAUAN OBI
PULAU MISOOL
Ceram Sea

Tenjung D'Urville

SEMENANJUNG BOMBERAI
Teluk Cenderawasih

Mamberamo

Jayapura

Tanjung Aru
Banjarmasin
Martapura
Bulu Rantekombola
11,335 Ft.
Danau Towuti
Teluk Bone

BURU
CERAM
Ambon

PEGUNUNGAN MAOKE
Puncak Jaya
16,503 Ft.
Puncak Trikora
15,584 Ft.

Tanjung Selatan
Parepare
Singkang
Watampone
Kendari
O   N   E   S   I   A
MOLUCCAS
Puncak Mandala
15,617 Ft.

NEW GUINEA

Ujungpandang
Tual

BANDA SEA

KEPULAUAN ARU

Tanjung De Jongs
Digul

DA ISLANDS
KEPULAUAN BARAT DAYA

PULAU YAMDENA

PULAU YOS SUDARSO

Bali Sea
BALI
Gunung Rinjani
Gunung Tambora
9,350 Ft.
Flores Sea
Mataram 12,224 Ft
Raba
Ende

ARAFURA SEA

Tanjung Vals

Copyright by Rand McNally & Co.
Made in U.S.A.
N-CMW60098-P1- -3-2-2

pasar
SUMBAWA
LOMBOK
FLORES
Memboro
Tanjung Sasar
SUMBA

LESSER SUNDA
ISLANDS

⊛ **DILI**
EAST TIMOR
TIMOR

Timor Sea

Kupang

0   100   200   300   400   500 Miles
0   200   400   600   800 Kilometers

Scale 1:16,000,000; one inch to 252 miles

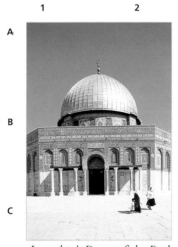

Jerusalem's Dome of the Rock is an important Muslim shrine.

Saudi Arabia's Ar Rub' al Khāli or "The Empty Quarter," contains mountainous sand ridges.

Map labels:

Al Qāmishlī · Khvoy · Marand · Ahar · Orūmīyeh · Tabrīz · Ardabīl

Al Lādhīqīyah · HALAB · Ar Raqqah · Al Mawşil · Mīāneh · Marāgheh · Rasht

Idlib · Dayr az Zawr · As Sulaymānīyah · Arbīl · Mahābād · Zanjān · Gonbad-e Qābūs · Qūchān

Tartus · Tarābulus · Hamāh · Karkūk · Sanandaj · Qazvīn · Karaj · Sārī · ELBURZ MTS. · Sabzevār · Qūchān · MASHH

LEBANON · Hims · SYRIA · Sanandaj · TEHRĀN · Āmol · Qolleh-ye Damāvand 18,386 Ft. · Neyshābūr

Saydā · Beirut · DAMASCUS · BAGHDĀD · Bākhtarān · Hamadān · Qom · IRAN · DASHT-E KAVĪR · Torbat-e Heydarīyeh

Haifa · Teverya · Ar Ramādī · Borūjerd · Arāk · Kāshān · Herā

ISRAEL · Tel Aviv-Yafo · Gaza · Az-Zarqā' · Amman · Khorramābād · Dezfūl · Najafābād · Eşfahān · Ardakān · Birjand

Be'ér Sheva' · Jerusalem · IRAQ · Al Hillah · An Najaf · Al 'Amārah · Mas'ed-e Soleymān · Qomsheh · Yazd

EGYPT · JORDAN · Jabal Ramm 5,755 Ft. · An Nāşirīyah · Ahvāz · Abādān · ZAGROS MTS. · Kermān

SINAI PEN. · Jabal Al Lawz 7,884 Ft. · Al Başrah · KUWAIT · BŪBīYĀN · Shīrāz · Zāhedān

Tabūk · AN NAFŪD · Al Jahrah · Kuwait · Bandar-e Būshehr · Jahrom · Bam

Ra's Abu Madd · Ha'il · Ad Dammām · BAHRAIN · Bandar-e 'Abbās

Buraydah · Al Khubar · Al Manāmah · Ra's al-Khaymah · OMAN

AL-ḤIJĀZ · SAUDI ARABIA · QATAR · Ash Shariqah · Dubayy

Medina · AD DAHNĀ · Al Hufūf · Ad Dawhah · Abu Dhabi · Al 'Ayn · Muscat

RIYADH · UNITED ARAB EMIRATES · Jabal ash-Shām 9,957 Ft. · Ra's al Hadd

JIDDAH · Mecca · At Tā'if · ARABIAN PENINSULA · Sūr

AS SIR · Jabal Sawdā' 10,522 Ft. · AR RUB' AL KHĀLI · OMAN · MAŞĪRAH

Abhā · Khamis Mushayt · Abā as Su'ūd · Khalīj Maşīrah

Şa'dah · Dawhat Şawqirah

an-Nabī Shu'ayb · Jabal 12,008 Ft. · Sanaa · YEMEN · Şalālah

Al Hudaydah · Al Mukallā

Ta'izz

Aden

SOUTH ASIA AND THE MIDDLE EAST

South Asia is separated from the rest of Asia by the highest mountains in the world: the Himalayas, the Karakoram Range, and the Hindu Kush. Nepal and Bhutan lie tilted along the southern slopes of the Himalayas, their land rising steeply from low plains and foothills up to the loftiest mountaintops. To the south is India, the second most populous country in the world after China. To the west of South Asia is the Middle East. Deserts cover much of this region, but beneath the desert sands lies a fortune in oil and natural gas. These resources have made many Middle Eastern countries wealthy but have also sparked conflict in the region.

Soldiers enjoy a meal in Afghanistan.

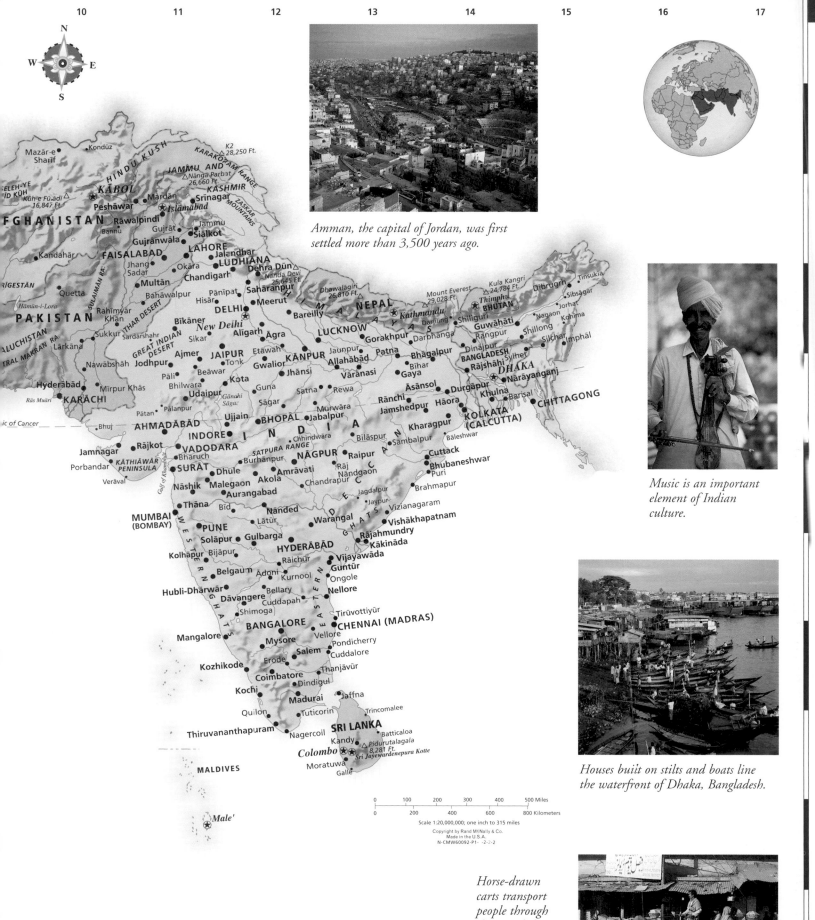

10   11   12   13   14   15   16   17

N
W   E
S

Amman, the capital of Jordan, was first
settled more than 3,500 years ago.

Music is an important
element of Indian
culture.

Houses built on stilts and boats line
the waterfront of Dhaka, Bangladesh.

Horse-drawn
carts transport
people through
the crowded
streets of Lahore,
Pakistan.

Mazār-e
Sharīf
Kondūz
HINDU KUSH
KARAKORAM RANGE
K2
28,250 Ft.
JAMMU AND
△Nanga Parbat
26,660 Ft.
TELEH-YE
FID KŪH
Kūh-e Fūādī
16,847 Ft.
KĀBOL
KASHMIR
Mardān
Srīnagar
Peshāwar
Islāmābād
ZASKAR
MOUNTAINS
AFGHANISTAN
Rāwalpindi
Jammu
Bannū
Gujrāt
Siālkot
Gujrānwāla
Kandahār
FAISALABAD
LAHORE
Jalandhar
Jhang
Sadar
Okāra
LUDHIANA
Dehra Dūn△
RĪGESTĀN
Quetta
Multān
Chandigarh
Nanda Devi
25,645 Ft.
Dhawalāgiri
26,810 Ft.
HIMALAYAS
Mount Everest
29,028 Ft.
Kula Kangri
△24,784 Ft.
Tinsukia
Dibrugrh
SULAIMAN RA.
Bahāwalpur
Hisār
Saharanpur
NEPAL
Thimphu
Sibsagar
Jorhat
Hāmūn-i-Lora
Rahīmyār
Khān
Pānīpat
Meerut
Kāthmandu
BHUTAN
Rāngpur
Nagaon
Kohima
PAKISTAN
DELHI
Bareilly
LUCKNOW
Darbhanga
Shiliguri
Guwāhāti
Shillong
Silchar
Imphāl
Sukkur
Sardārshahr
THAR DESERT
New Delhi
Sikar
Alīgarh
Āgra
Gorakhpur
Jaunpur
Patna
Dinājpur
BANGLADESH
Sylhet
Larkāna
Nawābshāh
GREAT INDIAN
DESERT
Ajmer
JAIPUR
Etāwah
KĀNPUR
Allahābād
Bhāgalpur
Rājshāhi
DHAKA
Mīrpur Khās
Jodhpur
Tonk
Gwalior
Jhānsi
Vārānasi
Gaya
Bīhar
Āsānsol
Durgāpur
Nārāyanganj
Hyderābād
Pāli
Beāwar
Bhilwāra
Guna
Satna
Rewa
Ranchi
Haora
Khulna
Barisal
KARĀCHI
Udaipur
Kota
Murwāra
Jamshedpur
KOLKATA
(CALCUTTA)
CHITTAGONG
Rās Muāri
Gāndhi
Sāgar
Pātan
Pālanpur
Ujjain
Sāgar
Jabalpur
Kharagpur
Bāleshwar
of Cancer
Bhuj
AHMADĀBĀD
BHOPĀL
INDIA
Chhindwāra
Bilāspur
Sambalpur
Jamnagar
INDORE
Raipur
Cuttack
VADODARA
SATPURA RANGE
NĀGPUR
Rāj
Nāndgaon
Bhubaneshwar
Rājkot
Bharuch
Burhānpur
Puri
KĀTHIĀWĀR
PENINSULA
SURĀT
Dhule
Amrāvati
Akola
Jagdalpur
Brahmapur
Porbandar
Nāshik
Malegaon
Chandrapur
Jaypur
Verāval
Gulf of Khambhāt
Aurangabad
Thāna
Bīd
Nānded
Warangal
Vizianagaram
Vishākhapatnam
MUMBAI
(BOMBAY)
PUNE
Lātūr
Rājahmundry
WESTERN
Solāpur
Gulbarga
HYDERĀBĀD
Kākināda
Kolhāpur
Bijāpur
Rāichūr
Vijayawāda
DECCAN
Belgaum
Ādoni
Kurnool
Guntūr
EASTERN
Hubli-Dhārwār
Dāvangere
Bellary
Ongole
Nellore
Shimoga
Cuddapah
GHATS
Tirūvottiyūr
BANGALORE
CHENNAI (MADRAS)
Mangalore
Mysore
Vellore
GHATS
Pondicherry
Salem
Cuddalore
Kozhikode
Erode
Thanjāvūr
Coimbatore
Dindigul
Kochi
Madurai
Jaffna
Quilon
Tuticorin
Trincomalee
Thiruvananthapuram
Nagercoil
SRI LANKA
Batticaloa
Kandy
△Pidurutalagala
8,281 Ft.
Colombo
Sri Jayewardenepura Kotte
MALDIVES
Moratuwa
Galle
Male'

100   200   300   400   500 Miles
200   400   600   800 Kilometers
Scale 1:20,000,000; one inch to 315 miles
Copyright by Rand McNally & Co.
Made in the U.S.A.
N-CMW60092-P1- -2-2-2

AUSTRALIA

& OCEANIA

Australia & Oceania Facts

Area: 3,300,000 square miles (8,500,000 square kilometers)

Highest Mountain: Mount Wilhelm, Papua New Guinea, 14,793 feet (4,509 meters)

Lowest Point: Lake Eyre North, Australia, -52 feet (-16 meters)

Longest River: Murray-Darling, 2,169 miles (3,491 kilometers)

Largest Lake: Lake Eyre North, Australia, 3,700 square miles (9,500 square kilometers)

Largest Desert: Great Victorian Desert, Australia, 104,000 square miles (270,000 square kilometers)

Largest Island: New Guinea, Oceania/Asia, 309,000 square miles (800,000 square kilometers)

ARAFURA SEA

MELVILLE ISLAND
Cape Croker
Cobourg Peninsula

IMOR SEA
Darwin

Arnhem Land

Cape Londonderry
Joseph Bonaparte Gulf

INDIAN OCEAN

Cape Leveque

Mt. Hann 2,556 Ft.
Mt. Ord 3,074 Ft.

Kimberley Plateau

King Leopold Ranges

Fitzroy

NORTHERN

Victoria

Barkly Tableland

GROOTE EYLANDT

Tanami Desert

TERRITORY

Eighty Mile Beach

Great Sandy Desert

A U S T R A L I A

Lake Auld

Mt. Leisler 2,943 Ft.
Mt. Liebig 5,000 Ft.
Mt. Zeil 4,957 Ft.

MacDonnell Ranges

North West Cape

Mt. Brockman 3,714 Ft.
Mt. Bruce 4,052 Ft.

Hamersley Range

Mt. Meharry 4,104 Ft.

Gibson Desert

Mt. Aloysius 3,560 Ft.
Lake Amadeus
Uluru 2,844 Ft.
Mt. Cockburn 3,734 Ft.
Mt. Woodroffe 4,724 Ft.

Mt. Augustus 3,625 Ft.

WESTERN

Lake Carnegie

Tropic of Capricorn

Shark Bay

DIRK HARTOG ISLAND

AUSTRALIA

Great Victoria Desert

SOUTH AUSTRALIA

Nullarbor Plain

Lake Gairdner

Darling Range

Great Australian Bight

West Po

Perth

Geographe Bay
Cape Naturaliste
Bluff Knoll 3,596 Ft.
Hood Point
Cape Arid
ARCHIPELAGO OF THE RECHERCHE

Cape Leeuwin
Point D'Entrecasteaux

INDIAN OCEAN

Australia's Aborigines believe that Uluru, also known as Ayers Rock (above), is sacred; Sydney, Australia (below) is built around one of the world's largest natural harbors.

"**A**ustralia" has two meanings. It is the name of both the world's smallest, flattest continent and the world's sixth largest country, which occupies the entire continent. It is the only inhabited continent that lies completely within the southern hemisphere; for this reason it has been nicknamed the "Land Down Under." Most of Australia's interior — the Outback — is barren desert, sparsely populated but ruggedly beautiful, with dramatic landforms such as Ayers Rock. Australia's best-known geographic feature, however, is the Great Barrier Reef, Earth's largest living structure, which stretches 1,250 miles (2,000 kilometers) through the Coral Sea off Australia's eastern coast.

To the north and east of Australia lies Oceania, which is made up of more than 25,000 volcanic islands and coral atolls scattered across the Pacific Ocean. A few of the islands, such as New Guinea and New Zealand's North and South Islands, are relatively large, but many others are too small to appear on any but the most detailed maps.

Torres Strait
Cape York
Cape York Peninsula
CORAL SEA
Gulf of Carpentaria
Great Barrier Reef
Gregory Range
Bartle Frere 5,322 Ft.
Halifax Bay
Clarke Range
Great Dividing Range
Mt. Dalrymple 4,131 Ft.
Selwyn Range
Great Artesian Basin
QUEENSLAND
Cape Capricorn
Tropic of Capricorn
Sandy Cape
FRASER ISLAND
Mt. Kiangarow 3,760 Ft.
Cooper Creek
PACIFIC OCEAN
impson Desert
Grey Range
Darling Downs
Brisbane
Southport
Cape Byron
Sturt Stony Desert
Lake Eyre North
Barwon
Lake Torrens
Darling
Barrier Range
Great Dividing Range
NORFOLK ISLAND
Mary Peak 3,871 Ft.
Murray
Lachlan
NEW SOUTH WALES
Penrith
Newcastle
Sydney
Gulf
Adelaide
Canberra A.C.T.
Wollongong
Jervis Bay
Encounter Bay
GAROO Bay
AND
VICTORIA
Snowy Mts.
Mt. Kosciuszko 7,313 Ft.
Great Dividing Range
Cape Jaffa
Cape Howe
North Cape
Cape Nelson
Melbourne
Wilsons Promontory
Needles Point
Cape Otway
Auckland
NORTH ISLAND
Bay of Plenty
KING ISLAND
Bass Strait
FLINDERS ISLAND
TASMAN SEA
Cape Egmont
East Cape
Cape Grim
Cape Portland
Mt. Ossa 5,305 Ft.
Cape Farewell
Mt. Ruapehu 9,177 Ft.
Freycinet Peninsula
TASMANIA
The Twins 5,990 Ft.
Wellington
NEW ZEALAND
Hobart
Aoraki 12,316 Ft.
Southern Alps
Christchurch
Banks Peninsula
South East Cape
SOUTH ISLAND
Cape Providence
Dunedin
CHATHAM ISLANDS
Foveaux
STEWART ISLAND
Strait

N
W E
S

| 0 | 100 | 200 | 300 | 400 | 500 Miles |
| 0 | 200 | 400 | 600 | 800 Kilometers |

Scale 1:20,000,000; one inch to 315 miles
Copyright by Rand McNally & Co.
Made in U.S.A.
N-CMW95000-A1- -1-1-2

Land Elevation
Feet (Meters)

9,840 and over (3,000 and over)
6,560 - 9,840 (2,000 - 3,000)
3,280 - 6,560 (1,000 - 2,000)
1,640 - 3,280 (500 - 1,000)
656 - 1,640 (200 - 500)
0 - 656 feet (0 - 200)

THE LAND

Desert wastelands of sand and rock blanket the central and western parts of Australia, while a broad band of dry grasslands surrounds the deserts. Only about six percent of Australia's land is suitable for farming. Most Australians live along the southeastern coast, between the ocean and the long chain of mountains and plateaus known as the Great Dividing Range. Manufacturing and service industries flourish in this region. New Zealand, Australia's neighbor to the southeast, includes mountains, fjords, glaciers, rain forests, and geysers. Thanks to its small population and lack of heavy industry, it is one of the least polluted countries in the world. New Guinea, which lies to the north of Australia, is the second largest island in the world. High, jagged mountains form a long spine across its width, wide swampy plains line its coasts, and tropical rain forests cover much of the island. Most of the other islands of Oceania were formed by volcanoes.

Environments

Besides desert and grassland, Australia also has forests, swamps, and mountains. Mountains cover two-thirds of New Zealand. New Guinea's dense rain forests, with their valuable hardwood trees, are an important natural resource, as are the palm trees that grow on many of the other islands of Oceania.

Environments

- Forest
- Swamp
- Crop and woodland
- Cropland
- Crop and grazing land
- Grassland
- Desert
- Tundra
- Barren
- Urban

Mineral processing facilities can be found throughout Australia.

Manufacturing

Manufacturing plays a central role in Australia's economy, with the refinement of metals and other natural resources topping the list of industries. The country also produces chemicals, plastics, textiles, and other durable goods. Traditionally, New Zealand has produced few manufactured goods, but its food-processing and paper manufacturing industries have been expanding. Most of the other countries in Oceania do not produce manufactured goods.

Sheep outnumber people in Australia by a ratio of seven to one. In New Zealand, the ratio is 14 to one.

Much of Australia's interior, called the Outback, consists of semiarid plains that harbor hearty plants and animals.

Wool

With more than 14 percent of the world's sheep, Australia produces more wool than any other country on Earth. The largest sheep stations, or ranches, cover more than 5,000 square miles (12,900 square kilometers). New Zealand ranks as the second largest wool producer; nearly half of its land is used as pasture.

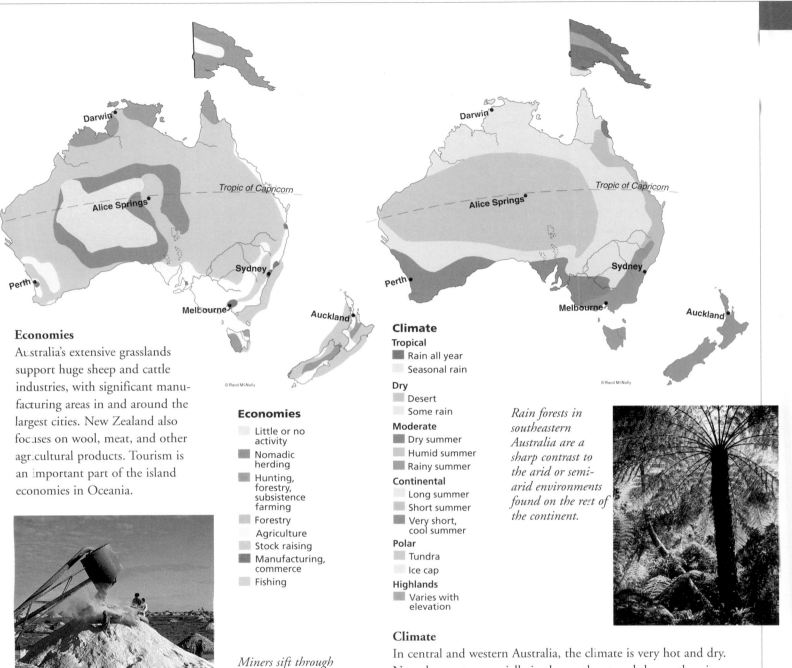

Economies

Australia's extensive grasslands support huge sheep and cattle industries, with significant manufacturing areas in and around the largest cities. New Zealand also focuses on wool, meat, and other agricultural products. Tourism is an important part of the island economies in Oceania.

Economies

- Little or no activity
- Nomadic herding
- Hunting, forestry, subsistence farming
- Forestry
- Agriculture
- Stock raising
- Manufacturing, commerce
- Fishing

Miners sift through mounds of sediment to uncover opals, iridescent gemstones that are exported.

Gems and Minerals

White, black, and fire opals mined in southern Australia are world-famous, but Australia is also an important source of diamonds: Its mines produce thirty percent of the world's supply. Australia's many other mineral resources include iron ore, coal, uranium, lead, zinc, copper, nickel, and natural gas. New Zealand has large reserves of coal, natural gas, and oil, while New Guinea's greatest sources of mineral wealth are copper, gold, and silver.

Not all diamonds become jewelry; industries use them to cut hard surfaces.

Climate

Tropical
- Rain all year
- Seasonal rain

Dry
- Desert
- Some rain

Moderate
- Dry summer
- Humid summer
- Rainy summer

Continental
- Long summer
- Short summer
- Very short, cool summer

Polar
- Tundra
- Ice cap

Highlands
- Varies with elevation

Rain forests in southeastern Australia are a sharp contrast to the arid or semi-arid environments found on the rest of the continent.

Climate

In central and western Australia, the climate is very hot and dry. Near the coasts, especially in the southeast and the north, rain is more abundant and temperatures are cooler. New Zealand's climate is generally milder and wetter than Australia's. New Guinea and most other parts of Oceania have hot tropical climates.

Tourism

Tourists are drawn to Australia's natural wonders as well as to the fun-loving, easygoing lifestyle of Australians. Scenic New Zealand also enjoys a booming tourist industry. The tropical islands of Oceania have long been popular vacation spots, especially for sun-seeking Europeans and Americans.

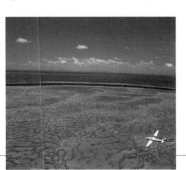

Airplanes provide a spectacular view of the Great Barrier Reef.

THE PEOPLE

Although Australia is one of the largest countries in the world, it has a relatively small population. Very few people live in its vast interior. Most Australians live near the coast, especially along the southeastern stretch that includes Sydney, Melbourne, Brisbane, and Adelaide. Although the Aborigines were the earliest humans to settle the continent, they make up only one percent of Australia's population today. Most Australians are descendants of British settlers, but in recent years immigrants from all over the world have added diversity to the continent's ethnic makeup. New Zealand's population is similar to Australia's, but its native people, the Maoris, represent ten percent of the population. Due to centuries of isolation, the island groups of Oceania have retained their distinct cultures. There has been little immigration there from other parts of the world.

A father and son ride around their farm in Australia.

Boating is a popular pastime for tourists in Australia and New Zealand.

The Aborigine culture includes many ceremonial dances and rituals.

Australia's large population of kangaroos often comes into contact with humans.

ARAFURA SEA

TIMOR SEA

MELVILLE ISLAND
Cape Croker
Van Diemen Gulf
Darwin
Arnhem Land
Pine Creek

GROOTE EYLAND

Cape Londonderry
Joseph Bonaparte Gulf

Cape Leveque
Wyndham
Victoria

Mataranka

Newcastle Waters
Hooker Creek

INDIAN OCEAN

Kimberley Plateau
Yeeda
Halls Creek
Broome
Fitzroy
Christmas Creek
Cape Latouche Treville

NORTHERN
TERRITORY
The Granites
Tennant Creek

Port Hedland
Marble Bar
Great Sandy Desert
Dampier
Nullagine
Lake Auld
Onslow
Yarralloola
Ethel Creek
North West Cape

AUSTRALIA

Alice Springs
Lake Amadeus
Uluru 2,844 Ft.

WESTERN

Tropic of Capricorn

Minilya
Carnegie
Carnarvon
Lake Carnegie
Wooramel
Wiluna
Shark Bay
Meekatharra
AUSTRALIA
DIRK HARTOG ISLAND
Sandstone
White Cliffs
Mount Magnet
Leonora
Mullewa
Paynes Find
Geraldton
Dongara
Kalgoorlie-Boulder
Coolgardie
Norseman
Darling Range
Balladonia
Wanneroo
Gosnells
Perth
Armadale
Newdegate
Fremantle
Wagin
Hopetoun
Cape Arid
Geographe Bay
Bunbury
Hood Point
ARCHIPELAGO OF THE RECHERCHE
Cape Naturaliste
Augusta
Point D'Entrecasteaux
Cranbrook
Albany

SOUTH AUSTRALIA

Great Victoria Desert
Mount Eba
Kingoonya

Eucla
Ceduna
Lake Gairdner
Streaky Bay
Great Australian Bight
Eyre Peninsula
Port Lincoln
Cape Carnot

INDIAN OCEAN

10   11   12   13   14   15   16   17

The Aborigines developed boomerangs to aid them in hunting animals.

Australia & Oceania Facts

Population: 32,170,000

Population Density: 9.7 people per square mile (3.8 per square kilometer)

Most Populous Country: Australia, 19,825,000 people

Largest City: Sydney, Australia, 4,400,000 people (metropolitan area)

These schoolgirls relax in Sydney.

Torres Strait
Bamaga
Cape York
Weipa
Duifken Point
Cape York Peninsula
CORAL SEA
N W E S
Gulf of Carpentaria
Cooktown
Cairns
Normanton
rketown
Camooweal
Mount Isa
Cloncurry
Hughenden
Halifax Bay
Townsville
Great Barrier Reef
Great Dividing Range
Winton
Blair Athol
Mackay
Great Artesian Basin
Longreach
Emerald
Rockhampton
Cape Capricorn
Barcaldine
Springsure
Gladstone
Tropic of Capricorn
Yaraka
Blackall
Theodore
Bundaberg
Copper Creek
QUEENSLAND
Charleville
Mitchell
Maryborough
Sandy Cape
FRASER ISLAND
Gympie
Innamincka
Thargomindah
Cunnamulla
Chinchilla
Toowoomba
Redcliffe
★Brisbane
Ipswich
Southport
Warwick
Cape Byron
Lismore
Grafton
Lake Eyre North
Marree
Barwon
Bourke
Armidale
Coffs Harbour
Darling
Tamworth
Lake Torrens
Milparinka
Wilcannia
Nyngan
Taree
Broken Hill
Dubbo
NEW SOUTH WALES
Cessnock
Newcastle
Port Augusta
Whyalla
Penrith
★Sydney
Murray
Mildura
Griffith
Campbelltown
Wollongong
Port Pirie
Elizabeth
Wagga Wagga
Goulburn
A.C.T.
★Adelaide
VICTORIA
Wangaratta
Albury
Canberra★
Jervis Bay
Encounter Bay
NGAROO BAY ISLAND
Horsham
Bendigo
Cooma
Mt. Kosciuszko 7,313 Ft.
Cape Jaffa
Hamilton
Ballarat
Great
Cape Howe
Mount Gambier
Geelong
★Melbourne
Moe
Sale
Portland
Cape Otway
Wilsons Promontory
KING ISLAND
Bass Strait
FLINDERS ISLAND
TASMAN SEA
Cape Grim
Burnie
Devonport
Zeehan
Launceston
TASMANIA
Hobart★
South East Cape

PACIFIC OCEAN

NORFOLK ISLAND (Austl.)

North Cape
NORTH ISLAND
Whangarei
East Coast Bays
Manukau
Auckland
Hamilton
Bay of Plenty
Tauranga
New Plymouth
Cape Egmont
Taupo
Rotorua
East Cape
Gisborne
Wanganui
Napier
Hastings
Cape Farewell
Palmerston North
Nelson
Cook Strait
Porirua
Greymouth
Wellington
NEW ZEALAND
Aoraki
12,316 Ft.
Haast
Southern Alps
Waiau
SOUTH ISLAND
Christchurch
Cape Providence
Manapouri
Ashburton
Oamaru
Invercargill
Foveaux Strait
Dunedin
CHATHAM ISLANDS (N.Z.)
STEWART ISLAND

0 100 200 300 400 500 Miles
0 200 400 600 800 Kilometers

Scale 1:20,000,000; one inch to 315 miles

PACIFIC ISLANDS

Scattered across a vast area in the Pacific Ocean, the islands of Oceania feature landscapes as varied as the alpine terrain of New Zealand's South Island, the mountain rain forests of Papua New Guinea, and the flower- and palm-strewn atolls of Polynesia. Papua New Guinea, which occupies the western portion of the island of New Guinea, is Oceania's largest country. It is a land of much ethnic variety: More than 700 dialects are spoken there, although English is the official language. To the east of Papua New Guinea lies the group of islands known as Melanesia, a name that means "black islands." To the north and east of Melanesia is Micronesia ("small islands"), and farther east lies Polynesia ("many islands"). These far-flung volcanic islands and coral atolls were originally settled by seafaring peoples from the Asian mainland who brought their plants, animals, and cultures with them as they ventured as far as Hawaii and Easter Island in huge canoes.

Snowcapped Aoraki, or Mount Cook, is New Zealand's highest mountain.

The seastar plays an important role in Oceania's reef systems.

10   11   12   13   14   15   16   17"

New Zealand, called Aoteraroa ("long white cloud") by its original Maori inhabitants, is the second largest country in Oceania (after Australia). Most people live on North Island in Auckland and Wellington. While South Island is known for its mountains and deep fjords, North Island has its share of wonders: Glowworms light deep cave chambers, while hot springs and geysers provide geothermal power and heat for the island's inhabitants. New Zealand has far more sheep than people, and wool and mutton are two of its leading exports.

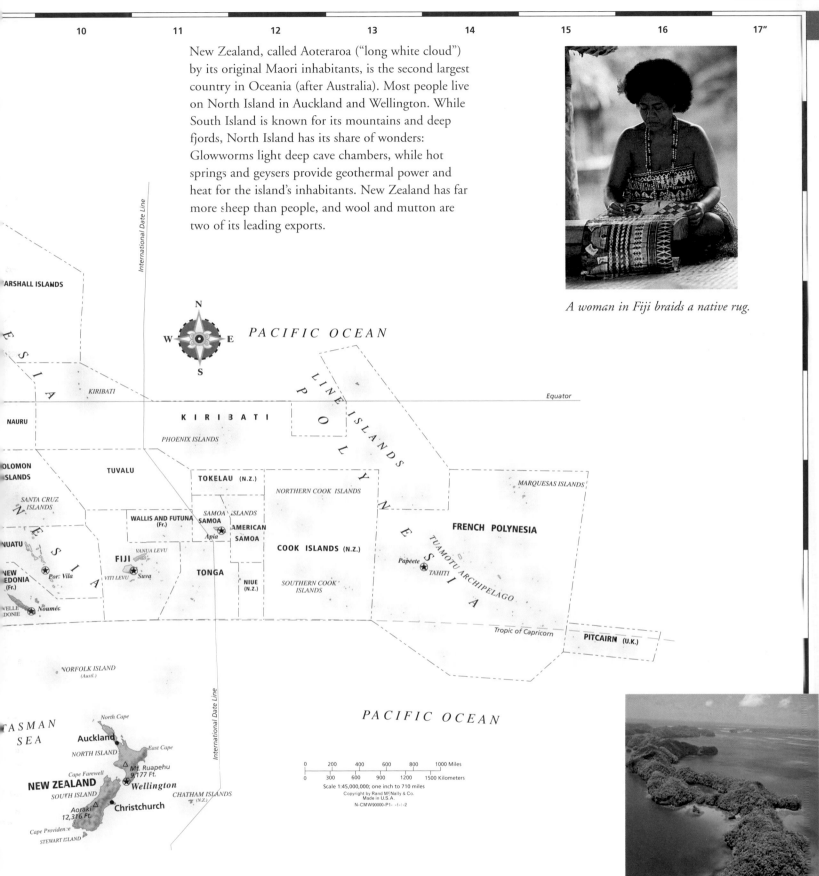

A woman in Fiji braids a native rug.

PACIFIC OCEAN

N
W   E
S

ARSHALL ISLANDS

ESIA

LINE ISLANDS

KIRIBATI

Equator

NAURU

KIRIBATI

PHOENIX ISLANDS

POLY

OLOMON ISLANDS

TUVALU

TOKELAU (N.Z.)

NORTHERN COOK ISLANDS

MARQUESAS ISLANDS

SANTA CRUZ ISLANDS

NESIA

SAMOA ISLANDS

WALLIS AND FUTUNA (Fr.)   SAMOA

AMERICAN SAMOA

NESIA

FRENCH POLYNESIA

NUATU

Apia

COOK ISLANDS (N.Z.)

TUAMOTU ARCHIPELAGO

FIJI

VANUA LEVU

Papeete

TAHITI

NEW EDONIA (Fr.)

Por. Vila

VITI LEVU   Suva

TONGA

NIUE (N.Z.)

SOUTHERN COOK ISLANDS

SI

VELLE DONIE

Nouméa

Tropic of Capricorn

PITCAIRN (U.K.)

NORFOLK ISLAND (Austl.)

International Date Line

PACIFIC OCEAN

TASMAN SEA

North Cape

Auckland

East Cape

NORTH ISLAND

Cape Farewell

Mt. Ruapehu 9,177 Ft.

NEW ZEALAND

SOUTH ISLAND

Wellington

CHATHAM ISLANDS (N.Z.)

Aoraki 12,316 Ft.

Christchurch

Cape Providence

STEWART ISLAND

0   200   400   600   800   1000 Miles
0   300   600   900   1200   1500 Kilometers
Scale 1:45,000,000; one inch to 710 miles
Copyright by Rand McNally & Co.
Made in U.S.A.
N-CMW90000-P1- -1-1-2

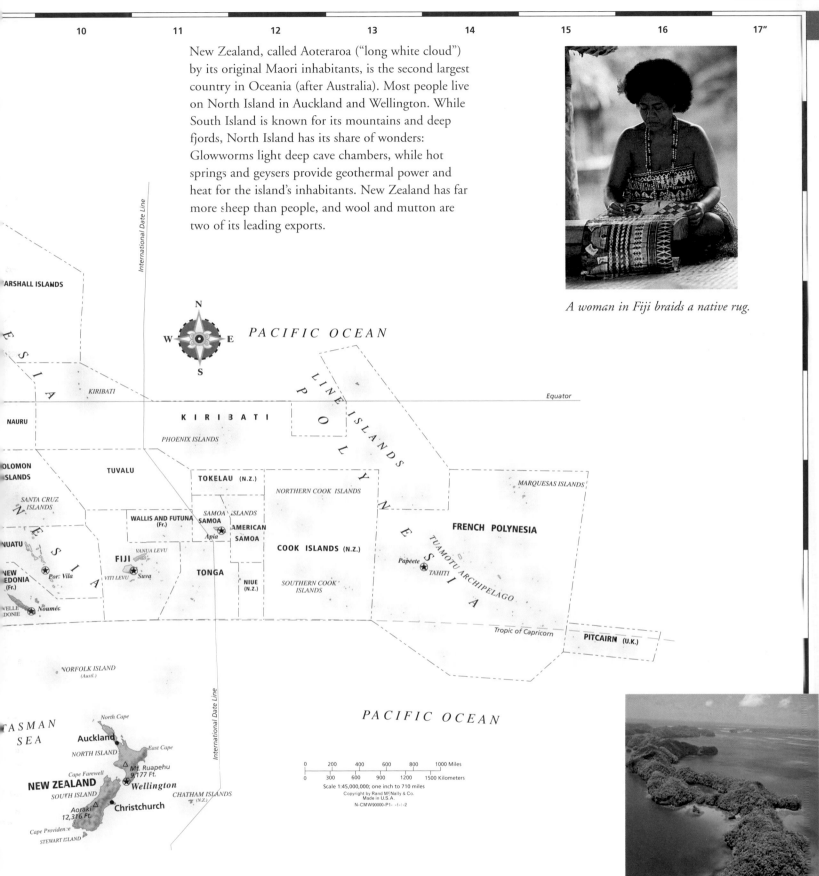

Reefs dominate the volcanic island of Palau.

ANTARCTICA

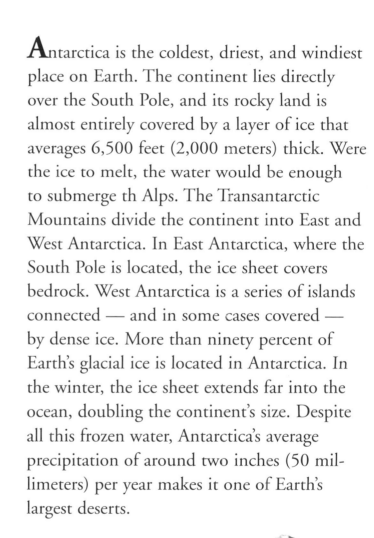

Antarctica is the coldest, driest, and windiest place on Earth. The continent lies directly over the South Pole, and its rocky land is almost entirely covered by a layer of ice that averages 6,500 feet (2,000 meters) thick. Were the ice to melt, the water would be enough to submerge th Alps. The Transantarctic Mountains divide the continent into East and West Antarctica. In East Antarctica, where the South Pole is located, the ice sheet covers bedrock. West Antarctica is a series of islands connected — and in some cases covered — by dense ice. More than ninety percent of Earth's glacial ice is located in Antarctica. In the winter, the ice sheet extends far into the ocean, doubling the continent's size. Despite all this frozen water, Antarctica's average precipitation of around two inches (50 millimeters) per year makes it one of Earth's largest deserts.

Antarctica Facts

Area: 5,400,000 square miles
(14,000,000 square kilometers)

Highest Mountain: Vinson Massif,
16,066 feet (4,897 meters)

Lowest Point: Deep Lake, -184 feet
(-56 meters)

Coldest Spot: Vostok, July 21, 1983,
-129° Fahrenheit (-89° Celsius)

Very little plant life can survive in such cold conditions, but certain lichens, molds, mosses, fungi, algae, and bacteria live in this arctic habitat.

Antarctica has no permanent residents. Instead, groups of researchers from all over the world come to visit scientific stations and to learn more about this forbidding, fascinating continent.

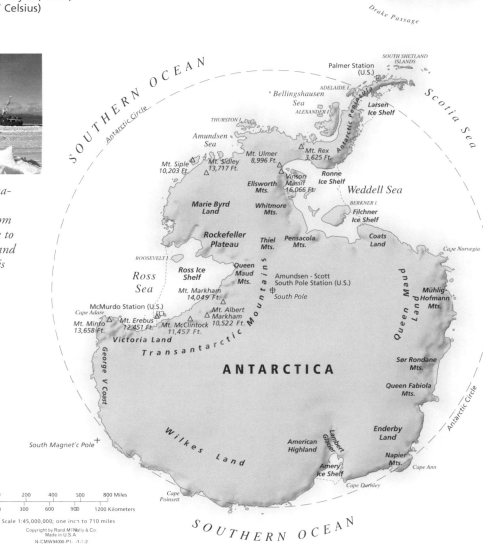

Drake Passage

SOUTHERN OCEAN

SOUTH SHETLAND ISLANDS

Palmer Station (U.S.)

ADELAIDE I.

Bellingshausen Sea

ALEXANDER I.

THURSTON I.

Antarctic Circle

Amundsen Sea

Antarctic Peninsula

Larsen Ice Shelf

Scotia Sea

Mt. Ulmer 8,996 Ft.

Mt. Rex 3,625 Ft.

Mt. Siple 10,203 Ft.

Mt. Sidley 13,717 Ft.

Ellsworth Mts.

Vinson Massif 16,066 Ft.

Ronne Ice Shelf

Weddell Sea

Marie Byrd Land

Whitmore Mts.

BERKNER I.

Filchner Ice Shelf

Cape Norvegia

Rockefeller Plateau

Thiel Mts.

Pensacola Mts.

Coats Land

SOUTHERN OCEAN

ROOSEVELT I.

Ross Sea

Ross Ice Shelf

Queen Maud Mts.

Amundsen - Scott South Pole Station (U.S.)

South Pole

Queen Maud Land

Mühlig Hofmann Mts.

Mt. Markham 14,049 Ft.

McMurdo Station (U.S.)

Cape Adare

Mt. Albert Markham 10,522 Ft.

Mt. Minto 13,658 Ft.

Mt. Erebus 12,451 Ft.

Mt. McClintock 11,457 Ft.

Sør Rondane Mts.

Victoria Land

Transantarctic Mountains

ANTARCTICA

George V Coast

Queen Fabiola Mts.

Enderby Land

South Magnetic Pole

Wilkes Land

American Highland

Lambert Glacier

Napier Mts.

Cape Ann

Antarctic Circle

Amery Ice Shelf

Cape Darnley

Cape Poinsett

SOUTHERN OCEAN

Seabirds flock to Antarctica to roost, and several different species of penguin (above left) live on the ice, near the coast (left). No land mammals live here, but an abundance of krill — tiny shrimplike creatures — provides food for a large population of aquatic mammals, including a variety of whales (below) and seals.

0 200 400 500 800 Miles
0 300 600 900 1200 Kilometers

Scale 1:45,000,000; one inch to 710 miles
Copyright by Rand McNally & Co.
Made in U.S.A.
N-CMW94000-P1- -1-1-2

Country Flag and Fact File

North America

Anguilla (U.K.)
Area: 37 sq mi (96 sq km)
Population: 13,000
Capital: The Valley

Antigua and Barbuda
Area: 171 sq mi (442 sq km)
Population: 68,000
Capital: St. John's

Bahamas
Area: 5,382 sq mi
  (13,939 sq km)
Population: 300,000
Capital: Nassau

Barbados
Area: 166 sq mi (430 sq km)
Population: 280,000
Capital: Bridgetown

Belize
Area: 8,867 sq mi
  (22,966 sq km)
Population: 270,000
Capital: Belmopan

Canada
Area: 3,855,103 sq mi
  (9,984,670 sq km)
Population: 32,360,000
Capital: Ottawa

Costa Rica
Area: 19,730 sq mi
  (51,100 sq km)
Population: 3,925,000
Capital: San José

Cuba
Area: 42,804 sq mi
  (110,861 sq km)
Population: 11,290,000
Capital: Havana

Dominica
Area: 290 sq mi (751 sq km)
Population: 69,000
Capital: Roseau

Dominican Republic
Area: 18,730 sq mi
  (48,511 sq km)
Population: 8,775,000
Capital: Santo Domingo

El Salvador
Area: 8,124 sq mi
  (21,041 sq km)
Population: 6,530,000
Capital: San Salvador

Greenland (Denmark)
Area: 836,331 sq mi
  (2,166,086 sq km)
Population: 56,000
Capital: Godthåb

Grenada
Area: 133 sq mi (344 sq km)
Population: 89,000
Capital: St. George's

Guatemala
Area: 42,042 sq mi
  (108,889 sq km)
Population: 14,095,000
Capital: Guatemala

Haiti
Area: 10,714 sq mi
  (27,750 sq km)
Population: 7,590,000
Capital: Port-au-Prince

Honduras
Area: 43,277 sq mi
  (112,088 sq km)
Population: 6,745,000
Capital: Tegucigalpa

Jamaica
Area: 4,244 sq mi
  (10,991 sq km)
Population: 2,705,000
Capital: Kingston

Mexico
Area: 758,452 sq mi
  (1,964,382 sq km)
Population: 104,340,000
Capital: Mexico City

Nicaragua
Area: 50,054 sq mi
  (129,640 sq km)
Population: 5,180,000
Capital: Managua

Panama
Area: 29,157 sq mi
  (75,517 sq km)
Population: 2,980,000
Capital: Panamá

Puerto Rico (U.S.)
Area: 3,515 sq mi
  (9,104 sq km)
Population: 3,890,000
Capital: San Juan

St. Kitts and Nevis
Area: 101 sq mi (261 sq km)
Population: 39,000
Capital: Basseterre

St. Lucia
Area: 238 sq mi (616 sq km)
Population: 165,000
Capital: Castries

St. Vincent and the Grenadines
Area: 150 sq mi (388 sq km)
Population: 115,000
Capital: Kingstown

Trinidad and Tobago
Area: 1,980 sq mi
  (5,128 sq km)
Population: 1,100,000
Capital: Port of Spain

United States
Area: 3,794,083 sq mi
  (9,826,630 sq km)
Population: 291,680,000
Capital: Washington

South America

Argentina
Area: 1,073,519 sq mi
(2,780,400 sq km)
Population: 38,945,000
Capitals: Buenos Aires

Bolivia
Area: 424,165 sq mi
(1,098,581 sq km)
Population: 8,655,000
Capitals: La Paz (seat of
government) and Sucre
(legal capital)

Brazil
Area: 3,300,172 sq mi
(8,547,404 sq km)
Population: 183,080,000
Capital: Brasília

Chile
Area: 291,930 sq mi
(756,096 sq km)
Population: 15,745,000
Capital: Santiago

Colombia
Area: 439,737 sq mi
(1,138,914 sq km)
Population: 41,985,000
Capital: Bogotá

Ecuador
Area: 109,484 sq mi
(283,561 sq km)
Population: 13,840,000
Capital: Quito

Guyana
Area: 83,000 sq mi
(214,969 sq km)
Population: 705,000
Capital: Georgetown

Paraguay
Area: 157,048 sq mi
(406,752 sq km)
Population: 6,115,000
Capital: Asunción

Peru
Area: 496,225 sq mi
(1,285,216 sq km)
Population: 28,640,000
Capital: Lima

Suriname
Area: 63,037 sq mi
(163,265 sq km)
Population: 435,000
Capital: Paramaribo

Uruguay
Area: 67,574 sq mi
(175,016 sq km)
Population: 3,425,000
Capital: Montevideo

Venezuela
Area: 352,145 sq mi
(912,050 sq km)
Population: 24,835,000
Capital: Caracas

Europe

Albania
Area: 11,100 sq mi
(28,748 sq km)
Population: 3,535,000
Capital: Tiranë

Andorra
Area: 181 sq mi
(468 sq km)
Population: 70,000
Capital: Andorra

Austria
Area: 32,378 sq mi
(83,858 sq km)
Population: 8,170,000
Capital: Vienna

Belarus
Area: 80,155 sq mi
(207,600 sq km)
Population: 10,315,000
Capital: Minsk

Belgium
Area: 11,787 sq mi
(30,528 sq km)
Population: 10,340,000
Capital: Brussels

Bosnia and Herzegovina
Area: 19,767 sq mi
(51,197 sq km)
Population: 4,000,000
Capital: Sarajevo

Bulgaria
Area: 42,855 sq mi
(110,994 sq km)
Population: 7,550,000
Capital: Sofia

Croatia
Area: 21,829 sq mi
(56,538 sq km)
Population: 4,430,000
Capital: Zagreb

Czech Republic
Area: 30,450 sq mi
(78,866 sq km)
Population: 10,250,000
Capital: Prague

Denmark
Area: 16,640 sq mi
(43,096 sq km)
Population: 5,405,000
Capital: Copenhagen

Estonia
Area: 17,462 sq mi
(45,227 sq km)
Population: 1,405,000
Capital: Tallinn

Finland
Area: 130,559 sq mi
(338,145 sq km)
Population: 5,210,000
Capital: Helsinki

France
Area: 208,482 sq mi
(539,965 sq km)
Population: 60,305,000
Capital: Paris

Germany
Area: 137,847 sq mi
(357,022 sq km)
Population: 82,415,000
Capital: Berlin

Greece
Area: 50,949 sq mi
(131,957 sq km)
Population: 10,635,000
Capital: Athens

Hungary
Area: 35,919 sq mi
(93,030 sq km)
Population: 10,045,000
Capital: Budapest

Iceland
Area: 39,769 sq mi
(103,000 sq km)
Population: 280,000
Capital: Reykjavík

Ireland
Area: 27,133 sq mi
(70,273 sq km)
Population: 3,945,000
Capital: Dublin

Italy
Area: 116,342 sq mi
(301,323 sq km)
Population: 58,030,000
Capital: Rome

Latvia
Area: 24,942 sq mi
(64,600 sq km)
Population: 2,340,000
Capital: Rīga

Liechtenstein
Area: 62 sq mi (160 sq km)
Population: 33,000
Capital: Vaduz

Lithuania
Area: 25,213 sq mi
(65,300 sq km)
Population: 3,590,000
Capital: Vilnius

Luxembourg
Area: 999 sq mi
(2,586 sq km)
Population: 460,000
Capital: Luxembourg

Macedonia
Area: 9,928 sq mi
(25,713 sq km)
Population: 2,065,000
Capital: Skopje

Malta
Area: 122 sq mi (316 sq km)
Population: 400,000
Capital: Valletta

Moldova
Area: 13,070 sq mi
(33,851 sq km)
Population: 4,440,000
Capital: Chişinău

Monaco
Area: 0.8 sq mi (2 sq km)
Population: 32,000
Capital: Monaco

Netherlands
Area: 16,164 sq mi
(41,864 sq km)
Population: 16,270,000
Capitals: Amsterdam
(designated) and The Hague
(seat of government)

Norway
Area: 125,050 sq mi
(323,877 sq km)
Population: 4,565,000
Capital: Oslo

Poland
Area: 120,728 sq mi
(312,685 sq km)
Population: 38,625,000
Capital: Warsaw

Portugal
Area: 35,516 sq mi
(91,985 sq km)
Population: 10,110,000
Capital: Lisbon

Romania
Area: 91,699 sq mi
(237,500 sq km)
Population: 22,370,000
Capital: Bucharest

San Marino
Area: 24 sq mi (61 sq km)
Population: 28,000
Capital: San Marino

Serbia and Montenegro
Area: 39,449 sq mi
(102,173 sq km)
Population: 10,660,000
Capital: Belgrade

Slovakia
Area: 18,924 sq mi
(49,012 sq km)
Population: 5,420,000
Capital: Bratislava

Slovenia
Area: 7,821 sq mi
(20,256 sq km)
Population: 1,935,000
Capital: Ljubljana

Spain
Area: 194,885 sq mi
(504,750 sq km)
Population: 40,250,000
Capital: Madrid

Sweden
Area: 173,732 sq mi
(449,964 sq km)
Population: 8,980,000
Capital: Stockholm

Switzerland
Area: 15,943 sq mi
(41,293 sq km)
Population: 7,430,000
Capital: Bern

Ukraine
Area: 233,090 sq mi
(603,700 sq km)
Population: 47,890,000
Capital: Kiev

United Kingdom
Area: 93,788 sq mi
(242,910 sq km)
Population: 60,185,000
Capital: London

Vatican City
Area: 0.2 sq mi (0.4 sq km)
Population: 1,000
Capital: Vatican City

FACT AND FLAG FILE 99

Africa

Algeria
Area: 919,595 sq mi
  (2,381,741 sq km)
Population: 33,090,000
Capital: Algiers

Angola
Area: 481,354 sq mi
  (1,246,700 sq km)
Population: 10,875,000
Capital: Luanda

Benin
Area: 43,484 sq mi
  (112,622 sq km)
Population: 7,145,000
Capitals: Porto-Novo
  (designated) and Cotonou
  (de facto)

Botswana
Area: 224,607 sq mi
  (581,730 sq km)
Population: 1,570,000
Capital: Gaborone

Burkina Faso
Area: 105,869 sq mi
  (274,200 sq km)
Population: 13,400,000
Capital: Ouagadougou

Burundi
Area: 10,745 sq mi
  (27,830 sq km)
Population: 6,165,000
Capital: Bujumbura

Cameroon
Area: 183,568 sq mi
  (475,440 sq km)
Population: 15,905,000
Capital: Yaoundé

Cape Verde
Area: 1,557 sq mi
  (4,033 sq km)
Population: 415,000
Capital: Praia

Central African Republic
Area: 240,536 sq mi
  (622,984 sq km)
Population: 3,715,000
Capital: Bangui

Chad
Area: 495,755 sq mi
  (1,284,000 sq km)
Population: 9,395,000
Capital: N'Djamena

Comoros
Area: 863 sq mi
  (2,235 sq km)
Population: 640,000
Capital: Moroni

Congo
Area: 132,047 sq mi
  (342,000 sq km)
Population: 2,975,000
Capital: Brazzaville

Cote d'Ivoire
Area: 124,504 sq mi
  (322,463 sq km)
Population: 17,145,000
Capitals: Abidjan and
  Yamoussoukro

Dem. Rep. of the Congo
Area: 905,446 sq mi
  (2,345,095 sq km)
Population: 57,445,000
Capital: Kinshasa

Djibouti
Area: 8,958 sq mi
  (23,200 sq km)
Population: 460,000
Capital: Djibouti

Egypt
Area: 386,662 sq mi
  (1,001,449 sq km)
Population: 75,420,000
Capital: Cairo

Equatorial Guinea
Area: 10,831 sq mi
  (28,051 sq km)
Population: 515,000
Capital: Malabo

Eritrea
Area: 45,406 sq mi
  (117,600 sq km)
Population: 4,390,000
Capital: Asmera

Ethiopia
Area: 426,373 sq mi
  (1,104,300 sq km)
Population: 67,210,000
Capital: Addis Ababa

Gabon
Area: 103,347 sq mi
  (267,668 sq km)
Population: 1,340,000
Capital: Libreville

The Gambia
Area: 4,127 sq mi
  (10,689 sq km)
Population: 1,525,000
Capital: Banjul

Ghana
Area: 92,098 sq mi
  (238,533 sq km)
Population: 20,615,000
Capital: Accra

Guinea
Area: 94,926 sq mi
  (245,857 sq km)
Population: 9,135,000
Capital: Conakry

Guinea-Bissau
Area: 13,948 sq mi
  (36,125 sq km)
Population: 1,375,000
Capital: Bissau

Kenya
Area: 224,961 sq mi
  (582,646 sq km)
Population: 31,840,000
Capital: Nairobi

Lesotho
Area: 11,720 sq mi
  (30,355 sq km)
Population: 1,865,000
Capital: Maseru

Liberia
Area: 43,000 sq mi
  (111,369 sq km)
Population: 3,345,000
Capital: Monrovia

Libya
Area: 679,362 sq mi
  (1,759,540 sq km)
Population: 5,565,000
Capital: Tripoli

Madagascar
Area: 226,658 sq mi
  (587,041 sq km)
Population: 17,235,000
Capital: Antananarivo

Malawi
Area: 45,747 sq mi
  (118,484 sq km)
Population: 11,780,000
Capital: Lilongwe

Mali
Area: 478,841 sq mi
  (1,240,192 sq km)
Population: 11,790,000
Capital: Bamako

Mauritania
Area: 397,956 sq mi
  (1,030,700 sq km)
Population: 2,955,000
Capital: Nouakchott

Mauritius
Area: 788 sq mi (2,040 sq km)
Population: 1,215,000
Capital: Port Louis

Morocco
Area: 172,414 sq mi
  (446,550 sq km)
Population: 31,950,000
Capital: Rabat

Mozambique
Area: 309,496 sq mi
  (801,590 sq km)
Population: 18,695,000
Capital: Maputo

Namibia
Area: 317,818 sq mi
  (823,144 sq km)
Population: 1,940,000
Capital: Windhoek

Niger
Area: 489,192 sq mi
  (1,267,000 sq km)
Population: 11,210,000
Capital: Niamey

Nigeria
Area: 356,669 sq mi
  (923,768 sq km)
Population: 135,570,000
Capital: Abuja

Rwanda
Area: 10,169 sq mi
  (26,338 sq km)
Population: 7,880,000
Capital: Kigali

Sao Tome and Principe
Area: 372 sq mi (964 sq km)
Population: 180,000
Capital: São Tomé

Senegal
Area: 75,951 sq mi
  (196,712 sq km)
Population: 10,715,000
Capital: Dakar

Seychelles
Area: 176 sq mi (455 sq km)
Population: 81,000
Capital: Victoria

Sierra Leone
Area: 27,699 sq mi
  (71,740 sq km)
Population: 5,815,000
Capital: Freetown

Somalia
Area: 246,201 sq mi
  (637,657 sq km)
Population: 8,165,000
Capital: Mogadishu

South Africa
Area: 470,693 sq mi
  (1,219,090 sq km)
Population: 42,770,000
Capitals: Pretoria
  (administrative), Cape
  Town (legislative), and
  Bloemfontein (judicial)

Sudan
Area: 967,500 sq mi
  (2,505,813 sq km)
Population: 38,630,000
Capital: Khartoum

Swaziland
Area: 6,704 sq mi
  (17,364 sq km)
Population: 1,165,000
Capitals: Mbabane
  (administrative) and
  Lobamba (legislative)

Tanzania
Area: 364,900 sq mi
  (945,087 sq km)
Population: 36,230,000
Capitals: Dar es Salaam
  (de facto) and Dodoma
  (legislative)

Togo
Area: 21,925 sq mi
  (56,785 sq km)
Population: 5,495,000
Capital: Lomé

Tunisia
Area: 63,170 sq mi
  (163,610 sq km)
Population: 9,980,000
Capital: Tunis

Uganda
Area: 93,065 sq mi
  (241,038 sq km)
Population: 26,010,000
Capital: Kampala

Zambia
Area: 290,586 sq mi
  (752,614 sq km)
Population: 10,385,000
Capital: Lusaka

Zimbabwe
Area: 150,873 sq mi
  (390,759 sq km)
Population: 12,630,000
Capital: Harare

Asia

Afghanistan
Area: 251,773 sq mi
 (652,090 sq km)
Population: 29,205,000
Capital: Kabul

Armenia
Area: 11,506 sq mi
 (29,800 sq km)
Population: 3,325,000
Capital: Yerevan

Azerbaijan
Area: 33,437 sq mi
 (86,600 sq km)
Population: 7,850,000
Capital: Baku

Bahrain
Area: 267 sq mi (691 sq km)
Population: 675,000
Capital: Al Manāmah

Bangladesh
Area: 55,598 sq mi
 (143,998 sq km)
Population: 139,875,000
Capital: Dhaka

Bhutan
Area: 17,954 sq mi
 (46,500 sq km)
Population: 2,160,000
Capital: Thimphu

Brunei
Area: 2,226 sq mi
 (5,765 sq km)
Population: 360,000
Capital: Bandar Seri Begawan

Cambodia
Area: 69,898 sq mi
 (181,035 sq km)
Population: 13,245,000
Capital: Phnum Pénh

China
Area: 3,690,045 sq mi
 (9,557,172 sq km)
Population: 1,298,720,000
Capital: Beijing

Cyprus
Area: 3,572 sq mi
 (9,251 sq km)
Population: 775,000
Capital: Nicosia

East Timor
Area: 5,743 sq mi
 (14,874 sq km)
Population: 1,010,000
Capital: Dili

Georgia
Area: 26,911 sq mi
 (69,700 sq km)
Population: 4,920,000
Capital: Tbilisi

India
Area: 1,222,510 sq mi
 (3,166,285 sq km)
Population: 1,057,415,000
Capital: New Delhi

Indonesia
Area: 735,310 sq mi
 (1,904,443 sq km)
Population: 236,680,000
Capital: Jakarta

Iran
Area: 636,372 sq mi
 (1,648,195 sq km)
Population: 68,650,000
Capital: Tehrān

Iraq
Area: 169,235 sq mi
 (438,317 sq km)
Population: 25,025,000
Capital: Baghdād

Israel
Area: 8,019 sq mi
 (20,770 sq km)
Population: 6,160,000
Capital: Jerusalem

Japan
Area: 145,850 sq mi
 (377,750 sq km)
Population: 127,285,000
Capital: Tōkyō

Jordan
Area: 34,495 sq mi
 (89,342 sq km)
Population: 5,535,000
Capital: 'Ammān

Kazakhstan
Area: 1,049,156 sq mi
 (2,717,300 sq km)
Population: 16,780,000
Capital: Astana

Kuwait
Area: 6,880 sq mi
 (17,818 sq km)
Population: 2,220,000
Capital: Kuwait

Kyrgyzstan
Area: 77,182 sq mi
 (199,900 sq km)
Population: 4,930,000
Capital: Bishkek

Laos
Area: 91,429 sq mi
 (236,800 sq km)
Population: 5,995,000
Capital: Viangchan

Lebanon
Area: 4,016 sq mi
 (10,400 sq km)
Population: 3,755,000
Capital: Beirut

Malaysia
Area: 127,320 sq mi
 (329,758 sq km)
Population: 23,310,000
Capital: Kuala Lumpur

Maldives
Area: 115 sq mi (298 sq km)
Population: 335,000
Capital: Male'

Mongolia
Area: 604,829 sq mi
 (1,566,500 sq km)
Population: 2,730,000
Capital: Ulan Bator

Myanmar
Area: 261,228 sq mi
 (676,578 sq km)
Population: 42,620,000
Capital: Yangon

Nepal
Area: 56,827 sq mi
(147,181 sq km)
Population: 26,770,000
Capital: Kathmandu

North Korea
Area: 46,540 sq mi
(120,538 sq km)
Population: 22,585,000
Capital: P'yŏngyang

Oman
Area: 119,499 sq mi
(309,500 sq km)
Population: 2,855,000
Capital: Muscat

Pakistan
Area: 339,732 sq mi
(879,902 sq km)
Population: 152,210,000
Capital: Islāmābād

Philippines
Area: 115,831 sq mi
(300,000 sq km)
Population: 85,430,000
Capital: Manila

Qatar
Area: 4,412 sq mi
(11,427 sq km)
Population: 830,000
Capital: Doha

Russia
Area: 6,592,849 sq mi
(17,075,400 sq km)
Population: 144,310,000
Capital: Moscow

Saudi Arabia
Area: 830,000 sq mi
(2,149,690 sq km)
Population: 24,680,000
Capital: Riyadh

Singapore
Area: 264 sq mi (683 sq km)
Population: 4,685,000
Capital: Singapore

South Korea
Area: 38,328 sq mi
(99,268 sq km)
Population: 48,450,000
Capital: Seoul

Sri Lanka
Area: 25,332 sq mi
(65,610 sq km)
Population: 19,825,000
Capitals: Colombo
(designated) and
Sri Jayawardenepura
(seat of government)

Syria
Area: 71,498 sq mi
(185,180 sq km)
Population: 17,800,000
Capital: Damascus

Taiwan
Area: 13,901 sq mi
(36,002 sq km)
Population: 22,675,000
Capital: T'aipei

Tajikistan
Area: 55,251 sq mi
(143,100 sq km)
Population: 6,935,000
Capital: Dushanbe

Thailand
Area: 198,115 sq mi
(513,115 sq km)
Population: 64,570,000
Capital: Bangkok

Turkey
Area: 302,541 sq mi
(783,577 sq km)
Population: 68,505,000
Capital: Ankara

Turkmenistan
Area: 188,457 sq mi
(488,100 sq km)
Population: 4,820,000
Capital: Ashgabat

United Arab Emirates
Area: 32,278 sq mi
(83,600 sq km)
Population: 2,505,000
Capital: Abu Dhabi

Uzbekistan
Area: 172,742 sq mi
(447,400 sq km)
Population: 26,195,000
Capital: Tashkent

Vietnam
Area: 128,066 sq mi
(331,689 sq km)
Population: 82,150,000
Capital: Hanoi

Yemen
Area: 203,850 sq mi
(527,968 sq km)
Population: 19,680,000
Capital: Sanaa

Australia and Oceania

Australia
Area: 2,969,910 sq mi
(7,692,030 sq km)
Population: 19,825,000
Capital: Canberra

Cook Islands (New Zealand)
Area: 91 sq mi (236 sq km)
Population: 21,000
Capital: Avarua

Fiji
Area: 7,056 sq mi
(18,274 sq km)
Population: 875,000
Capital: Suva

Kiribati
Area: 313 sq mi (811 sq km)
Population: 100,000
Capital: Bairiki

Marshall Islands
Area: 70 sq mi (181 sq km)
Population: 57,000
Capital: Majuro (island)

Federated States of Micronesia
Area: 271 sq mi (702 sq km)
Population: 110,000
Capital: Palikir

Nauru
Area: 8.1 sq mi (21 sq km)
Population: 13,000
Capital: Yaren District

New Zealand
Area: 104,454 sq mi
 (270,534 sq km)
Population: 3,975,000
Capital: Wellington

Niue (New Zealand)
Area: 100 sq mi (259 sq km)
Population: 2,000
Capital: Alofi

Northern Mariana Islands (U.S.)
Area: 179 sq mi (464 sq km)
Population: 77,000
Capital: Saipan (island)

Palau
Area: 188 sq mi (487 sq km)
Population: 20,000
Capitals: Koror (de facto)
 and Melekeok (future)

Papua New Guinea
Area: 178,704 sq mi
 (462,840 sq km)
Population: 6,115,000
Capital: Port Moresby

Samoa
Area: 1,093 sq mi
 (2,831 sq km)
Population: 180,000
Capital: Apia

Solomon Islands
Area: 10,954 sq mi
 (28,370 sq km)
Population: 515,000
Capital: Honaira

Tonga
Area: 251 sq mi
 (650 sq km)
Population: 110,000
Capital: Nuku'alofa

Tuvalu
Area: 10 sq mi (26 sq km)
Population: 11,000
Capital: Funafuti

Vanuatu
Area: 4,707 sq mi
 (12,190 sq km)
Population: 200,000
Capital: Port Vila

Other Territories and Dependencies

North America

Country Name	Area	Population	Capital
Aruba (Netherlands)	75 sq mi (193 sq km)	71,000	Oranjestad
Bermuda (U.K.)	21 sq mi (54 sq km)	65,000	Hamilton
Cayman Islands (U.K.)	102 sq mi (264 sq km)	43,000	George Town
Guadeloupe (France)	687 sq mi (1,780 sq km)	440,000	Basse-Terre
Martinique (France)	425 sq mi (1,100 sq km)	430,000	Fort-de-France
Montserrat (U.K.)	39 sq mi (102 sq km)	9,000	Plymouth
Netherlands Antilles (Netherlands)	309 sq mi (800 sq km)	215,000	Willemstad
St. Pierre and Miquelon (France)	93 sq mi (242 sq km)	7,000	Saint-Pierre
Turks and Caicos Islands (U.K.)	166 sq mi (430 sq km)	20,000	Grand Turk
Virgin Islands (U.S.)	134 sq mi (347 sq km)	110,000	Charlotte Amalie

South America

Falkland Islands (U.K.)	4,700 sq mi (12,173 sq km)	3,000	Stanley
French Guiana (France)	32,253 sq mi (83,534 sq km)	190,000	Cayenne
South Georgia and the South Sandwich Islands (U.K.)	1,450 sq mi (3,755 sq km)	none	Grytviken Harbour

Europe

Faroe Islands (Denmark)	540 sq mi (1,399 sq km)	47,000	Tórshavn
Gibraltar (U.K.)	2.3 sq mi (6.0 sq km)	28,000	Gibraltar
Guernsey (U.K.)	30 sq mi (78 sq km)	65,000	St. Peter Port
Isle of Man (U.K.)	221 sq mi (572 sq km)	74,000	Douglas
Jersey (U.K.)	45 sq mi (116 sq km)	90,000	St. Helier

Africa

British Indian Ocean Territory (U.K.)	23 sq mi (60 sq km)	none	none
Mayotte (France)	144 sq mi (374 sq km)	180,000	Mamoutzou
Reunion (France)	969 sq mi (2,510 sq km)	760,000	Saint-Denis
St. Helena (U.K.)	121 sq mi (314 sq km)	7,500	Jamestown
Spanish North Africa (Spain)	12 sq mi (32 sq km)	140,000	none

Australia and Oceania

American Samoa (U.S.)	77 sq mi (199 sq km)	58,000	Pago Pago
Christmas Island (Australia)	52 sq mi (135 sq km)	400	Settlement
Cocos (Keeling) Islands (Australia)	5.4 sq mi (14 sq km)	600	West Island
French Polynesia (France)	1,544 sq mi (4,000 sq km)	265,000	Papeete
Guam (U.S.)	212 sq mi (549 sq km)	165,000	Hagåtña (Agana)
Johnson Atoll (U.S.)	0.5 sq mi (1.3 sq km)	1,100	none
Midway Islands (U.S.)	2 sq mi (5.2 sq km)	none	none
New Caledonia (France)	7,172 sq mi (18,575 sq km)	210,000	Nouméa
Norfolk Island (France)	14 sq mi (36 sq km)	2,000	Kingston
Pitcairn (U.K.)	19 sq mi (49 sq km)	100	Adamstown
Tokelau (New Zealand)	4.6 sq mi (12 sq km)	1,500	none
Wake Island (U.S.)	3 sq mi (7.8 sq km)	none	none
Wallis and Futuna (France)	99 sq mi (255 sq km)	16,000	Mata-Utu

Glossary

A

agriculture Land use for the growing of crops and the raising of livestock; farming.

arid Extremely dry; lacking moisture.

B

border The region or line around the edge of a country, state, province, or territory that separates it from another country, state, province, or territory.

C

cape An expanse of land, shaped like a point, extending into water.

capital A city that is the seat of a country or state government.

cartographer A person who makes maps.

cash crop Crops grown to sell commercially, often to foreign countries.

climate Weather patterns within a region that happen over long periods of time.

continent A major landmass surrounded by water. Earth has seven continents.

country A nation with its own distinct name, land area, government, language, and culture.

crop Vegetables, grains, cotton, or other plants grown by farmers.

culture Customs, traditions, and a way of life that people share.

D

desert An area of hot or cold land that is dry, with little or no rainfall.

E

economy The organization and management of a country's resources, industries, and services.

elevation The height of land above sea level, measured in feet or meters.

environment The natural conditions of an area that include climate, land, and resources.

equator The imaginary line of 0° latitude that circles Earth at its center.

ethnic group People who share traits, such as language, culture, heritage, and lifestyle.

export To send or sell goods to other countries.

F

fertile Land with rich soil that is suitable for growing crops.

fjord A deep, narrow inlet of the sea bordered by steep cliffs; usually created by a glacier.

G

glacier A huge mass of slow-moving ice.

gulf A large bay; an area of a sea or ocean partly enclosed by land.

H

hemisphere A half of Earth that is divided East and West or North and South.

hydroelectric power The use of falling water to produce energy in the form of electricity.

I

iceberg A large floating ice block that has broken off a glacier or ice sheet.

import To bring goods in from a foreign country to use or sell.

L

latitude Imaginary horizontal lines measuring distance in degrees north or south of the equator.

longitude Imaginary vertical lines measuring distance in degrees east or west of the prime meridian.

M

mineral Naturally occurring substances within the earth, such as coal, copper, or iron ore.

N

nomads People who move from place to place in search of food, water, and pastures for themselves and animal herds.

O

ocean A huge body of salt water. Oceans cover nearly two-thirds of Earth's surface.

P

peninsula A narrow area of land surrounded on three sides by water.

permafrost Ground that is permanently frozen.

plain An area of land that is low and flat.

population The total number of people living in a region.

prime meridian The imaginary vertical line of 0° that runs through Greenwich, England from the North Pole to the South Pole.

R

rain forest Dense tropical forest with abundant rainfall and humidity.

resources Substances occuring naturally that have value, such as water and minerals.

rural Having to do with the countryside; opposite of urban.

S

savanna A tree-scattered grassland.

scale The measure of distance on a map as it compares to actual distance.

subsistence farming Farming that produces enough food for farmers, their families, and perhaps a local market, but not enough to sell commercially.

swamp A wetland, or marsh.

T

temperate A mild climate that is neither hot nor cold.

trade The buying, selling, and exchanging of goods within or between countries.

tundra The cold, frozen plains of the Arctic regions.

U

urban Having to do with cities; opposite of rural.

V

volcano An opening in Earth's crust through which lava, steam, and ash erupt.

Index of Major Places on the Maps

Place	Map Ref.	Page No.
A Coruña, Spain	F-2	55
Abidjan, Cote d'Ivoire	I-5	67
Abilene, Texas, U.S.	I-8	33
Abu Dhabi, United Arab Emirates	E-7	85
Abuja, Nigeria	H-8	67
Acapulco, Mexico	G-5	35
Accra, Ghana	I-6	67
Ad Dawḥah, Qatar	E-7	85
Adana, Turkey	C-3	77
Addis Ababa, Ethiopia	H-14	67
Adelaide, Australia	G-9	91
Aden, Yemen	G-5	85
Adirondack Mountains, New York, U.S.	E-13	33
Adriatic Sea, Europe	E-2	59
Aegean Sea	H-6	59
Afghanistan, Asia, country	C-9	85
Ahmadābād, India	E-11	85
Ajaccio, France	G-7	55
Akron, Ohio, U.S.	F-12	33
Al Manāmah, Bahrain	E-7	85
Alabama, United States, state	I-11	33
Alaska, United States, state	J-4	33
Albania, Europe, country	G-4	59
Albany, New York, U.S.	E-14	33
Al Baṣrah, Iraq	C-6	85
Alberta, Canada, province	G-8	31
Albuquerque, New Mexico, U.S.	H-7	33
Alexandria, Egypt	C-12	67
Algeria, Africa, country	C-7	67
Algiers, Algeria	B-7	67
Alice Springs, Australia	E-8	91
Allahābād, India	E-13	85
Almaty, Kazakhstan	I-6	79
Alps, Europe, mountains	E-7	55
Amazon, South America, river	E-7	43
American Samoa, Oceania, dependency	F-12	93
'Ammān, Jordan	C-4	85
Amsterdam, Netherlands	B-6	55
Amu Darya, Asia, river	H-4	79
Amur, Asia, river	B-12	81
Andes, South America, mountains	C-3	41
Andorra, Europe, country	G-4	55
Angel Falls, Venezuela	E-8	43
Angers, France	D-4	55
Angola, Africa, country	E-3	69
Anguilla, North America, country	F-15	35
Ankara, Turkey	C-3	77
Ann Arbor, Michigan, U.S.	F-12	33
Annapolis, Maryland, U.S.	G-13	33
Anshan, China	D-12	81
Antalya, Turkey	C-2	77
Antananarivo, Madagascar	G-9	69
Antigua and Barbuda, North America, country	F-15	35
Antsiranana, Madagascar	E-10	69
Antwerpen, Belgium	C-6	55
Apia, Samoa	F-11	93
Appalachian Mountains, United States	H-12	33
Appennines, Italy, mountains	F-8	55
Arabian Desert, Egypt	D-13	67
Arabian Peninsula, Asia	E-5	85
Aral Sea, Asia	G-4	79
Ararat, Mount, Turkey, volcano	C-5	77
Arctic Ocean	B-9	79
Argentina, South America, country	F-4	45
Arizona, United States, state	H-5	33
Arkansas, United States, state	H-10	33
Arkhangel'sk, Russia	C-13	53
Armenia, Asia, country	C-5	77
Aruba, North America, country	H-13	35
Ashgabat, Turkmenistan	H-4	79
Asmera, Eritrea	G-14	67
Astana (Aqmola), Kazakhstan	G-6	79
Asunción, Paraguay	C-5	45
At Ṭā'if, Saudi Arabia	E-4	85
Atacama Desert, Chile	B-3	45
Athens, Greece	H-6	59
Atlanta, Georgia, U.S.	H-12	33
Atlantic Ocean	H-14	33
Atlas Mountains, Africa	B-6	67
Auckland, New Zealand	I-10	93
Augsburg, Germany	D-8	55
Augusta, Maine, U.S.	E-14	33
Austin, Texas, U.S.	I-9	33
Australia, Oceania, country	H-6	93
Austria, Europe, country	E-8	55
Ayeyarwady, Myanmar, river	C-4	83
Azerbaijan, Asia, country	C-6	77
Baghdad, Iraq	C-6	85
Bahamas, North America, country	E-12	35
Bahía Blanca, Argentina	F-4	45
Bahrain, Asia, country	D-6	85
Baikal, Lake, Russia	G-10	79
Bākhtarān, Iran	C-6	85
Baku, Azerbaijan	B-6	77
Balearic Islands, Spain	H-4	55
Balikapan, Indonesia	I-10	83
Balkhash, Lake, Kazakhstan	H-6	79
Baltic Sea, Europe	I-9	53
Baltimore, Maryland, U.S.	F-13	33
Bamako, Mali	G-4	67
Bandar Lampung, Indonesia	J-7	83
Bandar Seri Begawan, Brunei	G-9	83
Bandung, Indonesia	K-7	83
Bangalore, India	H-12	85
Bangkok, Thailand	E-6	83
Bangladesh, Asia, country	E-14	85
Bangor, Maine, U.S.	D-15	33
Bangui, Central African Republic	I-10	67
Banjarmasin, Indonesia	J-9	83
Banjul, Gambia, The	G-2	67
Barbados, North America, country	H-16	35
Barcelona, Spain	G-5	55
Bareilly, India	D-12	85
Bari, Italy	H-9	55
Barquisimeto, Venezuela	B-7	43
Barranquilla, Colombia	A-6	43
Barrow Point, Alaska, U.S.	I-4	33
Basel, Switzerland	E-7	55
Baton Rouge, Louisiana, U.S.	I-10	33
Be'ér Sheva', Israel	C-4	85
Beijing, China	D-11	81
Beirut, Lebanon	B-4	85
Belarus, Europe, country	G-5	57
Belém, Brazil	D-11	43
Belfast, Northern Ireland, U.K.	I-3	53
Belgium, Europe, country	C-6	55
Belgrade, Yugoslavia	E-4	59
Belize, North America, country	G-8	35
Belize City, Belize	G-8	35
Belmopan, Belize	G-8	35
Belo Horizonte, Brazil	I-12	43
Benin, Africa, country	H-6	67
Bering Sea	K-4	33
Bering Strait	J-3	33
Berlin, Germany	B-8	55
Bern, Switzerland	E-7	55
Bhāgalpur, India	E-14	85
Bhopal, India	E-12	85
Bhubaneshwar, India	F-14	85
Bhutan, Asia, country	D-14	85
Białystok, Poland	G-4	57
Bielefeld, Germany	B-7	55
Bien Hoa, Vietnam	E-7	83
Bīkāner, India	D-11	85
Bilbao, Spain	F-3	55
Biloxi, Mississippi, U.S.	I-11	33
Birmingham, England, U.K.	J-4	53
Birmingham, Alabama, U.S.	H-11	33
Biscay, Bay of, Europe	F-3	55
Bishkek, Kyrgyzstan	I-6	79
Bismarck, North Dakota, U.S.	E-8	33
Bissau, Guinea-Bissau	G-3	67
Black, Asia, river	B-6	83
Black Forest, Germany	D-7	55
Black Hills, South Dakota, U.S., mountains	E-8	33
Black Sea	F-7	59
Blanc, Mont, Europe, mountain	E-6	55
Blue Nile, Africa, river	G-13	67
Blue Ridge, United States, mountains	H-12	33
Bogotá, Colombia	C-6	43
Boise, Idaho, U.S.	E-5	33
Bolivia, South America, country	G-8	43
Bologna, Italy	F-8	55
Bon, Cap, Tunisia, cape	A-9	67
Bonn, Germany	C-7	55
Bordeaux, France	E-4	55
Borneo, Asia, island	I-9	83
Bosnia and Herzegovina, Europe, country	E-3	59
Boston, Massachusetts, U.S.	E-14	33
Botswana, Africa, country	G-4	69
Boulder, Colorado, U.S.	F-7	33
Brahmaputra, Asia, river	D-15	85
Brasília, Brazil	H-11	43
Bratislava, Slovakia	I-2	57
Brazil, South America, country	F-10	43
Brazzaville, Congo	C-3	69
Bremen, Germany	B-7	55
Brest, France	D-3	55
Brisbane, Australia	F-12	91
Bristol, England, U.K.	J-4	53
British Isles, Europe, islands	H-3	53
British Columbia, Canada, province	F-7	31
British Virgin Islands, North America, dependency	F-14	35
Brno, Czech Republic	H-2	57
Brownsville, Texas, U.S.	K-9	33
Brunei, Asia, country	G-9	83
Brussels, Belgium	C-6	55
Bucharest, Romania	E-6	59
Budapest, Hungary	I-2	57
Buenos Aires, Argentina	E-5	45
Buffalo, New York, U.S.	E-13	33
Bujumbura, Burundi	C-6	69
Bulgaria, Europe, country	F-6	59
Burgas, Bulgaria	F-7	59
Burkina Faso, Africa, country	G-6	67
Bursa, Turkey	B-2	77
Burundi, Africa, country	C-6	69
Cádiz, Spain	I-2	55
Caen, France	D-5	55
Cagayan de Oro, Philippines	F-12	83
Cairo, Egypt	C-12	67
Calgary, Alberta, Canada	H-8	31
Cali, Colombia	C-5	43

Place	Map Ref.	Page No.
California, United States, state	F-4	33
Cambodia, Asia, country	E-7	83
Cameroon, Africa, country	I-8	67
Campos, Brazil	I-13	43
Canada, North America, country	G-9	31
Canaveral, Cape, Florida, U.S.	J-13	33
Canberra, Australia	H-11	91
Cannes, France	F-6	55
Cape Town, South Africa	J-4	69
Cape Verde, Africa, country	F-1	67
Caracas, Venezuela	B-7	43
Cardiff, Wales, U.K.	J-4	53
Caribbean Sea	H-12	35
Caroline Islands, Oceania	E-7	93
Carpathian Mountains, Europe	H-3	57
Carson City, Nevada, U.S.	F-4	33
Cartagena, Colombia	A-6	43
Casablanca, Morocco	B-5	67
Cascade Range, North America, mountains	E-4	33
Casper, Wyoming, U.S.	F-7	33
Caspian Sea	G-3	79
Catania, Italy	I-9	55
Caucasus, mountains	F-3	79
Cayenne, French Guiana	C-11	43
Cayman Islands, North America, dependency	F-10	35
Cebu, Philippines	F-12	83
Celebes, Indonesia, island	I-11	83
Central African Republic, Africa, country	I-10	67
Chad, Africa, country	G-10	67
Chad, Lake, Africa	G-9	67
Changchun, China	C-12	81
Changsha, China	G-10	81
Charleroi, Belgium	C-6	55
Charleston, South Carolina, U.S.	H-13	33
Charleston, West Virginia, U.S.	G-12	33
Charlotte, North Carolina, U.S.	H-13	33
Charlottetown, Prince Edward Island, Canada	I-16	31
Chattanooga, Tennessee, U.S.	H-12	33
Chelyabinsk, Russia	F-6	79
Chengdu, China	G-9	81
Chennai (Madras), India	H-13	85
Chesapeake Bay, North America	G-13	33
Cheyenne, Wyoming, U.S.	F-7	33
Chicago, Illinois, U.S.	F-11	33
Chile, South America, country	G-3	45
China, Asia, country	F-8	81
Chişinău, Moldova	J-5	57
Chittagong, Bangladesh	E-15	85
Chongqing, China	G-9	81
Christchurch, New Zealand	I-10	93
Cincinnati, Ohio, U.S.	G-12	33
Cleveland, Ohio, U.S.	F-12	33
Cluj-Napoca, Romania	D-5	59
Cod, Cape, Massachusetts, U.S.	E-14	33
Coimbatore, India	H-12	85
Colombia, South America, country	C-6	43
Colombo, Sri Lanka	I-13	85
Colorado, United States, state	G-7	33
Columbia, South Carolina, U.S.	H-13	33
Columbia, United States, river	D-5	33
Columbus, Ohio, U.S.	F-12	33
Comoros, Africa, country	E-9	69
Conakry, Guinea	H-3	67
Concepción, Chile	F-2	45
Concord, New Hampshire, U.S.	E-14	33
Congo, Africa, country	B-3	69
Congo, Democratic Republic of the, Africa, country	C-4	69
Connecticut, United States, state	F-14	33
Cook Islands, Oceania, dependency	G-12	93
Copenhagen, Denmark	I-8	53
Córdoba, Argentina	E-4	45
Córdoba, Spain	H-2	55
Corsica, France, island	G-7	55
Costa Rica, North America, country	I-10	35
Cote d'Ivoire, Africa, country	H-5	67
Cotonou, Benin	I-6	67
Coventry, England, U.K.	J-4	53
Cozumel, Isla, Mexico, island	F-9	35
Crete, Greece, island	J-6	59
Crimean Peninsula, Ukraine	J-8	57
Cristóbal Colón, Pico, Colombia, mountain	A-6	43
Croatia, Europe, country	E-3	59
Cuba, North America, country	F-11	35
Curaçao, Netherlands Antilles, island	H-13	35
Cuttack, India	F-14	85
Cyprus, Asia, country	D-3	77
Czech Republic, Europe, country	H-1	57
Da Nang, Vietnam	D-8	83
Dakar, Senegal	G-2	67
Dalian, China	E-12	81
Dallas, Texas, U.S.	I-9	33
Damascus, Syria	B-4	85
Danube, Europe, river	E-5	59
Dar es Salaam, Tanzania	D-8	69
Darling, Australia, river	F-10	91
Darwin, Australia	B-8	91
Davenport, Iowa, U.S.	F-10	33
Daytona Beach, Florida, U.S.	I-13	33
Dead Sea, Asia	C-4	85
Deccan, India, plateau	F-13	85
Dehra Dūn, India	D-12	85
Delaware, United States, state	G-14	33
Delhi, India	D-12	85
Denmark, Europe, country	H-7	53
Denver, Colorado, U.S.	G-7	33
Des Moines, Iowa, U.S.	F-10	33
Detroit, Michigan, U.S.	F-12	33
Devils Island, French Guiana	C-11	43
Dhaka, Bangladesh	E-14	85
Dhule, India	F-11	85
Dijon, France	E-6	55
Dili, East Timor	K-12	83
Djibouti, Africa, country	G-15	67
Djibouti, Djibouti	H-15	67
Dnieper, Europe, river	G-6	57
Dniprodzerzhyns'k, Ukraine	I-8	57
Dodoma, Tanzania	D-7	69
Dominica, North America, country	G-15	35
Dominican Republic, North America, country	G-13	35
Don, Russia, river	D-4	79
Donostia-San Sebastián, Spain	F-4	55
Dortmund, Germany	C-7	55
Douala, Cameroon	I-8	67
Dover, Delaware, U.S.	F-14	33
Dover, Strait of, Europe	K-5	53
Dresden, Germany	C-8	55
Dubayy, United Arab Emirates	E-7	85
Dublin, Ireland	I-3	53
Duluth, Minnesota, U.S.	E-10	33
Durban, South Africa	I-6	69
Dushanbe, Tajikistan	I-5	79
Düsseldorf, Germany	C-7	55
East China Sea, Asia	G-12	81
East Timor, Asia, country	K-12	83
Ecuador, South America, country	D-5	43
Edinburgh, Scotland, U.K.	H-4	53
Edmonton, Alberta, Canada	H-9	31
Egypt, Africa, country	D-12	67
El Aaiún, Western Sahara	D-4	67
El Mansûra, Egypt	C-12	67
El Paso, Texas, U.S.	I-7	33
El Salvador, North America, country	H-8	35
El'brus, gora, Russia, mountain	E-3	79
Elbe, Europe, river	B-8	55
England, United Kingdom, political division	J-4	53
English Channel, Europe	K-3	53
Equatorial Guinea, Africa, country	J-8	67
Erie, Pennsylvania, U.S.	F-12	33
Erie, Lake, North America	J-13	31
Eritrea, Africa, country	F-14	67
Eşfahān, Iran	C-7	85
Essen, Germany	C-7	55
Estonia, Europe, country	G-10	53
Ethiopia, Africa, country	H-14	67
Etna, Monte, Italy, volcano	I-9	55
Euphrates, Asia, river	B-5	85
Everest, Mount, Asia	D-14	85
Faisalabad, Pakistan	C-11	85
Falkland Islands, South America, dependency	I-5	45
Farewell, Cape, New Zealand	I-10	93
Fargo, North Dakota, U.S.	E-9	33
Faroe Islands, Europe, dependency	E-4	53
Fear, Cape, North Carolina, U.S.	H-13	33
Fès, Morocco	B-6	67
Fiji, Oceania, country	G-10	93
Finland, Europe, country	D-10	53
Flagstaff, Arizona, U.S.	H-6	33
Florence, Italy	F-8	55
Florida, United States, state	J-12	33
Florida Keys, Florida, U.S., islands	K-13	33
Formosa, Argentina	C-5	45
Fort Lauderdale, Florida, U.S.	J-13	33
Fort Worth, Texas, U.S.	I-9	33
France, Europe, country	E-5	55
Frankfort, Kentucky, U.S.	G-12	33
Frankfurt, Germany	C-7	55
Fredericton, New Brunswick, Canada	I-15	31
Freetown, Sierra Leone	H-3	67
French Guiana, South America, dependency	C-10	43
French Polynesia, Oceania, dependency	F-14	93
Fuji, Mount, Japan, volcano	E-15	81
Fukuoka, Japan	F-13	81
Fushun, China	D-12	81
Gabon, Africa, country	C-2	69
Gaborone, Botswana	H-5	69
Galapagos Islands, Ecuador	D-2	43
Galveston, Texas, U.S.	J-9	33
Gambia, The, Africa, country	G-2	67
Ganges, Asia, river	E-13	85
Gaza, Gaza Strip	C-4	85
Geneva, Switzerland	E-6	55
Genoa, Italy	F-7	55
Gent, Belgium	C-6	55
George Town, Malaysia	G-5	83
Georgetown, Guyana	B-9	43
Georgia, Asia, country	B-5	77
Georgia, United States, state	H-12	33
Germany, Europe, country	C-7	55
Ghana, Africa, country	H-6	67
Gibraltar, Europe, dependency	I-2	55
Gibraltar, Strait of	B-5	67
Giza, Egypt	C-12	67
Glasgow, Scotland, U.K.	H-4	53
Gobi, Asia, desert	I-9	79
Good Hope, Cape of, South Africa	J-4	69

Place	Map Ref.	Page No.
Göteborg, Sweden	H-8	53
Gran Chaco, South America, plain	C-4	45
Granada, Spain	I-3	55
Grand Bahama, Bahamas, island	D-11	35
Grand Forks, North Dakota, U.S.	D-9	33
Great Bear Lake, Northwest Territories, Canada	E-9	31
Great Britain, United Kingdom, island	H-5	53
Great Dividing Range, Australia, mountains	D-10	91
Great Indian Desert, Asia	D-11	85
Great Plains, North America	F-8	33
Great Salt Lake, Utah, U.S.	F-6	33
Great Sandy Desert, Australia	E-6	91
Great Slave Lake, Northwest Territories, Canada	F-9	31
Great Victoria Desert, Australia	F-7	91
Greater Antilles, North America, islands	F-11	35
Greater Sunda Islands, Asia	J-8	83
Greece, Europe, country	H-5	59
Green Bay, Wisconsin, U.S.	E-11	33
Greenland, North America, dependency	B-7	29
Grenada, North America, country	H-15	35
Guadalajara, Mexico	F-5	35
Guadeloupe, North America, country	G-15	35
Guam, Oceania, dependency	C-7	93
Guangzhou, China	H-10	81
Guatemala, Guatemala	H-8	35
Guatemala, North America, country	G-8	35
Guayaquil, Ecuador	D-5	43
Guernsey, United Kingdom, island	K-4	53
Guinea-Bissau, Africa, country	G-3	67
Guiyang, China	G-9	81
Guyana, South America, country	B-9	43
Ha Noi, Vietnam	C-7	83
Hai Phong, Vietnam	C-7	83
Haiti, North America, country	F-12	35
Halab, Syria	B-4	85
Halifax, Nova Scotia, Canada	I-16	31
Halle, Germany	C-8	55
Hamburg, Germany	B-7	55
Hamilton, Ontario, Canada	J-13	31
Hangzhou, China	G-12	81
Hannover, Germany	3-7	55
Harare, Zimbabwe	F-6	69
Harbin, China	C-12	81
Harrisburg, Pennsylvania, U.S.	F-13	33
Hartford, Connecticut, U.S.	F-14	33
Hatteras, Cape, North Carolina, U.S.	H-14	33
Hawaii, United States, state	J-7	33
Helena, Montana, U.S.	D-6	33
Helsinki, Finland	F-10	53
Himalayas, Asia, mountains	D-12	85
Hindu Kush, Asia, mountains	C-10	85
Hiroshima, Japan	E-14	81
Hispaniola, North America, island	G-12	35
Hobart, Australia	I-11	91
Honduras, North America, country	H-9	35
Hong Kong (Xianggang), China	H-10	81
Honiara, Solomon Islands	F-9	93
Honolulu, Hawaii, U.S.	J-6	33
Hormuz, Strait of, Asia	E-8	85
Horn, Cape, Chile	J-4	45
Hot Springs, Arkansas, U.S.	H-10	33
Houston, Texas, U.S.	J-9	33

Place	Map Ref.	Page No.
Hudson, United States, river	F-14	33
Hudson Bay, Canada	G-12	31
Hue, Vietnam	D-8	83
Hungary, Europe, country	J-2	57
Huron, Lake, North America	J-13	31
Hyderābād, India	G-12	85
Hyderābād, Pakistan	E-10	85
Ibadan, Nigeria	H-7	67
Iceland, Europe, country	C-2	53
Idaho, United States, state	E-6	33
Illinois, United States, state	F-10	33
Inch'on, South Korea	E-12	81
India, Asia, country	E-12	85
Indian Ocean	G-5	93
Indiana, United States, state	F-11	33
Indianapolis, Indiana, U.S.	G-11	33
Indonesia, Asia, country	J-7	83
Indore, India	E-11	85
Indus, Asia, river	D-10	85
Innsbruck, Austria	E-8	55
Iowa, United States, state	F-10	33
Iqaluit, Nunavut, Canada	E-13	31
Iran, Asia, country	C-7	85
Iraq, Asia, country	C-5	85
Ireland, Europe, country	I-3	53
Irtysh, Asia, river	F-7	79
Islamabad, Pakistan	C-11	85
Israel, Asia, country	C-4	85
İstanbul, Turkey	B-2	77
Italy, Europe, country	G-8	55
İzmir, Turkey	C-2	77
Jackson, Mississippi, U.S.	I-11	33
Jacksonville, Florida, U.S.	I-13	33
Jaipur, India	E-11	85
Jakarta, Indonesia	J-7	83
Jamaica, North America, country	G-11	35
Jambi, Indonesia	I-6	83
Jammu and Kashmir, Asia, region	B-11	85
Jamnagar, India	F-10	85
Jamshedpur, India	E-13	85
Japan, Asia, country	D-15	81
Japan, Sea of, Asia	D-13	81
Java, Indonesia, island	K-8	83
Jayapura, Indonesia	I-16	83
Jefferson City, Missouri, U.S.	G-10	33
Jersey, United Kingdom, island	K-4	53
Jerusalem, Israel	C-4	85
Jiddah, Saudi Arabia	E-4	85
Jilin, China	C-12	81
Jinan, China	E-11	81
Johannesburg, South Africa	H-5	69
Jordan, Asia, country	C-4	85
Juneau, Alaska, U.S.	K-5	33
K2, Asia, mountain	B-11	85
Kabol, Afghanistan	C-10	85
Kalahari Desert, Africa	H-4	69
Kalgoorlie-Boulder, Australia	G-6	91
Kaliningrad, Russia	I-10	53
Kampala, Uganda	B-6	69
Kano, Nigeria	G-8	67
Kansas, United States, state	G-9	33
Kansas City, Missouri, U.S.	G-10	33
Kaohsiung, Taiwan	H-12	81
Kara Kum, Turkmenistan, desert	H-4	79
Karāchi, Pakistan	E-10	85
Kathmandu, Nepal	D-13	85
Katowice, Poland	H-3	57
Kaunas, Lithuania	I-11	53
Kazakhstan, Asia, country	G-5	79
Kazan', Russia	E-5	79
Kentucky, United States, state	G-11	33
Kenya, Africa, country	B-7	69
Khartoum, Sudan	G-13	67

Place	Map Ref.	Page No.
Kiev, Ukraine	H-6	57
Kigali, Rwanda	C-6	69
Kilimanjaro, Tanzania, mountain	C-7	69
Kingston upon Hull, England, U.K.	I-4	53
Kinshasa, Congo, Democratic Republic of the	C-3	69
Kiribati, Oceania, country	E-11	93
Kirov, Russia	D-16	53
Kitakyūshu, Japan	E-13	81
Kitwe, Zambia	E-5	69
Knoxville, Tennessee, U.S.	H-12	33
Kōbe, Japan	E-14	81
Kolkata (Calcutta), India	E-14	85
Köln, Germany	C-7	55
Kommunizma, Pik, Tajikistan, mountain	I-5	79
Koror, Palau	D-6	93
Kosciuszko, Mount, Australia	H-11	91
Kota, India	E-11	85
Kozhikode, India	H-12	85
Kraków, Poland	H-3	57
Kryvyi Rih, Ukraine	I-7	57
Kuala Lumpur, Malaysia	H-6	83
Kunming, China	H-8	81
Kursk, Russia	I-14	53
Kuwait, Asia, country	D-6	85
Kuwait, Kuwait	D-6	85
Kwangju, South Korea	E-13	81
Kyōto, Japan	E-14	81
Kyrgyzstan, Asia, country	I-6	79
La Paz, Bolivia	H-7	43
La Plata, Argentina	E-5	45
Lagos, Nigeria	I-7	67
Lahore, Pakistan	C-11	85
Land's End, England, U.K., cape	K-3	53
Lansing, Michigan, U.S.	F-12	33
Lanzhou, China	E-9	81
Laos, Asia, country	C-6	83
Lapland, Europe, historic region	C-9	53
Laredo, Texas, U.S.	J-8	33
Las Vegas, Nevada, U.S.	G-5	33
Latvia, Europe, country	H-10	53
Lausanne, Switzerland	E-6	55
Le Mans, France	D-5	55
Lebanon, Asia, country	B-4	85
Leipzig, Germany	C-8	55
Lena, Russia, river	G-10	79
León, Mexico	F-5	35
Lesotho, Africa, country	I-5	69
Lesser Antilles, North America, islands	H-14	35
Lexington, Kentucky, U.S.	G-12	33
Leyte, Philippines, island	E-12	83
Liberia, Africa, country	I-4	67
Libreville, Gabon	B-1	69
Libya, Africa, country	D-10	67
Libyan Desert, Africa	D-11	67
Liechtenstein, Europe, country	E-7	55
Liège, Belgium	C-6	55
Lille, France	C-6	55
Lilongwe, Malawi	F-6	69
Lima, Peru	G-5	43
Lincoln, Nebraska, U.S.	F-9	33
Lipetsk, Russia	H-15	53
Lisbon, Portugal	H-1	55
Lithuania, Europe, country	H-10	53
Little Rock, Arkansas, U.S.	H-10	33
Liverpool, England, U.K.	I-4	53
Ljubljana, Slovenia	D-2	59
Llanos, South America, plain	C-7	43
Lobamba, Swaziland	I-6	69
Loire, France, river	D-4	55
Lomé, Togo	I-6	67
London, England, U.K.	J-4	53

Place	Map Ref.	Page No.
Long Beach, California, U.S.	H-4	33
Los Angeles, California, U.S.	H-4	33
Louisiana, United States, state	I-10	33
Louisville, Kentucky, U.S.	G-11	33
Luanda, Angola	D-2	69
Lublin, Poland	H-4	57
Lucknow, India	D-12	85
Ludhiana, India	C-11	85
Lusaka, Zambia	F-5	69
Luxembourg, Luxembourg	D-6	55
Luxembourg, Europe, country	C-6	55
Luzon, Philippines, island	D-11	83
L'viv, Ukraine	H-4	57
Lyon, France	E-6	55
Macedonia, Europe, country	G-4	59
Mackinaw City, Michigan, U.S.	E-11	33
Madagascar, Africa, country	G-9	69
Madison, Wisconsin, U.S.	F-11	33
Madrid, Spain	G-3	55
Magellan, Strait of, South America	J-3	45
Maine, United States, state	D-14	33
Makassar Strait, Indonesia	I-10	83
Malabo, Equatorial Guinea	I-8	67
Malacca, Strait of, Asia	G-5	83
Malang, Indonesia	K-9	83
Malawi, Africa, country	E-6	69
Malay Peninsula, Asia	G-6	83
Malaysia, Asia, country	G-6	83
Maldives, Asia, country	I-11	85
Male', Maldives	J-11	85
Mali, Africa, country	F-6	67
Mallorca, Spain, island	H-5	55
Malta, Europe, country	J-9	55
Man, Isle of, United Kingdom	I-3	53
Managua, Nicaragua	H-9	35
Manaus, Brazil	E-9	43
Manchester, England, U.K.	I-4	53
Manchuria, China, historic region	C-12	81
Mandalay, Myanmar	B-5	83
Manila, Philippines	D-11	83
Manitoba, Canada, province	H-10	31
Mannheim, Germany	D-7	55
Maputo, Mozambique	H-6	69
Maracaibo, Venezuela	A-6	43
Mariana Islands, Oceania	C-8	93
Mariupol', Ukraine	I-9	57
Marrakech, Morocco	C-5	67
Marseille, France	F-6	55
Marshall Islands, Oceania, country	D-9	93
Martinique, North America, dependency	G-15	35
Maryland, United States, state	G-14	33
Maseru, Lesotho	I-5	69
Mashhad, Iran	B-8	85
Massachusetts, United States, state	E-14	33
Massif Central, France, mountains	F-5	55
Matterhorn, Europe, mountain	E-7	55
Mauritania, Africa, country	E-4	67
Mayotte, Africa, dependency	F-9	69
Mbabane, Swaziland	H-6	69
McKinley, Mount, Alaska, U.S.	J-4	33
Mecca, Saudi Arabia	E-4	85
Medan, Indonesia	H-5	83
Medellín, Colombia	B-6	43
Medina, Saudi Arabia	E-4	85
Mediterranean Sea	I-5	55
Meerut, India	D-12	85
Meknes, Morocco	B-6	67
Mekong, Asia, river	E-7	83
Melanesia, Oceania, islands	F-9	93
Melbourne, Australia	H-11	91
Melbourne, Florida, U.S.	J-13	33
Memphis, Tennessee, U.S.	H-11	33
Mendoza, Argentina	E-3	45
Menorca, Spain, island	H-5	55
Mérida, Mexico	F-8	35
Messina, Italy	I-9	55
Mexicali, Mexico	B-2	35
Mexico, North America, country	E-5	35
Mexico City, Mexico	F-6	35
Mexico, Gulf of, North America	E-8	35
Miami, Florida, U.S.	J-13	33
Michigan, United States, state	E-11	33
Michigan, Lake, United States	J-12	31
Micronesia, Oceania, islands	D-9	93
Micronesia, Federated States of, Oceania, country	D-8	93
Milan, Italy	F-7	55
Milwaukee, Wisconsin, U.S.	F-11	33
Mindanao, Philippines, island	F-12	83
Minneapolis, Minnesota, U.S.	E-10	33
Minnesota, United States, state	E-9	33
Minot, North Dakota, U.S.	D-8	33
Minsk, Belarus	F-5	57
Mississippi, United States, state	I-10	33
Mississippi, United States, river	I-10	33
Missouri, United States, state	G-10	33
Missouri, United States, river	F-9	33
Mobile, Alabama, U.S.	I-11	33
Mogadishu, Somalia	J-16	67
Moldova, Europe, country	I-5	57
Moluccas, Indonesia, islands	J-13	83
Mombasa, Kenya	C-8	69
Monaco, Europe, country	F-7	55
Mongolia, Asia, country	I-9	79
Monrovia, Liberia	I-4	67
Montana, United States, state	D-6	33
Monterrey, Mexico	D-6	35
Montevideo, Uruguay	E-5	45
Montgomery, Alabama, U.S.	I-11	33
Montpelier, Vermont, U.S.	E-14	33
Montréal, Québec, Canada	I-14	31
Montserrat, North America, dependency	G-15	35
Moorhead, Minnesota, U.S.	E-9	33
Morocco, Africa, country	C-5	67
Moscow, Russia	G-13	53
Mountain Nile, Sudan, river	H-13	67
Mozambique, Africa, country	G-6	69
Mumbai (Bombay), India	F-11	85
Munich, Germany	D-8	55
Münster, Germany	B-7	55
Murmansk, Russia	B-11	53
Muscat, Oman	E-8	85
Myanmar (Burma), Asia, country	B-5	83
Mysore, India	H-12	85
N'djamena, Chad	G-9	67
Nagoya, Japan	E-14	81
Nairobi, Kenya	C-7	69
Namibia, Africa, country	G-3	69
Nanjing, China	F-11	81
Nantucket Island, Massachusetts, U.S.	F-15	33
Naples, Italy	H-9	55
Nashville, Tennessee, U.S.	H-11	33
Nasser, Lake, Africa	E-13	67
Natal, Brazil	E-14	43
Natchez, Mississippi, U.S.	I-10	33
Nauru, Oceania, country	E-9	93
Ndola, Zambia	E-5	69
Nebraska, United States, state	F-8	33
Nepal, Asia, country	D-13	85
Netherlands, Europe, country	B-6	55
Netherlands Antilles, North America, dependency	H-14	35
Nevada, United States, state	F-5	33
New Brunswick, Canada, province	I-15	31
New Caledonia, Oceania, dependency	G-9	93
New Delhi, India	D-12	85
New Guinea, island	E-7	93
New Hampshire, United States, state	E-14	33
New Jersey, United States, state	F-14	33
New Mexico, United States, state	H-7	33
New Orleans, Louisiana, U.S.	I-11	33
New Providence, Bahamas, island	E-11	35
New York, New York, U.S.	F-14	33
New York, United States, state	E-13	33
New Zealand, Oceania, country	I-10	93
Newark, New Jersey, U.S.	F-14	33
Newfoundland and Labrador, Canada, province	G-15	31
Niagara Falls, North America	E-12	33
Niamey, Niger	G-7	67
Nicaragua, North America, country	H-9	35
Nice, France	F-6	55
Nicosia, Cyprus/North Cyprus	D-3	77
Niger, Africa, country	F-8	67
Niger, Africa, river	H-4	67
Nigeria, Africa, country	H-8	67
Nile, Africa, river	D-13	67
Niue, Oceania, dependency	G-12	93
Nizhniy Novgorod, Russia	D-5	79
Nordkapp, Norway, cape	A-9	53
Norfolk, Virginia, U.S.	G-13	33
Norfolk Island, Oceania, island	H-10	93
North Carolina, United States, state	H-13	33
North Cyprus, Asia, country	D-3	77
North Dakota, United States, state	D-8	33
North Korea, Asia, country	D-12	81
North Sea, Europe	I-6	53
Northern Ireland, United Kingdom, political division	I-3	53
Northern Mariana Islands, Oceania, dependency	C-8	93
Northwest Territories, Canada	D-8	31
Norway, Europe, country	F-7	53
Nouakchott, Mauritania	F-3	67
Nouméa, New Caledonia	G-9	93
Nova Scotia, Canada, province	I-16	31
Novosibirsk, Russia	G-8	79
Nunavut, Canada, territory	E-11	31
Nürnberg, Germany	D-8	55
Oakland, California, U.S.	F-4	33
Ob', Russia, river	E-7	79
Oder, Europe, river	G-1	57
Odesa, Ukraine	J-6	57
Ogden, Utah, U.S.	F-6	33
Ohio, United States, state	F-12	33
Ohio, United States, river	G-11	33
Okeechobee, Florida, U.S., lake	J-13	33
Okhotsk, Sea of, Asia	E-14	79
Okinawa-Jima, Japan, island	G-13	81
Oklahoma, United States, state	H-8	33
Oklahoma City, Oklahoma, U.S.	H-9	33
Olympia, Washington, U.S.	D-4	33
Omaha, Nebraska, U.S.	F-9	33
Oman, Asia, country	F-8	85
Oman, Gulf of, Asia	E-8	85
Omdurman, Sudan	F-13	67
Omsk, Russia	F-7	79
Ontario, Canada, province	I-12	31
Ontario, Lake, North America	J-14	31
Oregon, United States, state	E-4	33
Orel, Russia	H-14	53
Orlando, Florida, U.S.	J-13	33
Orléans, France	D-5	55
Ōsaka, Japan	E-14	81

Place	Map Ref.	Page No.
Oslo, Norway	G-7	53
Ostrava, Czech Republic	H-2	57
Ottawa, Ontario, Canada	J-14	31
Ouagadougou, Burkina Faso	G-6	67
Pacific Ocean	D-12	93
Padang, Indonesia	I-5	83
Pakistan, Asia, country	D-9	85
Palau, Oceania, country	D-7	93
Palembang, Indonesia	J-7	83
Pamir, Asia, mountains	I-5	79
Pampa, Argentina, region	F-4	45
Panamá, Panama	I-11	35
Panama, North America, country	I-11	35
Panamá, Golfo de, Panama, gulf	J-11	35
Panamá, Istmo de, Panama, isthmus	I-10	35
Papeete, French Polynesia	G-13	93
Papua New Guinea, Oceania, country	E-7	93
Paracel Islands, Asia	D-9	83
Paraguay, South America, country	B-5	45
Paraná, South America, river	D-5	45
Paris, France	D-5	55
Patagonia, Argentina, region	I-3	45
Pecos, United States, river	I-8	33
Pennsylvania, United States, state	F-13	33
Pensacola, Florida, U.S.	I-11	33
Perm', Russia	E-6	79
Persian Gulf, Asia	D-6	85
Perth, Australia	G-5	91
Peru, South America, country	G-6	43
Peshāwar, Pakistan	C-10	85
Philadelphia, Pennsylvania, U.S.	F-13	33
Philippine Sea	C-6	93
Philippines, Asia, country	E-11	83
Phnum Pénh, Cambodia	E-7	83
Phoenix, Arizona, U.S.	H-6	33
Pierre, South Dakota, U.S.	E-8	33
Pisa, Italy	F-7	55
Pitcairn, Oceania, dependency	G-15	93
Pittsburgh, Pennsylvania, U.S.	F-13	33
Platte, United States, river	F-8	33
Play Cu, Vietnam	E-8	83
Po, Italy, river	F-8	55
Pocatello, Idaho, U.S.	E-6	33
Poland, Europe, country	G-3	57
Poltava, Ukraine	H-8	57
Polynesia, Oceania, islands	E-12	93
Port Augusta, Australia	G-9	91
Port Harcourt, Nigeria	I-7	67
Port Moresby, Papua New Guinea	F-8	93
Port Said, Egypt	C-12	67
Port Vila, Vanuatu	G-10	93
Portland, Maine, U.S.	E-14	33
Portland, Oregon, U.S.	D-4	33
Porto, Portugal	G-2	55
Porto Alegre, Brazil	K-11	43
Porto-Novo, Benin	I-7	67
Portugal, Europe, country	G-1	55
Poznań, Poland	G-2	57
Prague, Czech Republic	H-1	57
Praia, Cape Verde	G-1	67
Pretoria, South Africa	H-5	69
Prince Edward Island, Canada, province	I-15	31
Providence, Rhode Island, U.S.	E-14	33
Provo, Utah, U.S.	F-6	33
Puebla, Mexico	F-6	35
Puerto Princesa, Philippines	F-10	83
Puerto Rico, North America, dependency	F-14	35
Pune, India	F-11	85
Pusan, South Korea	E-13	81
P'yongyang, North Korea	D-12	81
Pyrenees, Europe, mountains	F-4	55
Qacentina, Algeria	B-8	67
Qatar, Asia, country	E-7	85
Qingdao, China	E-11	81
Qiqihar, China	C-12	81
Qom, Iran	C-7	85
Québec, Canada, province	H-14	31
Québec, Québec, Canada	I-14	31
Quezon City, Philippines	D-11	83
Quito, Ecuador	D-5	43
Rabat, Morocco	B-5	67
Rainier, Mount, Washington, U.S.	D-4	33
Raipur, India	F-13	85
Rājahmundry, India	G-13	85
Rajkot, India	F-10	85
Rājshāhi, Bangladesh	E-14	85
Raleigh, North Carolina, U.S.	G-13	33
Rānchi, India	E-13	85
Rasht, Iran	B-7	85
Rawalpindi, Pakistan	C-11	85
Recife, Brazil	F-14	43
Red, Asia, river	B-7	83
Red, United States, river	H-8	33
Red Sea	F-4	85
Regina, Saskatchewan, Canada	I-10	31
Reims, France	D-6	55
Reno, Nevada, U.S.	F-4	33
Reykjavik, Iceland	C-1	53
Rhine, Europe, river	C-7	55
Rhode Island, United States, state	F-14	33
Rhône, Europe, river	F-6	55
Richmond, Virginia, U.S.	G-13	33
Rift Valley, Africa	I-14	67
Rio de Janeiro, Brazil	I-12	43
Rio Grande, North America, river	H-5	29
Riyadh, Saudi Arabia	E-6	85
Rīga, Latvia	H-10	53
Rocky Mountains, North America	E-4	29
Romania, Europe, country	E-5	59
Rome, Italy	G-8	55
Rosario, Argentina	E-5	45
Rostov-na-Donu, Russia	E-3	79
Roswell, New Mexico, U.S.	H-7	33
Rotterdam, Netherlands	B-6	55
Russia, Europe, country	F-9	79
Rwanda, Africa, country	C-6	69
Ryazan', Russia	G-14	53
Rybinsk, Russia	F-14	53
Ryukyu Islands, Japan	G-13	81
Sacramento, California, U.S.	F-4	33
Sahara, Africa, desert	D-8	67
Saint Helens, Mount, Washington, U.S., volcano	D-4	33
Saint John's, Newfoundland, Canada	H-17	31
Saint Joseph, Missouri, U.S.	G-10	33
Saint Kitts and Nevis, North America, country	G-15	35
Saint Louis, Missouri, U.S.	G-10	33
Saint Lucia, North America, country	G-16	35
Saint Paul, Minnesota, U.S.	E-10	33
Saint Petersburg, Florida, U.S.	J-13	33
Saint Petersburg, Russia	F-12	53
Saint Vincent and the Grenadines, North America, country	H-16	35
Sakhalin, Russia, island	F-14	79
Salem, Oregon, U.S.	D-4	33
Salt Lake City, Utah, U.S	F-6	33
Salvador, Brazil	G-13	43
Salzburg, Austria	D-8	55
Samara, Russia	E-5	79
Samoa, Oceania, country	F-11	93
San Antonio, Texas, U.S.	J-9	33
San Diego, California, U.S.	H-4	33
San Francisco, California, U.S.	F-4	33
San José, Costa Rica	I-10	35
San Juan, Argentina	E-3	45
San Luis Potosí, Mexico	E-5	35
San Marino, Europe, country	F-8	55
San Miguel de Tucumán, Argentina	C-4	45
San Salvador, El Salvador	H-8	35
Sanaa, Yemen	G-5	85
Santa Fe, Argentina	E-5	45
Santa Fe, New Mexico, U.S.	H-7	33
Santiago, Chile	E-3	45
Santiago, Dominican Republic	F-13	35
Santiago de Cuba, Cuba	F-12	35
Santos, Brazil	I-12	43
São Paulo, Brazil	I-12	43
Sao Tome and Principe, Africa, country	J-7	67
Sapporo, Japan	C-14	81
Sarajevo, Bosnia and Herzegovina	F-3	59
Sarasota, Florida, U.S.	J-12	33
Saratov, Russia	H-17	53
Sardinia, Italy, island	H-7	55
Saskatchewan, Canada, province	H-9	31
Saudi Arabia, Asia, country	D-5	85
Scotland, United Kingdom, political division	H-4	53
Seattle, Washington, U.S.	D-4	33
Seine, France, river	D-5	55
Semarang, Indonesia	K-8	83
Senegal, Africa, country	G-3	67
Seoul, South Korea	E-13	81
Serbia and Montenegro, Europe, country	E-4	59
Serengeti Plain, Tanzania	C-7	69
Sevastopol', Ukraine	K-8	57
Sevilla, Spain	H-2	55
Shanghai, China	F-12	81
Shasta, Mount, California, U.S., volcano	E-4	33
Sheffield, England, U.K.	I-4	53
Shenyang, China	D-12	81
Shetland Islands, Scotland, U.K.	F-5	53
Siberia, Russia, region	E-9	79
Sicily, Italy, island	I-9	55
Sierra Nevada, United States, mountains	F-4	33
Sierra Leone, Africa, country	H-3	67
Sinai Peninsula, Egypt	C-13	67
Singapore, Asia, country	H-6	83
Singapore, Singapore	H-6	83
Siracusa, Italy	I-9	55
Skopje, Macedonia	F-5	59
Slovakia, Europe, country	I-2	57
Slovenia, Europe, country	E-2	59
Smolensk, Russia	H-13	53
Snake, United States, river	E-6	33
Sofia, Bulgaria	F-5	59
Solomon Islands, Oceania, country	F-9	93
Somalia, Africa, country	H-16	67
South Africa, Africa, country	I-4	69
South Carolina, United States, state	H-12	33
South China Sea, Asia	I-10	81
South Dakota, United States, state	E-8	33
South Korea, Asia, country	E-13	81
Spain, Europe, country	G-3	55
Split, Croatia	F-3	59
Spokane, Washington, U.S.	D-5	33
Spratly Islands, Asia	F-9	83
Springfield, Illinois, U.S.	G-11	33
Sri Jayewardenepura Kotte, Sri Lanka	I-13	85
Sri Lanka, Asia, country	I-13	85

Place	Map Ref.	Page No.
Stanley, Falkland Islands	I-5	45
Stockholm, Sweden	G-9	53
Strasbourg, France	D-7	55
Stuttgart, Germany	D-7	55
Sucre, Bolivia	H-8	43
Sudan, Africa, country	G-12	67
Sudan, Africa, region	F-9	67
Suez, Egypt	C-13	67
Sulu Sea, Asia	F-11	83
Sumatra, Indonesia, island	I-6	83
Superior, Lake, North America	J-12	31
Surabaya, Indonesia	K-9	83
Suriname, South America, country	C-10	43
Suva, Fiji	G-10	93
Swaziland, Africa, country	I-6	69
Sweden, Europe, country	F-8	53
Switzerland, Europe, country	E-7	55
Sydney, Australia	G-12	91
Syr Darya, Asia, river	G-5	79
Syria, Asia, country	B-5	85
T'aipei, Taiwan	H-12	81
Tacoma, Washington, U.S.	D-4	33
Taegu, South Korea	E-13	81
Tagus, Europe, river	G-2	55
Tahiti, French Polynesia, island	G-14	93
Tahoe, Lake, United States	F-4	33
Taiwan, Asia, country	H-12	81
Taiwan Strait, Asia	H-11	81
Taiyuan, China	E-10	81
Tajikistan, Asia, country	I-5	79
Tallahassee, Florida, U.S.	I-12	33
Tallinn, Estonia	F-10	53
Tampa, Florida, U.S.	J-12	33
Tampico, Mexico	E-6	35
Tanger, Morocco	B-6	67
Tangshan, China	D-11	81
Tanzania, Africa, country	D-6	69
Tarsus, Turkey	C-3	77
Tashkent, Uzbekistan	H-5	79
Tasmania, Australia, island	I-11	91
Tbilisi, Georgia	B-5	77
Tegucigalpa, Honduras	H-9	35
Tehrān, Iran	B-7	85
Tel Aviv-Yafo, Israel	C-4	85
Tennessee, United States, state	H-11	33
Texas, United States, state	I-8	33
Thailand, Asia, country	D-6	83
Thames, England, U.K., river	J-4	53
Thana, India	F-11	85
Thanh Pho Ho Chi Minh, Vietnam	F-7	83
The Hague, Netherlands	B-6	55
Thessaloníki, Greece	G-5	59
Thimphu, Bhutan	D-14	85
Thunder Bay, Ontario, Canada	I-12	31
Tianjin, China	E-11	81
Tibet, Plateau of, China	E-5	81
Tien Shan, Asia, mountains	C-6	81
Tierra del Fuego, South America, island	J-4	45
Tigris, Asia, river	B-6	85
Timor, Asia, island	K-12	83
Tiranë, Albania	G-4	59
Tiruvottiyur, India	G-13	85
Togo, Africa, country	H-6	67
Tokelau, Oceania, dependency	F-11	93
Tōkyō, Japan	D-15	81
Toledo, Ohio, U.S.	F-12	33
Toledo, Spain	H-3	55
Tonga, Oceania, country	G-11	93
Tonkin, Gulf of, Asia	C-7	83
Topeka, Kansas, U.S.	G-9	33
Toronto, Ontario, Canada	J-13	31
Tórshavn, Faroe Islands	E-4	53
Toulouse, France	F-5	55
Trento, Italy	E-8	55
Trenton, New Jersey, U.S.	F-14	33
Trieste, Italy	E-8	55
Trinidad and Tobago, North America, country	H-16	35
Tripoli, Libya	B-9	67
Tucson, Arizona, U.S.	I-6	33
Tula, Russia	H-14	53
Tulsa, Oklahoma, U.S.	H-9	33
Tunis, Tunisia	B-8	67
Tunisia, Africa, country	B-8	67
Turin, Italy	F-7	55
Turkey, Asia, country	C-3	77
Turkmenistan, Asia, country	H-4	79
Turks and Caicos Islands, North America, dependency	F-13	35
Tutupaca, Volcán, Peru, volcano	H-7	43
Tuvalu, Oceania, country	F-10	93
Tver', Russia	G-13	53
Ufa, Russia	E-5	79
Uganda, Africa, country	B-6	69
Ujungpandang, Indonesia	J-11	83
Ukraine, Europe, country	H-6	57
Ulan Bator, Mongolia	I-10	79
Uluru, Australia, mountain	E-8	91
United Arab Emirates, Asia, country	E-7	85
United Kingdom, Europe, country	H-4	53
Ural Mountains, Russia	E-6	79
Uruguay, Europe, country	E-5	45
Ürümqi, China	C-6	81
Utah, United States, state	F-6	33
Uzbekistan, Asia, country	H-4	79
València, Spain	H-4	55
Valletta, Malta	J-9	55
Valparaíso, Chile	E-3	45
Vancouver, British Columbia, Canada	H-7	31
Vanuatu, Oceania, country	F-9	93
Varna, Bulgaria	F-7	59
Vatican City, Europe, country	G-8	55
Venezuela, South America, country	B-7	43
Venice, Italy	F-8	55
Veracruz, Mexico	F-6	35
Vermont, United States, state	E-14	33
Verona, Italy	F-8	55
Vesuvius, Italy, volcano	H-9	55
Viangchan, Laos	C-6	83
Victoria, British Columbia, Canada	H-7	31
Vienna, Europe	D-9	55
Vietnam, Asia, country	C-7	83
Vilnius, Lithuania	I-11	53
Virgin Islands, North America, dependency	F-14	35
Virginia, United States, state	G-13	33
Virginia Beach, Virginia, U.S.	G-14	33
Vladivostok, Russia	I-13	79
Volga, Russia, river	F-4	79
Volgograd, Russia	I-17	53
Wahran, Algeria	B-6	67
Wales, United Kingdom, political division	J-3	53
Wallis and Futuna, Oceania, dependency	F-11	93
Walvis Bay, Namibia	H-3	69
Warsaw, Poland	G-3	57
Washington, District of Columbia, U.S.	G-13	33
Washington, United States, state	D-5	33
Wellington, New Zealand	I-10	93
West Indies, islands	E-11	35
West Virginia, United States, state	G-12	33
Western Sahara, Africa, country	D-3	67
Wheeling, West Virginia, U.S.	F-12	33
White Nile, Sudan, river	H-13	67
White Sea, Russia	C-12	53
Whitehorse, Yukon, Canada	E-7	31
Whitney, Mount, California, U.S.	G-4	33
Wichita, Kansas, U.S.	G-9	33
Wiesbaden, Germany	C-7	55
Wilmington, Delaware, U.S.	F-13	33
Wilmington, North Carolina, U.S.	H-13	33
Windhoek, Namibia	H-3	69
Winnipeg, Manitoba, Canada	I-11	31
Winston-Salem, North Carolina, U.S.	G-13	33
Wisconsin, United States, state	E-10	33
Woods, Lake of the, North America	D-9	33
Wrocław, Poland	H-2	57
Wuhan, China	G-10	81
Wuppertal, Germany	C-7	55
Wyoming, United States, state	E-7	33
Xi'an, China	F-9	81
Yalu, Asia, river	D-12	81
Yamoussoukro, Cote d'Ivoire	H-5	67
Yangon, Myanmar	D-4	83
Yaoundé, Cameroon	I-8	67
Yekaterinburg, Russia	E-6	79
Yellowknife, Northwest Territories, Canada	F-9	31
Yellowstone, United States, river	E-7	33
Yemen, Asia, country	G-5	85
Yerevan, Armeria	C-5	77
Yogyakarta, Indonesia	K-8	83
Yokohama, Japan	E-15	81
York, Cape, Australia	B-10	91
Yucatan Peninsula, North America	F-8	35
Yukon Territory, Canada	D-7	31
Yukon, North America, river	J-4	33
Zagreb, Croatia	E-3	59
Zambia, Africa, country	F-5	69
Zanzibar, Tanzania	D-8	69
Zaragoza, Spain	G-4	55
Zhengzhou, China	F-10	81
Zimbabwe, Africa, country	G-5	69
Zürich, Switzerland	E-7	55